# Theological Commentary

Barcode
PTO

# Theological Commentary

## Evangelical Perspectives

Edited by R. Michael Allen

t&t clark

**Published by T&T Clark International**
*A Continuum Imprint*
The Tower Building,          80 Maiden Lane,
11 York Road,               Suite 704,
London SE1 7NX              New York, NY 10038

www.continuumbooks.com

© R. Michael Allen, with contributors, 2011

R. Michael Allen and contributors have asserted their right under the Copyright, Designs and Patents Act, 1988, to be identified as the Author of this work.

**British Library Cataloguing-in-Publication Data**
A catalogue record for this book is available from the British Library

ISBN: 978–0–567–64805–1 (hardback)
         978–0–567–42329–0 (paperback)

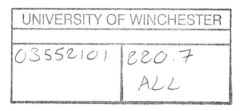

Typeset by Newgen Imaging Systems Pvt Ltd, Chennai, India
Printed and bound in India

# Contents

# Acknowledgments

There are many persons to thank for their help in preparing this volume. Most importantly, a number of able contributors submitted chapters of excellent quality ranging over the whole canon of Scripture and engaging a wide host of doctrinal topics. Geoff Ziegler played a pivotal role in the conceptualization and planning of the volume. My assistant Jason Paugh compiled the index. Tom Kraft, Anna Turton, and the capable staff of T & T Clark guided the manuscript to completion. It is always a pleasure to work with them. My wife Emily was ever supportive during the course of this project.

The editor and contributors dedicate this book to Prof. Henri Blocher, until recently the Gunther Knoedler Professor of Theology at Wheaton College in Wheaton, Illinois, and the longtime Professor of Systematic Theology at the Faculté Libre de Théologie Évangélique in Vaux-sur-Seine, France. For us, he has been many things—teacher, colleague, collaborator—and beyond any of these formal roles, a model of humble and rigorous theological scholarship in service of the church. His own service to theological studies can be captured well by pointing to his own "theological commentary": especially his *In the Beginning: The Opening Chapters of Genesis* (Downers Grove, IL: InterVarsity, 1984) and his exegesis of Romans 5 in *Original Sin: Illumining the Riddle* (New Studies in Biblical Theology; Downers Grove, IL: InterVarsity, 1997). It is a delight to include his essay on John 1 in this volume as a representative example of his theological work. He has exemplified careful and patient listening to the self-revelation of God through the testimony of these prophetic and apostolic witnesses, always as a member of an interpretive company that ranges through the centuries and around the globe. He has never been stuck in hermeneutical debates about exegesis; rather he has consistently read the Bible with theological and churchly passion. We thank him and pray that his example might be imitated by many.

Fort Lauderdale, Florida
January 2011

# Contributors

**Michael Allen** is Assistant Professor of Systematic Theology at Knox Theological Seminary in Fort Lauderdale, Florida. He is the author of *Reformed Theology* and *The Christ's Faith: A Dogmatic Account.* His writings have appeared in scholarly journals such as *International Journal of Systematic Theology, Scottish Journal of Theology, Horizons of Biblical Theology,* and *Journal of Theological Interpretation.* He serves as general editor of the forthcoming T&T Clark International Theological Commentary series.

**Henri Blocher** was the Gunther Knoedler Professor of Theology at Wheaton College in Wheaton, Illinois, and Professor of Systematic Theology at the Faculte Libre de Theologie Evangelique in Vaux-sur-Seine, France. He is the author of *Original Sin: Illumining the Riddle, Evil and the Cross: An Analytical Look at the Problem of Pain,* and *In the Beginning: The Opening Chapters of Genesis,* as well as many articles and a number of books in French. He has served as President of the Fellowship of European Evangelical Theologians.

**D. A. Carson** is Research Professor of New Testament at Trinity Evangelical Divinity School in Deerfield, Illinois. He is the author of dozens of books, most recently of *Christ and Culture Revisited* and *Scandalous: The Death and Resurrection of Jesus.* He has also written commentaries on the Gospel of Matthew and the Gospel of John. He is a founding member of the GRAMCORD Institute and the Gospel Coalition.

**Michael Horton** is the J. Gresham Machen Professor of Systematic Theology and Apologetics at Westminster Seminary in Escondido, California. He has authored numerous books, most recently *The Christian Faith: A Systematic Theology for Pilgrims on the Way.* He serves as host for the White Horse Inn radio program and as editor-in-chief for *Modern Reformation* magazine.

**Kelly Kapic** is Professor of Theological Studies at Covenant College in Lookout Mountain, Georgia. He is the author of *God So Loved He Gave* and *Communion with God: The Divine and the Human in the Theology of John Owen.* He has also edited a number of contemporary editions of the works of John Owen and the Puritan theologians.

**Andrew McGowan** is Minister of Inverness East Church in Scotland and was formerly Principal of Highland Theological College in Aberdeen, Scotland. He is author of *The Divine Spiration of Scripture: Challenging Evangelical Perspectives* and *The Federal Theology of Thomas Boston.*

**Walter Moberly** is Professor of Theology and Biblical Interpretation at Durham University in Durham, England. He is the author of numerous books, most recently of *The Theology of the Book of Genesis, Prophecy and Discernment,* and *The Bible, Theology, and Faith: A Study of Abraham and Jesus.* His writings have appeared in scholarly journals such as *Vetus Testamentum, Journal of Theological Studies, Harvard Theological Review,* and *Journal of Theological Interpretation.*

**Ryan Peterson** is Assistant Professor of Theology at Cedarville University in Cedarville, Ohio. His Wheaton Ph.D. dissertation on the doctrine of the image of God was awarded the 2011 Dissertation Prize by the Center for Catholic and Evangelical Dialogue.

**Scott Swain** is Associate Professor of Systematic Theology at Reformed Theological Seminary in Orlando, Florida. He is author of *Trinity, Revelation, and Reading* and (with Andreas Köstenberger) *Father, Son, and Spirit: The Trinity and John's Gospel.* He serves as general editor for the forthcoming T & T Clark International Theological Commentary series.

**Daniel Treier** is Associate Professor of Theology at Wheaton College in Wheaton, Illinois. He is the author of *Proverbs and Ecclesiastes, Introducing Theological Interpretation of Scripture: Recovering a Christian Practice* and *Virtue and the Voice of God: Toward Theology as Wisdom.* His writings have appeared in scholarly journals such as *International Journal of Systematic Theology, Scottish Journal of Theology,* and *Journal of Theological Interpretation.* He has edited numerous books, most notably serving as associate editor for the acclaimed *Dictionary for Theological Interpretation of Scripture.*

**Kevin Vanhoozer** is the Blanchard Professor of Theology at Wheaton College in Wheaton, Illinois. He has previously taught at Trinity Evangelical Divinity School and the University of Edinburgh. He is the author of many books, most recently of *Remythologizing Theology: Divine Action, Passion, and Authorship* and *The Drama of Doctrine: A Canonical-Linguistic Approach to Christian Theology.* He served as general editor of the acclaimed *Dictionary for Theological Interpretation of Scripture.*

Chapter 1

# Theological Commentary

## Michael Allen

### I

The essays in this book are offered as part of an ongoing conversation—attempts among the communion of saints to do justice to God's written Word. They are ventures in theological commentary on the Bible for the sake of the church's worship, witness, and wisdom. A number of questions deserve attention in this introduction, namely, what are the nature, the manner, and the resources employed by such work? Each of these three questions must be addressed briefly.

Our first question must be, then, what makes this *theological* commentary? Here we consider its nature. We should consider this important question in two stages.

First, we are offering *commentary upon Holy Scripture*. Each essay expands upon a given text found in the Bible. To be sure, theological texts take many forms: the sermon, the tract, the catechism, the encyclopedia, and the commentary. Each genre may witness to biblical truth. This last format, however, is most explicit in its desire to be shaped by not only that matter of the Bible, but also by its material shape and outline. Commentary allows the contours of the Scriptural text to guide its own texture. The breadth of commentary will match that of the text itself—taking in no more and no less than the prophets and apostles saw fit to say. Similarly, the emphases of commentary are patterned after the canonical focus. In this way, the very architecture of theology can be reshaped by canonical practice.

Of course, commentary is not opposed to dogmatics or any other genre. Every contributor to this book (and virtually every commentator in church history) has also written other forms of theology: thematic studies of biblical topics, sermons, or systematic theologies. Healthy theological culture flourishes when all guns are firing, when biblical reasoning expresses itself in dogmatic and commentarial forms. One cannot imagine John Calvin's reputation apart from both the *Institutes of Christian Religion* and his many biblical commentaries. Similarly, the brilliant theological pursuit of Origen is only seen when one lingers over *On First Principles* as well as his own commentaries; the same could be said of Thomas's *Summa Theologiae* and the fruits of his day job: biblical commentaries on Job, Romans, Hebrews, the Gospel of John, and other books. Dogmatics and commentary are best viewed as mutually enriching activities.[1] Yet in our own day, perhaps, it is especially important for biblical commentaries to be written by theologians. Much dogmatic work has proceeded far removed from the verbiage (much less the breadth and emphases) of the biblical writings. Surely the need of the day, more than anything else, is for theological commentary on the Bible.

Second, we are pursuing *theological* commentary on the Bible. Commentary is theological inasmuch as it views the act of reading within the economy of sinful reason's redemption in Christ Jesus. Thus, theological reflection on the Bible performs all the necessary linguistic and grammatical analysis as part of modern consideration of ancient texts, but it does so ever aware that the reader is addressed by the text. Furthermore, it locates the reader within the communion of saints—that trans-national and trans-generational body of believers who have gathered around this Word. So it seeks to gain from their collective wisdom, listening to the "great cloud of witnesses" and taking their witness a step further and a day longer. Not only does it glean from the past, but it also acknowledges the pull of the urgent: naming the tyrannies of the present that shape the reader's own self and seeking their resurrection in the life offered by the gospel. Again, biblical reading is a spiritual enterprise, a part of the ongoing fellowship of Christ with his brothers and sisters. We believe the ascended Lord ministers to his people as they attend to his book: as the apostle tells the Ephesians, the exalted one gives gifts to lead his people into the fullness of knowledge about his love—its "breadth and length and height and depth" (Eph. 3:18; see also Eph. 4:7-16).

The Bible should be read as the Word of God, a means by which God draws us from death to life and into the eternal fellowship that he has purposed in Christ Jesus. The essays in this volume offer commentary on various passages of the Bible, explicating how they fit within this broader vision of the canon of Scripture. Each essay, then, seeks to help Christians think more clearly and cogently, that is, more biblically and more Christianly, about their own lives in light of the works of God.

## II

How shall such theological reading proceed? In other words, our second question is, what will its manner be? What intellectual struggles does it engage?

---

[1] The mutually enriching nature of exegetical reasoning and dogmatic reasoning is well captured by John Webster, "Biblical Reasoning," *Anglican Theological Review* 90, no. 4 (2008), pp. 733–751.

Sometimes it is worth pointing out hurdles and harangues right at the start. *The Bible can be exceedingly difficult to read.* We often hear about the doctrine of *claritas scripturae*, that is, the clarity or luminosity of the Bible. Indeed, it is crucial to see that the gospel is portrayed blatantly and boldly throughout the canon—Jesus is clearly the central figure of this history of God amid Israel and the nations. God desires to be known, and he speaks powerfully, lovingly, compellingly. His Word is light, illumining the dark places of this world and our lives. The very Word of God is indeed clear.[2] Yet even the revered apostle Peter notes that the Scriptures can be downright difficult at times (2 Pet. 3:16). With Augustine, we must see that the living words are clear and yet not necessarily easy to interpret.[3] But we must also understand the nature of difficulty in reading the Bible. Its difficulty is not simply akin to that of Faulkner or Joyce. It is not mere grammatical structure or plot analysis that is so perplexing. There surely are lexical and grammatical issues to be investigated and argued, but they do not make up the whole or the principal part of the Bible's difficulty. Rather, thinking clearly about the nature of its difficulty might be helped by considering some words from an early letter of Franz Kafka:

> If the book we are reading does not wake us, as with a fist hammering on our skull, why then do we read it? Good God, we would also be happy if we had no books, and such books as make us happy we could, if need be, write ourselves. But what we must have are those books which come upon us like ill-fortune, and distress us deeply, like the death of one we love better than ourselves, like suicide. A book must be an ice-axe to break the sea frozen inside us.[4]

The Bible is difficult for many reasons. It involves characters and linguistic patterns from times long past. It surveys centuries and spans a number of political eras. Its language parallels other religions, though with its own distinctive tilt. It does require intellectual effort to interpret this book. Above all, though, reading the Bible is a thorny practice, because it is so penetrating. It cuts through the thick of things, like a hammering fist or an ice-axe or, as the anonymous writer to the Hebrews says, by "piercing to the division of soul and of spirit, of joints and of marrow, and discerning the thoughts and intentions of the heart" (Heb. 4:12). Biblical difficulty is largely a corollary of its doctrinal and moral judgment—this book involves the most profound and pervasive of

---

[2] For helpful reflection on the clarity of Scripture, see John Webster, "On the clarity of holy scripture," in *Confessing God: Essays in Christian Dogmatics II* (London: T & T Clark, 2005), pp. 33–67; Mark D. Thompson, *A Clear and Present Word: The Clarity of Scripture* (New Studies in Biblical Theology 21; Downers Grove, IL: InterVarsity, 2006).

[3] Augustine, *On Christian Teaching*, II. pp. 14–15.

[4] A letter from Franz Kafka (cited by George Steiner, *Language and Silence* [New York: Atheneum, 1970], p. 67).

judgments, drawing all reality into its theological register. It makes profound declarations about reality, separating the good from the bad, the beautiful from the grim, and the true from the false. Most crucial, however, is that this verbal illumination of reality shines upon the reader: "And no creature is hidden from his sight, but all are naked and exposed to the eyes of him to whom we must give account" (Heb. 3:13). This text will grab hold of you—it is difficult because it does not let you be.

Reading the Bible is a spiritual enterprise. As John Webster has reminded us, it is a part of the Spirit's work in mortifying our sinful reason and vivifying biblical reason within us.[5] Any attempt, then, to approach the texts neutrally is doomed from the start; a century ago, Adolf Schlatter observed that claims to objective neutrality result from a lack of self-awareness: "If he claims to be an observer, concerned solely with his object, then he is concealing what is really happening. As a matter of fact, he is always in possession of certain convictions, and these determine him not simply in the sense that his judgments derive from them, but also in that his perception and observation is molded by them."[6] As those marred by the power of sin, readers are going to resist and flee. Yet as those hampered by the penalty of sin, these very same readers need the grace and mercy spoken of in these pages. Engaging this book is a spiritual exercise, an occasion within the economy of sin and redemption.

# III

We shall consider next the resources and partnerships involved in theological commentary. More specifically, this third question focuses on what use we shall make of modern and ancient biblical reading practices.

If nothing else, modern biblical criticism has served to dull the edge of the ice-axe. Stanley Hauerwas has said that historical criticism serves to give us reasons not to be convicted by the text. We can see such intent expressed in the programmatic manifesto of John J. Collins, *The Bible after Babel: Historical Criticism in a Postmodern Age*. Collins argues that historical criticism—and now postmodern criticism too—functions primarily to foster suspicion of all ideals, complicating certainties and creating space for peaceful dialogue.[7] He asks what two hundred years of modern biblical studies have achieved, and he claims that "ongoing criticism has tended to highlight the tensions and differences within the biblical texts. Consequently, it is difficult to regard the

---

[5] John Webster, *Holiness* (Grand Rapids, MI: Eerdmans, 2003), Chapter 1.
[6] Adolf Schlatter, "The theology of the new testament and dogmatics," in *The Nature of New Testament Theology: The Contribution of William Wrede and Adolf Schlatter* (ed. and trans. Robert Morgan; *Studies in Biblical Theology* 2, no. 25; Naperville, IL: Allenson, 1973), p. 124.
[7] John J. Collins, *The Bible after Babel: Historical Criticism in a Postmodern Age* (Grand Rapids, MI: Eerdmans, 2005).

Bible . . . as a whole, as a coherent guide to life."[8] Coming from a senior and internationally renowned practitioner of historical criticism, these are enlightening words.

The approach of the modern critic is self-defeating. Again, Schlatter is helpful: "According to the skeptical position, it is true that the historian explains; he observes the New Testament neutrally. But in reality this is to begin at once with a determined struggle against it. The Word with which the New Testament confronts us intends to be believed, and so rules out once and for all any sort of neutral treatment."[9] The text itself calls for a passionate, self-involving reading. In short, it calls for faith working itself out in understanding.[10] Modern criticism, to the extent that it overlooks, denies, or mocks such self-investment, fails to let the matter shape the method of biblical study.[11] The proper objectivity in any discipline is shaped by its object of study—and the study of theology (focusing on the exposition of biblical texts) surely calls for a more personal and spiritual investment than the consideration of quarks or nebulae. Disciplinary parameters in theology, set by its object of study, cannot exclude the spiritual and the personal (though, of course, that does not mean that they can be reduced to such).

Yet it is not as though the discipline of modern biblical studies has nothing to show for itself. Indeed, we have learned much about the biblical text through the efforts of these practitioners.[12] For example, we can point to a couple of benefits in the way we read the very first chapter of the Bible. First, scholars note the presence of temple imagery in Genesis 1, apparent now that we can compare this text with other ancient near-Eastern texts.[13] Creation itself is for the sake of fellowship between God and those made in his image—while texts in Isaiah 40–48 may say this, it is drawn all the way from Genesis 1 itself. Second, comparative study of other ancient religions allows us to see the polemical nature of Genesis 1 as well. Whereas many religions ascribed divinity to the sun, moon, and stars, the biblical text emphasizes that they

---

[8]  Ibid., p. 10 (cf. pp. 25, 37, 62, 67, 131 fn 1, 141–142, 148).

[9]  Adolf Schlatter, "The Theology of the New Testament and Dogmatics," p. 122.

[10]  This phrase—faith working itself out in understanding—is a confluence of Gal. 5:6 and the famous lined from Augustine and Anselm, "faith seeking understanding" (*fides quarens intellectum*).

[11]  Of course, there is no monolithic entity called "historical criticism," a point made forcibly by James Barr, *History and Ideology in the Old Testament: Biblical Studies at the End of a Millenium* (New York: Oxford University Press, 1997), Chapter 1. Yet there are certain moods, values, and practices that can accurately go by the name of "modern biblical critism," on which see R. W. L. Moberly, "Biblical Criticism and Religious Belief," *Journal of Theological Interpretation* 2, no. 1 (2008), pp. 71–100.

[12]  For example, see the many gains conveyed in the lively history of modern biblical studies by Stephen Neill and Tom Wright, *The Interpretation of the New Testament, 1861–1986* (2nd edn; New York: Oxford University Press, 1989).

[13]  See, for example, Jon D. Levenson, "The temple and the world," *Journal of Religion* 64, no. 3 (1984), pp. 275–298.

are created things. In short, the Bible puts idols in their place. We may have gleaned these truths apart from biblical studies in the modern setting, but in God's providence that is where they have been developed most fully.

Theological commentary may make use of many modern insights into the historical nature of the texts. (Some would say it *must* do so.) Indeed, contributors to this volume will exhibit differing degrees of reliance upon such practices. Such proposals and discoveries will need to be assessed individually on the basis of whether or not they help the reading of God's Word.[14] Perhaps some modern theories are good ways to account for biblical data and fit with its own self-understanding. Other hypotheses may fail to do justice to the data or run aground on the Scripture's teaching about itself. Again, case-by-case investigation is required. We must appropriate without capitulating. Historical method is a wonderful handmaid and a terrible master. Too frequently it locates difficulty at exactly the wrong place, denying the spiritual nature (and struggle) of reading in the economy of grace and amplifying or magnifying the lexical, historical, and grammatical work of interpretation. There are doctrinal deficiencies in these modern tendencies.

This uneasy relationship with modern biblical criticism is similar to the continuing relevance of patristic and medieval exegesis as well. Again, there are many blessings to be found in consulting this storehouse of interpretive wisdom. From Irenaeus we learn to see patterns of recapitulation and strands of redemptive-historical development. From Origen we begin to see words and images picked up and expanded upon throughout the canon. From Augustine we are reminded that the virtues shape our reading of the text, and the words are meant to increase our exercise of love.

Yet honoring the fathers does not require slavishly repeating them or overlooking their warts and wounds. Surely we must be wise as serpents, assessing their exegesis by its canon sense—does it illumine our reading of the Bible or does it distract from the text's breadth and its particular emphases? Frequently theological commentators will need to diverge from long revered reading practices, believing that God's Word has broken through afresh. In so doing this is not to divert from the expectations of the fathers themselves, for they thought biblical study was an ascetic discipline and a portrait in itself of the life of cross-bearing. They expected the long-cherished paths of the past to turn and twist as we journey upward in a pilgrim-like progress.

Because the Bible names our sin and declares the path of life, it will exceed our grasp. We are limited and finite, sinful and skewed. We will frequently fly

---

[14] For one notable attempt to consider a number of modern scholarly insights alongside many traditional exegetical practices, see R. W. L. Moberly, *The Theology of the Book of Genesis* (Old Testament Theology; Cambridge: Cambridge University Press, 2009). By and large, Moberly seeks to assimilate the results of modern biblical criticism without allowing them to limit the scope of theological reading of the biblical text.

to the dark and hunker down. Yet our best approach to treasure the life-giving oracles of God is to glean from the witness of the saints in centuries past as well as in our own day. We must faithfully appropriate the wisdom of the ancient fathers as well as the gleanings of the modern scholars—always returning to the Bible again with whatever interpretive goods we have received.

# IV

Finally, a few words should be said about the contributions to this volume.

First, this book offers evangelical approaches to the necessary task of theological commentary on the Bible. Contributors have been selected for several reasons, tied to their proficiency as evangelical theologians and their demonstrated facility in close reading of texts. Many have not yet published in the realm of "biblical studies" or "biblical commentary" per se; yet, their ability to interpret theological texts from the Christian tradition and their passionate concern for "theological commentary" give credibility to their exemplary place in the contemporary scene.

These essays are evangelical, coming from authors who stand within the world of British and American evangelicalism.[15] Most live and move and have their being within some Reformed community, though this is not true of all. As you will note from our narrative regarding the fall and rise of theological commentary, we would insist that many theologian-pastors from the evangelical world, as well as a number of theologians and exegetes in this context, have maintained a vibrant practice of faithful reading of the Bible. Of course, evangelicalism is about as difficult to define as pornography or time, so we would be the first to admit that it is identified with many who do not practice theological commentary, indeed who are not interested in anything theological or even in the genre of commentary. Nonetheless, we believe that the demise of historical–critical methods as the hegemonic practice in the academy ought to lead many outside evangelicalism to consider the intellectually rigorous, theologically cogent practice of commentary practiced by pastors and theologians within the various evangelical and Reformed churches.

These essays are approaches to theological commentary, and the pluralism implied in the term "approaches" should not be missed. The editor has imposed no method upon the contributors. While some follow traditional readings, others protest such mainstays based on exegetical reasoning. While a few employ detailed historical–critical methodology in their work, many find this theologically vacuous and strategically fruitless. On top of such formal

---

[15] See Timothy Larsen, "Defining and locating evangelicalism," in *The Cambridge Companion to Evangelical Theology* (eds Timothy Larsen and Daniel J. Treier; Cambridge: Cambridge University Press, 2007), pp. 1–14.

concerns, social backgrounds as well as ecclesial and academic contexts necessarily affect the conversation partners with whom each contributor concerns themselves. Furthermore, the editor has not required any particular position regarding hermeneutical theory as a sine qua non for participation in this project. All contributors share basic spiritual and theological convictions regarding the role of the Bible in the economy of salvation, as an auxiliary of the life-giving Holy Spirit. Nevertheless, we trust that practitioners will vary in their assessment of philosophical schemes for making sense of this spiritual reality and, therefore, we have not made use of any hermeneutical *shibboleths* in selecting contributors.

Second, essays are also diverse in that they engage texts from across the canon of Scripture. Commentary on the first chapter of Genesis is likely to look different from that on Paul's Letter to the Colossians, and essays related to texts of various literary genres do not disappoint in this regard. In this way, this book can serve as a staging post of sorts for those baffled and/or curious about theological commentary, showing approaches to different types of biblical witness. Whereas a book-length commentary offers needed depth, this book offers a sampling of wider breadth. Best of all, one might turn from essays here to read the (forthcoming) commentaries by some of our contributors or even to other commentaries on these very biblical books.

Nonetheless, there is a coherence to be found in these diverse contributions from across the evangelical spectrum and, indeed, the Atlantic Ocean. We have asked each contributor to deal with three intellectual moves: (1) careful exegesis of the actual text in its own literary and historical context, (2) engagement of canonical texts related to their primary text, highlighting any varying emphases, supplementary concerns, and developmental comments, and (3) analysis of the dogmatic implications of the text, particularly by showing its use in the history of interpretation and its relevance in contemporary debates. Obviously, essays will emphasize one or another component based on a number of factors, yet all show concern for these three facets of theological commentary. And, we pray, such analysis may still be done in a manner approved by John Calvin: clearly (*claritas*) and to the point (*brevitas*).

Two essays have been commissioned to take stock of current efforts at theological commentary. Walter Moberly and Don Carson consider this movement from the vantage point of Old and New Testament studies, respectively. It should be noted that they did so cheerfully without having read the contributions to this volume. Moberly offers case study examples to show what a theological commentary might look like. Carson sees six major *foci* in the movement, to each of which he offers a vibrant reply: "Yes, But . . . " If any movement is to flourish, it must engage the serious concerns of its sympathetic yet critical near neighbors in the faith; the success of the chapters in this volume may be weighed against the suggestions of Moberly and Carson as one possible barometer of their value. That much remains for the reader to judge.

If these essays provoke your exegetical imagination or stoke your theological passions, we point to series of theological commentary currently in progress (for example, the forthcoming T & T Clark International Theological Commentary or similar series published by Brazos, Eerdmans, and Westminster John Knox), as well as to notable examples found in major journals and books. We hope that this proves useful in the development of a scholarly and ecclesial community of those who pursue the spiritual and intellectual practice of theological commentary on the life-giving testimony of the prophets and apostles, the very Word of God. Thus, we join with the saints of past years in offering this prayer: *O God of Truth, write thy own words upon our hearts and inscribe them on our lips; so shall all glory be to thee in our reading of thy Word.*

Chapter 2

# Genesis 1

Ryan S. Peterson

In Genesis 1 God is identified as the maker of all things who orders all things toward their proper ends. Creation is identified as a reality wholly dependent upon God for its existence, the various parts of which are directed diversely toward the ends that will bring about the flourishing of the whole of creation.

These theological identifications and a portrayal of the relationship between God and creation are communicated in four moves. The first move involves the particular identification of God, known through God's action (including speech-acts) in Genesis 1. The second involves the proper identification of created things as creatures. The third move involves a recognition of the good ends toward which created things are ordered; the unfolding of these ends is a *theological* statement that exposes various aspects of God's character. The fourth involves the proper identification of one particular creature within creation—humanity. Genesis 1 gives God's people the tools necessary for rightly identifying God and creatures. Furthermore, God's character and God's intention for humanity within creation are tied to one another by the particular end God has given to the human creature.

In this chapter I argue that Genesis 1 provides the narrative identifications (identities) necessary for the canonical unfolding of God's self-revelation to humanity. This particular narrative is given to Israel and the church but is ultimately portrayed as the appropriate way for all people to understand themselves within creation before God. The argument will be supported in two ways: first, through a brief analysis of Genesis 1 as a whole in which divine identity takes precedence; second, through a more careful analysis of Gen. 1:26-28 in which human identity is explicated in relation to divine identity.

## I. Divine Identity

God's narrative identity in Genesis 1 is established through the careful depiction of God's sovereignty over all that he brings into existence, God's Word through whom God brings all things into existence, and God's Spirit whose immanence in the creation narrative communicates God's active presence in all that occurs.[1]

Robert Jenson's description of the way in which God's identity is known through narrative is useful for further explicating the significance of God's identity as revealed in Genesis 1. Jenson argues that God is "identified by narrative," and because of this God's self-identity is "constituted by dramatic coherence."[2] For Israel, God's identity centers on the Exodus. "Asked who God is, Israel's answer is, 'Whoever rescued us from Egypt.' "[3] For the church, God's identity follows from Jesus Christ's resurrection. "To the question 'Who is God?' the New Testament has one new descriptively identifying answer: 'Whoever raised Jesus from the dead.' "[4] Therefore, "God is whoever raised Jesus from the dead, having before raised Israel from Egypt."[5]

What is left out of this account is that both the Old and the New Testaments also identify God as: "Whoever created all things." "In the beginning God created the heavens and the earth" (Gen. 1:1). It is possible that Jenson intentionally overlooked this identification because it did not suit his particular purpose, which was to show how God is identified in history (while *creatio ex nihilo* is pre-history). Nevertheless, creation is given dramatic shape in Genesis 1, and it therefore contributes to the canonical identification of God. Moreover, canonical references to God's identity as creator abound.[6] *What* must be said of God's identity from Genesis 1 is complex, but it is necessary *that* we say something. Due attention must be given to the manner in which God is identified in Genesis 1 so that the God of the gospel can be rightly identified by the church, for the God who raised Jesus from the dead, having raised Israel from Egypt, had already created all things. As the maker of all things, God is not merely a god but *the only true God*. By ordering everything toward its proper end, God determines not only the existence of creation but also its good shape.

God's identity as maker of all things has been a fixed pole in Christian theological reflection; the church's confessions begin with this identification, and the significance of the doctrine of creation for Christian theological reflection

---

[1] See, for example, Augustine, *De Genesi ad litteram*, 1.6.

[2] Robert W. Jenson, *Systematic Theology*, vol. 1: *The Triune God* (Oxford: Oxford University Press, 1997), p. 64. Jenson's assertion that God's identity is *constituted* by dramatic coherence is problematic, but the claim that God's identity is *known* to us by dramatic coherence is a necessary one. See Kevin J. Vanhoozer, *Remythologizing Theology: Divine Action, Passion, and Authorship* (Cambridge: Cambridge University Press, 2010), pp. 107–109; 184–185. For Vanhoozer's attractive alternative, see pp. 181–240.

[3] Ibid., 1:44.

[4] Ibid., 1:44.

[5] Ibid., 1:63.

[6] See, for example, Ps. 115:15; 121:2; 124:8; 134:3; 146:6; Prov. 14:31 cf. 17:5; Eccl. 11:5 with 12:1; Isa. 17:7; 44:24; 45:1-25; 51:13; 54:5; Jer. 10:12-16 cf. 51:15-19; Jonah 1:9; John 1:1-3; Acts 4:24; 14:15; 17:24; Eph. 3:9; Col. 1:16; Rev. 4:11; 10:6; 14:7.

can hardly be overstated.[7] The doctrine of creation influences a range of issues including debates regarding God's providence, divine attributes, and theological method. Much of the debate between classical theism and process theology turns on the doctrine of creation. Interpretation of God's actions elsewhere in the Old Testament, such as divine repentance, is also hinged to particular notions of how God relates to the world—notions upon which Genesis 1 has a bearing.

Before proceeding to such issues, however, it is necessary to briefly note the various contexts (i.e., linguistic, cultural–historical, literary, religious, scientific, etc.) that help situate various readings of Genesis 1.[8] As R. W. L. Moberly has noted, it has not helped interpretations of Genesis 1 that "many of the debates that surround it tend to bear either on particular parts of it, such as humanity in the image of God, or on particular issues whose relation to the text is in fact rather oblique, such as the nature of Jewish and Christian understandings of creation ex nihilo or the implications of modern creationism."[9] We may add that comparative efforts to discover the meaning of Genesis 1 through analysis of other ancient Near Eastern creation accounts have had a similar effect. Any of these concerns may help angle light onto the text. But if these extra-canonical interests are allowed to delimit interpretation of Genesis 1, then the relevant narrative identities become clouded as the canonical context for Genesis 1 is traded for a different context altogether. A theological reading of Genesis 1 provides relevant material for addressing such issues, but only *a posteriori*. My goal in this chapter is to provide a canonical reading of Genesis 1 that has constructive theological implications; however, the implications themselves will have to be explored elsewhere.

## II. Divine Identity in Genesis 1

בְּרֵאשׁ ית בָּרָ א אֱלֹה ים אֵ ת הַשָּׁמַ יִם וְאֵ ת הָאָרֶץ׃

When the opening verse of Genesis 1 is read as such—as the opening words of the biblical canon—the first temptation is to ask who, exactly, אֱלֹהִים is. The temptation is to look elsewhere for a description of אֱלֹהִים and then to

---

[7]  So the Apostles' Creed: "*credo in deum patrem omnipotentem, creatorem cæli et terræ*" and the Nicene-Constantinopolitan Creed: "Πιστεύομεν εἰσ ἕνα Θεὸν πατέρα παντοκράτορα ποιητὴν οὐρανοῦ καὶ γῆς ὁρατῶ ν τε πάντων καὶ ἀοράτων."

     For three different dogmatic and methodological uses of the doctrine of creation that have had profound influence, see Irenaeus' *Adversus Haereses*, Athanasius' *De Incarnatione Verbi Dei*, esp. §1–14, Thomas Aquinas' *Summa Theologiae*, especially the *prima pars*. Examples could easily be multiplied.

[8]  For a helpful survey of the significant contexts see R. W. L. Moberly, *The Theology of the Book of Genesis* (Old Testament Theology; Cambridge: Cambridge University Press, 2009), pp. 42–69.

[9]  Ibid., p. 42.

conclude that Genesis 1 refers the reader to this deity. But this is to be impatient with the text *as a narrative*. Genesis 1 exists to tell the reader who אֱלֹהִים is. It is significant that אֱלֹהִים is used rather than יהוה since Genesis 1 does not pretend to entertain the particular covenantal relationship God has with humanity.[10] Only the creational context is explored—God orders humanity toward its proper end in Genesis 1, but God has not yet entered into a covenant with humanity. Thus, the use of אֱלֹהִים allows for patterns of speech about God and creation to develop on the basis of the diverse actions of God within the narrative.

God is identified in Genesis 1 as the maker of each sphere of creation and each creature within each sphere. Days 1–6 clarify the content of the initial claim that he is the maker of all things (heaven and earth). Genesis 1 is composed in two literary panels. The first panel contains days 1–3. On these days God makes the various spaces or regions of existence. This is accomplished by "divine acts of separation."[11] The second panel contains days 4–6. On these days God peoples or fills these regions with living or mobile beings.[12] The course of these panels is symmetrical: "Day 1 corresponds to Day 4, Day 2 to Day 5, Day 3 to Day 6."[13] Genesis 2:1 summarizes the divine accomplishment according to the acts recorded in the two panels: "Thus the heavens and the earth were finished," [Days 1–3] "and all their multitude" [Days 4–6].[14]

Israel's monotheism is an important distinctive feature of Genesis 1. There is only one God, the creator. There are no other gods mentioned in the creation narrative.[15] The רוּחַ אֱלֹ־הִים is mentioned in 1:2 due to the Spirit's being

---

[10] It is unnecessary, it seems to me, to allow source criticism to control how we understand the significance of God's names in Genesis 1–2. Source criticism may prove useful for interpretation. Or, as in this case, it may prove to be a red herring when it comes to a text's *meaning*, regardless of whether or not it can rightly identify a text's *source*. Surely a theologically interested editor could have adjusted references to God in Genesis 1–2 to make them uniform if the differences between אֱלֹהִים and יהוה were theologically insignificant to the particular contexts of Genesis 1:1-2:4a and 2:4bff.

[11] Henri Blocher, *In the Beginning: The Opening Chapters of Genesis* (Downers Grove, IL: InterVarsity, 1984), p. 51.

[12] Ibid., p. 51; J. Richard Middleton, *The Liberating Image: The Imago Dei in Genesis 1* (Grand Rapids, MI: Brazos, 2005), p. 74.

[13] Blocher, *In the Beginning*, p. 51.

[14] Ibid., pp 51–52; Middleton, *The Liberating Image*, pp. 75–76.

[15] Some have argued that the plural in Gen. 1:26 ("Let us") should be read as God's address to a heavenly court. Despite the fact that several OT texts refer to a heavenly court of created angels, it is problematic to suppose that the plural is an address to the heavenly court in this case. As David J. A. Clines noted, "If 'we' includes the heavenly court, man must be made in the image of the *elohim*." But in the very next verse the author of Genesis 1 writes in the singular: "So God created humankind in his image" (Gen. 1:27). The other problem with this explanation is that it introduces other beings into the creative act. Again Clines's comment is useful: "The Old Testament quite consistently represents creation as the act of Yahweh alone, and we cannot avoid the force of 'let us' by explaining it as a mere consultation before the work of creation begins" ("The Image of God in Man," *TynBul* 19 [1968]: pp. 53–103 [67]). Others have understood the plural as an address from

*of God*—this is God's Spirit, participating in God's work. And God creates through his Word. There are no other participants in the creative act; only אֱלֹהִים creates. Second, none of the created realities shares in God's divinity. There are no divine or semi-divine creatures. Creation is no emanation from God. The creation is given its own being, distinct from God yet related to him. Objects in the cosmos that were worshipped as deities in the ancient Near East (i.e., the sun and moon) are called into existence by the fiat of Israel's God. God has no competitors; he did not need to conquer any other gods in order to stake his claim over the world. This radical monotheism establishes the uniqueness of God and his position over all other realities. As Richard Bauckham has demonstrated, "creator of all things" is an identifying characteristic uniquely ascribed to God in each layer of the biblical material in both Testaments.[16] God's identity as creator is presupposed by all subsequent Jewish and Christian thought.

Identifying God as creator is understood in coordination with identifying God as ruler. In Genesis 1, there is no aspect of creation outside of God's purview. God's governance over creation is first indicated in Genesis 1 by his creative act; since God has the authority to make the cosmos what it is, then it continues to exist under God's authority. Creation "obeys" God's Word as he pronounces and so determines creation's existence.[17] God's rule is also indicated by his prerogative to name the beings under his rule, and the whole cosmos (day, night, sky, sea, earth) is named by God.

Therefore, in Genesis 1, the narrative identity of God as creator and ruler of all things is established. Genesis 1 "encourages us to read forward . . . as it aims toward the fulfillment of the Word that is eternally spoken by the Father 'in the beginning.'"[18] It is the beginning, not merely of chronology, but of

one god to another, drawn unassimilated from an ancient Near Eastern myth. Again, I agree with Clines: "[W]e think it extremely unlikely, in spite of the superficial similarity of these texts, that the use of the plural in Genesis 1:26 is in any way dependent on such mythological descriptions. If the author of Genesis 1 was in every other instance able to remove all trace of polytheism from the traditional material he was handling, as he is generally agreed to have done, why did he not manage to expunge the plural of 'let us'? Did he not realize the contradiction between 'let us' and 'God created?'" (p. 64). It is generally agreed now that the author of Genesis 1 was too careful and deliberate in his work to have missed such an obvious contradiction. As Blocher asserts, "the author is not the kind of man to make a blunder!" (*In the Beginning*, p. 84).

Cf. Middleton, *The Liberating Image*, p. 56. He lists the following texts as those which refer to a heavenly court: Job 1:6; 2:1; 5:1; 15:8; 38:7; Ps. 29:1; 82:1; 89:5-7 (MT 89:6-8); 95:3; 96:4 (= 1 Chron. 16:25); Ps. 97:7; Exod. 15:11; 2 Sam. 5:22-25; 1 Kgs 22.19; Isa. 6:2, 8; Jer. 23:18, 21–22; Ezek. 1; 3:12-13; 10; Dan. 4:17 (MT 4.14). None of these texts necessarily has a direct bearing on the meaning of Gen. 1:26, however.

[16] Richard Bauckham, *God Crucified: Monotheism and Christology in the New Testament* (Grand Rapids, MI: Eerdmans, 1998).

[17] Middleton, *The Liberating Image*, p. 72.

[18] R. R. Reno, *Genesis* (Brazos Theological Commentary on the Bible; Grand Rapids, MI: Brazos, 2010), p. 38.

the identification of the God known through the biblical narratives. A further theological suggestion may be made on the basis of this narrative reading of Genesis 1: God is known along with the particular narratives presented in Scripture. Moreover, human identification of God is tied to time—God is known diachronically through God's relation to the world and action in the world's history.

Reading Genesis 1 as primarily a text about God's identity opens up new possibilities for interpreting the nature of human identity as the *imago Dei* in Gen. 1:26-28. It is to these possibilities that I will now turn.

## III. Human Identity in Genesis 1

Recently, Richard Briggs argued that the image of God should be understood "as a relatively underdetermined place-holder for something that can only be more clearly defined by seeing how the canonical narrative develops, beyond Genesis, and indeed beyond the OT."[19] I will argue along similar lines. Further, I will argue that the image of God is humanity's *identity* within the created order. Humans are permanently identified as the image of God, and realization of this identity occurs diachronically through relationship with God. So, as Gregory of Nyssa asserted, the "[o]ne who is made in the image of God has the task of becoming who he is."[20] In the following paragraphs, this reading is justified through a careful reading of Gen. 1:26-28 and an exploration of one way the meaning of the image of God unfolds canonically. Then, I will conclude with a brief dogmatic reflection demonstrating the benefit of a canonical reading of the image of God in at least one case. Due to space constraints, I must hope the benefits of interpreting the image of God as human identity will suggest themselves on the basis of these examples.

If the above reading of Genesis 1—as a text primarily about God's divine identity and the various identities of God's creatures—is fitting, then further attention to the identity of humanity as God's image is warranted. My argument is based on one formal and three material propositions. First the formal proposition: there exists in Genesis 1 a formal similarity between God's identity and human identity. The implications of this claim will be explored below. The three material propositions are as follows: first, as Briggs recently noted, "the notion of humanity as being in 'the image of God' in Genesis is one that consists in giving humans a significant place in the narrative that follows, not just in

[19] Richard S. Briggs, "Humans in the Image of God and Other Things Genesis Does Not Make Clear," *Journal of Theological Interpretation* 4 (2010): 111–126.
[20] Gregory of Nyssa, *On the Making of Man* (Nicene and Post-Nicene Fathers, Second Series), vol. 5, p. 405.

Genesis but in the whole of the OT (and, for Christians, the NT too)"[21]; second, the claim that humanity is God's image is a claim about humanity's identity within creation that is revealed and realized diachronically in relation to God's identity as God's identity is revealed in history and narrated in Scripture; third, if humanity is God's creature, and God has determined to make humanity in the image of God, then the full revelation of what it means for humanity to be God's image will only be known when humanity has reached its *telos*. This final point has Christological implications that press back into my reading of Genesis 1. At this point, it is important to attend to the text of Gen. 1:26-28 directly.

The text reads as follows:

Then God said, "Let us make humankind in our image, according to our likeness (בְּצַלְמֵנוּ כִּדְמוּתֵנוּ); and let them have dominion over the fish of the sea, and over the birds of the air, and over the cattle, and over all the wild animals of the earth, and over every creeping thing that creeps upon the earth."

So God created humankind in his image,

in the image of God he created them;

male and female he created them.

God blessed them, and God said to them, "Be fruitful and multiply, and fill the earth and subdue it; and have dominion over the fish of the sea and over the birds of the air and over every living thing that moves upon the earth."

There are, of course, a number of interpretive issues encountered in Gen. 1:26-28, and they have received an abundance of attention. Gordon Wenham highlights three issues in particular, all pertaining initially to 1:26: (1) the use of the plural; (2) the meaning of the prepositions בְ and כְ; (3) the meaning of צלם and דמות.[22] The debates surrounding these issues tend to eclipse the larger theological statement that is made in Genesis 1 concerning creation and humanity's place within it. Moreover, in the end, it is not altogether clear what exactly should be concluded about any of these three issues merely on the basis of critical exegesis of Gen. 1:26-28. The meaning of the text is in some measure ambiguous even upon close inspection.

James Barr goes so far as to say that "[t]here is no reason to believe that this writer had in his mind any definite idea about the content or the location of the image of God."[23] If this is even partly true, then the immediate context of Gen. 1:26 should not be expected to provide the needed information for

[21] Briggs, "Humans in the Image of God", p. 122.

[22] Gordon Wenham, *Genesis 1–15* (Word Biblical Commentary 1; Nashville, TN: Thomas Nelson, 1987), pp. 27–29.

[23] James Barr, "The Image of God in the Book of Genesis: A Study of Terminology," *Bulletin of the John Rylands Library* 51 (1968): 11–26 (13).

understanding the meaning of the image of God. Barr came to this conclusion by examining the lexical stock of Hebrew words that could have been chosen by the author or editor of Gen. 1:26 to say that humanity is made in God's image. Barr is hopeful that comparing צלם to other possible word choices will shed light on the choice made by the author. "[I]t is the choice, rather than the word itself, which signifies."[24] Barr argues that צלם is an opaque word, ambivalent in meaning. It is this ambivalence which makes the word suitable. The term indicates the relation between God and humanity but, since the term is ambiguous, it does not come with the conceptual "baggage" that would have been carried by other terms, especially terms used regularly of idols.[25] Barr concludes, "What I suggest is that . . . the choice of *selem* as a major word for the relation between God and man becomes intelligible, even at a stage at which we have still not determined what entity constituted the image of God in man, and even granting the possibility that the P writer himself did not know."[26] Barr argues that דמות limits the meaning of צלם since it indicates "that the sense intended for *selem* must lie within that part of its range which overlaps with the range of *demut*."[27]

When reflecting on the image of God in his Gifford lectures some years later, Barr summarizes his interpretation: "The image of God in humanity is not something that can be *defined*, as if we could point out this or that characteristic which clearly exists and to which the phrase expressly refers."[28] But Barr adds that the image of God might refer the reader to God: "It may thus be possible to say that, though the image of God is attached to the story of the creation of humanity, its primary function and purpose is to say something about God. Its dynamics develop from the need to clarify speech about *him*. Precisely for that reason one cannot necessarily locate the elements in human existence to which it applies."[29]

Barr perhaps succeeded in demonstrating what the author of Genesis 1 was not saying, but he did not offer an explanation of what the author may have meant by the image. Barr's method led to excessive attention to discrete terms rather than attending to the theological use to which these terms were put.

Claus Westermann's study, cited in Barr's Gifford lectures, offers an alternative. Westermann notes the remarkable lack of attention to the whole creation narrative when interpreting Gen. 1:26-30: "As far as I know there has been no attempt to derive the principles for the understanding

---

[24] Ibid., p. 15.
[25] See Ibid., pp. 21–22.
[26] Ibid., p. 22.
[27] Ibid., p. 24.
[28] James Barr, *Biblical Faith and Natural Theology* (Oxford: Clarendon, 1993), p. 169 (emphasis original).
[29] Ibid., p. 170 (emphasis original).

of Gen. 1:26f. from the passage as a whole. It is usually said: the immediate
context says nothing about the meaning of the image and likeness; the text
presumes it and the hearers knew what was meant."[30] The question he puts
to the text is helpful: "What can a narrative mean that wants to tell about
the creation of humanity and which has as its kernel the creation of a
human being in the image of God? What is the purpose of the creator God
when he decides to create a person in his image?" Westermann contrasts
this question with the possibility of asking a question disconnected from
the creation narrative, the narrative context in which the claim about
humanity being made in the image of God is embedded. The mere question of how humanity is described in Gen. 1:26 does not take the creation
narrative seriously enough since "When it is said in the context of prime-
val event that 'God created man. . . . ,' then something is being said about
the beginning of humanity that is not accessible to our understanding."[31]
We have no experience of the beginning that would yield the divine perspective pronounced by Gen. 1:26.

Juxtaposing Westermann's concern with Barr's conclusions yields a helpful insight. While, as Barr concludes, the terms צלם and דמות are somewhat
ambiguous, this does not necessarily imply that the narrative is ambiguous regarding what one ought to think of humanity in light of the fact that
God decided to make an image of himself and that God created humanity
to be that image. To begin with, the image of God provides a context for
understanding the relationship between God and humanity. This is the case
because God's decision to make an earthly image of himself is intimately
related to God's decision to create humanity. The logic flows from God's willing that an image of himself should exist to God's act of creation in bringing
humanity into existence. God was not faced with a pre-existent humanity
that was then determined to be God's image. Nor did God make humankind
and subsequently add his image to it. Rather, to contextualize the language
further, God decided to put an image of himself into the cosmic sanctuary
to serve as God's representative.[32] Therefore, God created humanity as this
image.[33] Because God has determined that humanity be God's image, the
relationship between God and humanity determines the very form of human

---

[30] Claus Westermann, *Genesis 1–11: A Commentary* (trans. John J. Scullion; London: SPCK, 1984), p. 156.
[31] Westermann, *Genesis 1–11*, p. 156.
[32] Middleton, *The Liberating Image*, pp. 81–88.
[33] The fittingness of the existence of an earthly image of God is only known to us after God makes this decision. Nevertheless, the fact that God did make this decision is a sign of its fittingness. Even more important to note is the shape of God's determination that humanity be the image. No particular human attribute has a priori likeness to divinity. Humanity is known to be God's image only insofar as humanity is understood in relation to the divine creator.

existence; this particular creature is what it is because it is identified as God's image by God. "Made in God's image," then, is the identity of humanity.[34]

Since God is revealed in Genesis 1 as the maker and ruler of all things, this has implications for the creature intended to image God. J. Richard Middleton rightly draws attention to the relationship between God's rule and human rule.[35] But for the functional interpretation, the shape of this relationship determines *in toto* the shape of the *imago Dei*.

My suggestion is that the relationship between God's rule and human rule *illustrates* the *imago Dei* and establishes one of its aspects. Gen. 1:26 does not say, "let humanity image me *only* in this . . . let him rule." Rather, "Let us make humankind in our image, according to our likeness; *and* let them have dominion over the fish of the sea, and over the birds of the air, and over the cattle, and over all the wild animals of the earth, and over every creeping thing that creeps upon the earth" (italics mine).[36] The connection between image and ruling is not one of definition.[37] On the contrary, the connection is paradigmatic. The logic of the text seems to be thus: God is creator and ruler of all things; let God's image rule over the earth. Divine self-revelation suggests something about the shape of human existence because humanity is God's image. The text leaves room for fuller understanding of what it means to be God's image *as more about God is revealed*. In Gen 1:26-28 humanity is called to image God by having dominion over the earth precisely because it is God's dominion over the earth that has been made known thus far.[38]

---

[34] Most interpretations of the *imago Dei* start with humanity as the given and inquire about the content of the image. The procedure suggested here is to start with the image as the given and wonder about the being of the human creature identified as God's image. The case for this reading is strengthened by the claim that creation is portrayed in Genesis 1 as a cosmic temple in which the existence of an image of God is appropriate.

[35] Middleton, *The Liberating Image*, pp. 88–90.

[36] Even if one chooses to translate וְיִרְדּוּ "so that they may rule," the text does not say that humanity is made in the image of God *only* for the purpose of ruling. God may have additional purposes in mind.

[37] Humanity is the object of creation in Gen. 1:26-27, and we are told three things about it: (1) Humanity is made in the image of God; (2) Humanity is intended to rule; (3) Humanity is made to be male and female. These descriptive terms are not interchangeable in content. So, the text does not imply: the image of God is to rule; the image of God is male and female; the rulers are the image of God; the rulers are male and female; the male and female are the image of God (together); or the male and female are the rulers. To the question "who is the image of God?" the only answer that can be given is: the human creature. But to the question "what is humanity?" three answers must be given: humanity is the image of God, humanity is the creaturely ruler of the earth, and humanity exists as two sexes.

To what do these various descriptions refer? The *imago Dei* is human identity. Rule is an activity, a consequence of the image. Regarding humanity's sexual differentiation, Gen. 1:27 states, "Male and female he created them." The pronoun אתם refers back to האדם, describing the distinct but complementary ways of existing as a human being. The comment relates specifically to the manner by which humans will be fruitful and multiply in accordance with God's command and blessing in 1:28.

[38] It is important to note that humanity is not invited to share in creating. The creaturely image of God should imitate God's character and actions, but is ontologically distinct from God and is identified fully as a creature.

God, in giving humanity the identity "image of God," leaves humanity with-out a self-directed definition or goal. Humans can only know themselves in light of God as God is for the world. One could even say that God makes dis-ciples out of humanity so that through attending to God's Being-for-the-world humanity will learn what it is to image God in its being-in-the-world.

Therefore, the Genesis narrative establishes that God, as creator of all things, has determined that the human creature be "in his image." In Genesis 1, the implication drawn from this fact is that humanity, male and female, will rule over the non-human creatures on earth. But human identity is also under-determined to the extent that God, the one imaged, is not yet fully revealed in his being creator.[39]

There are several advantages to interpreting the image of God as human identity. First of all, it is doubly fitting in the broader context. This interpreta-tion fits Genesis 1 in that this chapter as a whole is interested in the identity of God as maker of all things and the identity of all created things as crea-tures. The identity interpretation also fits the rest of Genesis (including the continuation of the image of God after the fall), the Old Testament texts that refer to human identity, and the relevant New Testament texts. The reader of Genesis 1 is directed to the rest of the Scriptures to see how it is that human-ity's existence as God's image takes shape and is realized. Second, the identity interpretation provides a coherent alternative to the substantive, relational, and functional interpretations, none of which is fully satisfactory on its own.[40] Yet, the identity interpretation affirms the importance of human ontology and relationality as conditions of possibility for the *imago Dei*. Human rule over the earth is considered one aspect of imaging God. Third, the identity

---

[39] This interpretation of the image of God is dependent upon a particular notion of identity and by a particular doctrine of revelation that need further elaboration. All I can provide here is a list of helpful sources on these points. For identity, see Richard Bauckham, *God Crucified: Monotheism and Christology in the New Testament* (Grand Rapids, MI: Eerdmans, 1998); Hans Frei, *The Identity of Jesus Christ* (Eugene, OR: Wipf and Stock, 1997); Robert W. Jenson, *The Triune Identity: God According to the Gospel* (Minneapolis, MN: Fortress, 1982); Paul Ricoeur, *Oneself as Another* (trans. Kathleen Blamey; Chicago, IL: University of Chicago Press, 1992); Kevin J. Vanhoozer, "Does the Trinity Belong in a Theology of Religions?" in *The Trinity in a Pluralistic Age: Theological Essays on Culture and Religion.* (ed. Kevin J. Vanhoozer; Grand Rapids, MI: Eerdmans, 1997), pp. 41–71. For the doc-trine of revelation, see Gabriel Fackre, *The Doctrine of Revelation: A Narrative Interpretation* (Edinburgh Studies in Constructive Theology; Edinburgh: Edinburgh University Press, 1997); Colin E. Gunton, *A Brief Theology of Revelation* (Edinburgh: T&T Clark, 1995); Ronald Thiemann, *Revelation and Theology: The Gospel as Narrated Promise* (Notre Dame: University of Notre Dame Press, 1985).

[40] For an examination of the exegetical and conceptual problems with substantive, rela-tional, and functional interpretations, see Karl Barth, *Church Dogmatics* III/1, pp. 183–206; Clines, "The Image of God in Man", pp. 56–61; Nathan MacDonald, "The *Imago Dei* and Election: Reading Genesis 1:26-28 and Old Testament Scholarship with Karl Barth," *International Journal of Systematic Theology* 10 (2008): pp. 303–327; Middleton, *The Liberating Image*, pp. 15–29; Westermann, *Genesis 1–11*, pp. 147–158.

interpretation accommodates doctrinal insights from the Christian tradition regarding theological anthropology, but it also provides new possibilities for solving difficult doctrinal puzzles.

In the final two sections of this chapter, therefore, I will present an interpretation of one NT passage to express how interpreting the *imago Dei* as human identity can open up fruitful avenues for interpretation of other canonical texts. Then, I will offer a brief explanation of how interpreting the *imago Dei* as human identity can aid dogmatic reflection by considering one doctrinal problem in particular.

## IV. Canonical Development

Several New Testament texts are relevant to the foregoing discussion, but space constraints must limit this exploration. Therefore, I will provide one example of how interpreting the image of God as human identity aids and is aided by canonical interpretation. I am hopeful that this example will suggest the kind of benefits that can be enjoyed as the *imago Dei* is interpreted as human identity and informed canonically.

The Christian tradition has often turned to 1 John 3:2 to further understand human identity as God's image.[41] There are three reasons why this text is especially appropriate here. First, it refers directly to the realization of human identity—what humanity will be. If the *imago Dei* is human identity, then the realization of human identity will have some relation to the *imago Dei* interpreted canonically, whether or not the term εἰκών is used. Second, 1 John 3:2 indicates that full transformation into the likeness of God will take place when God or Christ is fully revealed to humanity through his presence. This coheres with my suggestion that human identity is dependent upon divine revelation. Third, the ambiguity of 1 John 3:2 regarding the one into whose likeness God's people will be changed, whether the Father or the Son, is instructive about the relation between the Father, the Son, and God's other children.

1 John 3:2 reads as follows:

"Beloved, we are God's children now; what we will be has not yet been revealed. What we do know is this: when he is revealed, we will be like him, for we will see him as he is."

The material shape of 1 John 3:2 is similar to Gen. 1:26-28. The subject of both texts is human identity in relation to God and, specifically, to God's self-revelation. In Genesis 1, the illustration of the relationship between God and

---

[41] For example, see Origen, *De Principiis*, 3:6:1; Augustine, *De Trinitate*, XIV.23.

humanity is demonstrated through dominion. God rules all things; God's earthly image rules the earth. The principal teaching is that the image of God will reflect a likeness to God. In 1 John 3:2, this principle is extended eschatologically. Even now, it is not yet known *what* the fullness of human likeness to God will be, but *that* the Christian's participation in likeness to God will be completed upon the fullness of divine revelation is foundational to Christian hope. In Genesis 1, humanity is tasked to have dominion over the earth because God's dominion over all things had been disclosed. Likewise, in 1 John 3:2, the fullness of human identity will be known when God in Jesus is seen "as he is" since knowledge of human identity is dependent upon divine revelation.[42]

As the children of God are formed by the Spirit into the likeness of Christ, they are *for that reason* formed in the likeness of God. Jesus is the image of God because he is the very Son of God who in relation to the Father is the "exact imprint of God's very being" (Heb. 1:3) who "has made the Father known" (John 1:18). Because of the nature of the relations of the Son to the Father and God's children to the Son, a child of God realizes the image of God insofar as they are conformed to the image of Christ.

1 John 3:2 represents the eschatological hope of the complete realization of the *imago Dei* in God's children, and as such it points toward the perfection of human identity. Genesis 1:26-28 is the initial canonical indication that human identity is tied to God's self-revelation. Conceptually, these are the beginning

---

[42] It is linguistically unclear whether it is Jesus or the Father who will appear and be seen by God's children. In another Johannine text, John 17:25, Jesus prays for his disciples acknowledging that the world does not know the Father but that Jesus himself knows the Father and the disciples have believed that the Father has sent him. In John 17:25, then, Jesus mediates the knowledge of the Father to his disciples (Judith Lieu, *I, II, & III John: A Commentary* [New Testament Library; Louisville: Westminster John Knox, 2008], p. 124n61). Lieu argues that 1 John differs from John 17:25 at this point, since "the transformation that 1 John anticipates may be likeness to God" (Lieu, *I, II, & III John*, p. 125). Stephen Smalley argues that the "αὐτόν" at the end of 1 John 3:1 probably refers to the Father. Nevertheless, he allows that a secondary reference to Jesus may be included. Smalley suggests that the logic of 1 John 3:1; 13 is parallel to Jesus's teaching that the world hates his disciples because the world first hated Jesus (John 15:18-19) (Stephen Smalley, *1, 2, 3 John* [Word Biblical Commentary 51; Waco, TX: Word, 1984], pp. 142–43). While a difference can be discerned between the fact that the world does not know God and the fact that the world hates Jesus, there is a theological link between the world's lack of knowledge and the world's lack of proper loves. In any case, it is probable that the "αὐτόν" in 3:2 has the same referent as "αὐτῷ" in 2:28 since this also is the one who will appear. In 2:28, the author's use of παρουσία suggests that Jesus is in view. Moreover, the fact that Jesus is spoken of in 3:5 as the one who "was revealed" (ἐφανερώθη) further suggests that likeness to Jesus is discussed in 3:2. Taking a clue from 2:23, however, it may very well be the case that the author has no interest in separating likeness to the Father and likeness to the Son. "No one who denies the Son has the Father; everyone who confesses the Son has the Father also." The author binds the Son to the Father and the Father to the Son. So, likeness to the Son implies likeness to the Father as God's people are also included as children of God.

and end points of a theological interpretation of the *imago Dei*. In between these points, there is a line of theological development.

There are formal theological indicators that designate the relevant biblical texts constituting this line. The texts can be identified in one of two ways: (1) the image of God is directly referred to or clearly alluded to; (2) an ethical command is based on and justified by an appeal to God's own character as demonstrated through God's economy. If (1), then further inquiry must be undertaken in order to discern the nature of the reference. If (2), then the rationale is based on the principle of the *imago Dei*—that human identity, and therefore human action, is determined by God's self-revelation.

## V. Dogmatic Implications

As with the previous section, there is only space for one brief example of how the identity interpretation of Genesis 1 informs dogmatic reflection. Because of its volatile relationship with the doctrine of the image of God, the doctrine of sin is a suitable choice.

Is it proper to say that people have the identity "made in God's image" even when they live sinfully? If Scripture suggests that the *imago Dei* is the permanent identity of humanity, then it follows that the entrance of sin does not change this fact. In diverse parts of the biblical canon, Gen. 9:6 and Jas 3:9, ethical directives are based on humanity's identity as God's image and likeness. If the *imago Dei* continues to bear ethical implications after Genesis 3, this is because humanity retains its created status as the creature made in the image and likeness of God.

But how is this so, when humanity practices a sinful form of life? Sin is, indeed, a betrayal of humanity's station, a perversion of humanity's God-given identity and its place in God's properly ordered creation. And yet, humanity's identity as *imago Dei* ensures that humanity continues to represent God on the earth. Humanity continues to bear witness to that which it worships. Vanhoozer argues that "The human creature is called above all to be a witness. It is the vocation of human being to be echoes of God's evocative creative, reconciling and redeeming action."[43] But the identity interpretation suggests that being a witness is not a chosen vocation—it is the assigned vocation of humanity. Humans are witnesses. Therefore, it is not a question of whether humans are or are not witnesses but whether or not humans are witnessing faithfully or unfaithfully, whether in fact humans are true or false witnesses. After the fall, humanity practices a form of life that amounts to a lie about the Creator. The

---

[43] Kevin Vanhoozer, "Human Being, Individual and Social," in *The Cambridge Companion to Christian Doctrine* (ed. Colin Gunton; Cambridge Companions to Religion; Cambridge University Press, 1997), p. 183.

fallen way of life is a false image, the result of idolatries. And since humanity imitates its objects of worship, "those who make [idols] are like them, so are all who trust in them" (Ps. 115:8).[44]

But God intervenes in human history. God judges the false images of himself. And God establishes a truthful image on the earth through his Son. This truthful image of God is Christ and his church. The effect of this determination is that humanity, having had its identity realized in Jesus Christ, will represent God in the world such that creation is made to flourish in "the freedom of the glory of the children of God" (Rom. 8:21).

## VI. Conclusion

Genesis 1 is ultimately interested in aiding the reader to rightly identify God and God's creation. It serves as the narrative entry point into the biblical canon where God's identity is disclosed through God's relationship with his people and human identity is disclosed through humanity's relationship with God. In the end, Jesus Christ is the fullest revelation of both God and humanity. Therefore, by binding divine and human identities to one another, Genesis 1 sets the biblical narratives moving toward their proper end.

---

[44] See G. K. Beale, *We Become What We Worship: A Biblical Theology of Idolatry* (Downers Grove, IL: IVP Academic, 2008), pp. 141–160 for a detailed study of Ps. 115:4-8 in conversation with other relevant texts.

Chapter 3

# Exodus 3

## Michael Allen

Theological commentary seeks to make plain and accessible the breadth and emphases of the biblical text, with special concern to show its canonical and confessional implications. Certain texts are packed densely with doctrinal content. Exodus 3 must rank at the forefront of such a list. In his magisterial commentary, Brevard Childs observed that "the amazing fact is how seminal this one passage continues to be for each generation." Thus, he thought that both biblical and dogmatic theologians must partner together in a quest to glean the truths of this text. To that end, he claimed that "it lies in the nature of dogmatic theology to go beyond the biblical witness and to draw out the critical implications of its testimony for the modern church in the language of its culture. Perhaps the biblical theologian can best serve in this case by attempting to sketch some of the parameters of the two testaments."[1] As an exercise in theological commentary, this chapter seeks to engage exegesis, biblical theology, the history of interpretation, and contemporary dogmatic formulation. These disciplines may be usefully distinguished, though here they will not be separated. Owing to the constraints of space, some areas will be given less attention than others—those interested in the nest of issues related to source criticism and the history of interpretation will have to look elsewhere for satisfaction (even if some of these issues are briefly considered here).[2]

I will examine three major areas of concern: the setting of the text (in Exodus as well as in the biblical canon), the naming of God in the text, and the implications of this revelation. Thus, this chapter focuses especially

---

[1] Brevard S. Childs, *The Book of Exodus: A Critical, Theological Commentary* (Old Testament Library; Louisville, KY: Westminster, 1974), p. 88.

[2] For engagement of source critical issues, see R. W. L. Moberly, *The Old Testament of the Old Testament: Patriarchal Narratives and Mosaic Yahwism* (Overtures to Biblical Theology; Minneapolis: Fortress, 1992), chapter 1. In addition, development of the history of interpretation will be piecemeal and minimal. For such considerations, see my "Exodus 3 after the Hellenization Thesis," *JTI* 3, no. 2 (2009), pp. 179–196. For the history of interpretation in not only Christian, but also Jewish and Muslim traditions, see Paul Vignaux (ed.), *Dieu et l'être: Exégèses d'Exode 3,14 et de Coran 20,11–24* (Paris: Etudes Augustiniennes, 1978); Alain de Libera and Emilie Zum Brunn (eds), *Celui qui est: interpretations juives et chrétiennes d'Exode 3.14* (Paris: Cerf, 1986).

on the material found in vv. 13–15, though it seeks to locate these verses
within its wider settings.[3] There are contextual reasons for focusing on these
verses, inasmuch as the identity of God is most fully revealed here. It is this
revelation that seems to add gravity to Moses' calling and to make sense of
the miracles soon to come Israel's way. Only the presence of the sovereign
creator in her midst can account for the defeat of Pharaoh and the freedom
of the Jews.

# I. The Setting

Understanding the text requires grasping its context. As part of God's Word,
we can and must think of contexts near and far. Exodus 3 resides within a
particular book: the Exodus. This book makes up a sizable chunk of the larger
cadre of texts within the canon known as the Pentateuch or the Law. The Law
is one of three major parts of the Old Testament, and thus an early entry into
the Christian Bible. With this elementary survey in mind, we can quickly see
that context can be multilayered. In doing theological commentary, we are
reading this account within a whole economy of God's revelatory work. For the
sake of brevity, we will focus on two basic contexts, within which Exodus 3 must
be viewed: in Exodus and in the whole Bible.

## I.a. In Exodus

The book of the Exodus portrays the freedom given to the Israelites. The first
chapter recounts the struggles of Israel under the reign of a new Pharaoh: the
workload is increased and the innocents are to be killed. Moses is introduced
in Chapter 2, kept from slaughter by the cunning of his mother and the ironic
generosity of Pharaoh's daughter. There are conflicting realities here in these
first chapters. On the one hand, Israel has flourished: they "were fruitful and
increased greatly; they multiplied and grew exceedingly strong, so that the
land was filled with them" (1:7). In other words, they were fulfilling the man-
date originally given to Adam and reiterated time and again throughout the
Pentateuch (see Gen. 1:26ff. et al). They were multiplying and spreading out
as far as possible. On the other hand, little movement was possible. They were
slaves. Not only that, but they quickly became oppressed slaves, just as soon as
the influence of Joseph in the royal court died out (1:8). With the loss of this
sway, the Israelites were seen as a threat and a curse (1:9), and the Egyptians
began to constrict their freedoms.

---

[3]  For textual argument for the distinctiveness of these verses within the wider account, see
    R. W. L. Moberly, *The Old Testament of the Old Testament*, pp. 17–21.

The entry of Moses into the story suggests a remedy or divine response to the guile and ruthlessness of this new Pharaoh. Just as soon as Hebrew sons are ordered dead, we are told that a son is born. His very name alludes to the fact that he was "drawn out" from the mass killings (2:10). The miraculous birth sets the stage for an Israelite triumph, and Stephen's sermon in Acts 7 accentuates the sense of hope that pervades this early phase of Exodus. He refers to Moses as "beautiful in God's sight" (Acts 7:20) and as "mighty in his words and deeds" (7:22). Yet such optimism is tempered immediately. The boy, Moses, is born, saved from death, and eventually grows up to be a man, yet he kills an Egyptian in defense of an Israelite. He must flee the scene, leaving for Midian and anonymity (Exod. 2:15). By the time he meets the first Midianites, they identify him not as a miraculous survivor of the murder of the Hebrew sons, but as an Egyptian (2:19). When his Midianite wife bears a son, Moses names him Gershon, "for he said, 'I have been a sojourner in a foreign land'" (2:22).[4] Moses—and, through him, the readers of Exodus—are aware that this hero is far from home. It is this story that provides a preface to Exodus 3.

What does Exodus 3 do within the book of Exodus? In this immediate context, its point is to explain the call of Moses to serve as God's ambassador to the Egyptian Pharaoh. Though his birth was miraculous, and his deeds would be mighty, it is only when he encounters God that he becomes useful and effective. Exodus 3:2 offers a superscription: "And the angel of the LORD appeared to him in a flame of fire out of the midst of the bush." Exodus 3–4 recounts a lengthy conversation between the angel (identified as the LORD himself from 3:4 onward) and Moses, when this sojourner is called and commissioned for prophetic service. Not only that, but Moses is given instructions as to his modus operandi. He is to perform miracles, pass along the LORD's demand that Pharaoh free the Hebrews, and persevere through the slow process of a hardened ruler only gradually succumbing to the divine summons (4:21-23). This encounter makes all the difference, for Moses has experienced the presence of God and learned much about the character of God. Indeed, the people of Israel immediately accept Moses as a truth-telling ruler when he returns to their fold (4:31). Previously, the Hebrews doubted Moses' capacity to adjudicate their own internal disputes (2:14; cf. Acts 7:35), but now they seem to encourage his representation of them on the stage of foreign affairs—in Pharaoh's court.

Not only does the call of Moses occur here, but it happens at "Horeb, the mountain of God" (v. 1). Thus, this passage must be viewed as continuous

---

[4] Jon D. Levenson believes the Exodus is really a response to exile, not slavery, inasmuch as it changed the status of Israelites but not of Egypt itself ("Exodus and Liberation," in *The Hebrew Bible, the Old Testament, and Historical Criticism: Jews and Christians in Biblical Studies* (Louisville, KY: Westminster John Knox, 1993), p. 138). In this case, Gershon would be a microcosm for the whole of Israel, though this is not altogether obvious in the text.

with the later events at Horeb (Exod. 19–40). In both Exodus 3–4 and 19–40, the nearness and dwelling of God provides authority: now, to the ministry of Moses; later, to the book of the covenant. There are verbal links as well; in both cases God "calls out" of a bush or a mountain (3:4; 19:3). The main character of Exodus 3, then, is actually the LORD. At every point, the wherewithal of Moses is minimized: he doubts, he makes excuses, he eventually needs a spokesperson to articulate his own thoughts and words (cf. the commissioning of Aaron in 4:14-16). As Childs comments, "grounds for his being sent do not rest on Moses' ability, but on his being a vehicle for God's plan."[5] It must be clarified, though, that the notable factor here is that talent or ability or even exceptional character is not required to be a vehicle for God's plan. Moses is remarkably underwhelming.[6] Yet God promises: "I will be with your mouth and with his mouth and will teach you both what to do" (4:15). So this chapter speaks of God's commitment to reveal, to commission, to redeem the Israelites from captivity.

## I.b. In the canon

The burning bush incident recurs throughout the canon. In other words, it proves to be a crucial segment of Scripture, as evident by later references and allusions to its terminology and, more pervasively though less explicitly, by its formative influence upon the thought-forms of other biblical texts. As mentioned earlier, Stephen's sermon in Acts 7 shows that this was a turning point in the Moses narrative: "This Moses, whom they rejected, saying, 'Who made you a ruler and a judge?'—this man God sent as both ruler and redeemer by the hand of the angel who appeared to him in the bush" (Acts 7:35). Note that Stephen sees the burning bush encounter as the means by which Moses is transformed from joke to judge, from ruthless to redemptive. Stephen clearly articulates the historical and narrative function of the text as part of the broader history of God's redemption of Israel.

How does Exodus 3 function within the wider canon? "At different levels and in various ways" must be our first reply. Whereas the immediate focus of Exodus 3–4 is upon the call and authority of Moses as spokesperson for Israel (and texts like Acts 7 pick up on this), the text's wider resonance involves

---

[5] Childs, *The Book of Exodus*, p. 74.
[6] Moses raises four objections or questions to his calling by God. Whether or not these are legitimate questions, signs of unbelief or improper fear, or some combination thereof, is not very clear. We do know that Moses had an appropriate fear of God at the inception of the encounter (3:6), though it is evident that by the conclusion of the narrative he has taxed God's patience (4:14). Whether or not Moses sins in questioning, he surely proves unexceptional and unremarkable. While he also says "Here I am" when addressed by God (3:4), he fails to show the immediate courage and commitment displayed by Isaiah (Isa. 6:1-8) and Joshua (Josh. 1) in their commissioning accounts.

concern for speech about God. That is, the way in which its immediate concern occurs sheds light on a greater issue—deep knowledge of God's character. Israel needs a spokesperson and a savior. Moses was introduced on the scene earlier, yet it is only when he gains profound knowledge of the name of the LORD that things begin to move forward.

Huldrych Zwingli took the whole of Isaiah 40 to be commentary upon the divine name found in Exod. 3:14-15. Isa. 40, and the whole of Isa. 40–48, offers vivid description of God's transcendence and sovereign rule over the nations. Because he rules over and above all nations, God can employ various political powers for his purposes and then judge them for their sins. At every point, however, God's transcendent rule is linked to the course of human history and tangible experience. While God is not to be identified with history or anything therein (*a la* G. F. W. Hegel's *Geist*), God governs and guides history to his purposes. As has been shown by a number of biblical scholars, there are numerous lexical allusions to the exodus in Isaiah, where the deliverance of Israel is construed as an anticipated "new exodus."[7] Even more telling are thematic parallels that clearly exist: in both texts, the message is that God reigns over all threats, so God's people must trust him to provide.[8] The character of God instills the confidence of salvation to come and the credence of God's prophet (see repeated reference to YHWH in Isa. 45:14, 21–24).

Revelation 1:8 alludes also to the revelation of the name YHWH. The Apocalypse of Jesus Christ given to John first identifies God: "'I am the Alpha and the Omega,' says the Lord God, 'who is and who was and who is to come, the Almighty.'" The emphasis here is on the constancy and everlastingness of this God, signaled by comparing him to the first and last letters of the Greek alphabet. Indeed, at every point in history, he is "the Almighty," the "Lord God." Commentators throughout the centuries have observed consistently that this seems to restate the name from Exodus: "I AM who I AM" (3:14).[9] Not only are there lexical ties between Rev. 1:8 and the LXX rendering of Exod. 3:14, but both texts show a concern to emphasize that God does not change.[10] Taken with the intertextuality evident in Isaiah's use of Exodus, we see that

---

[7] Brevard S. Childs, *Isaiah: A Commentary* (Old Testament Library; Louisville, KY: Westminster John Knox, 2000), pp. 110–111; as well as a host of studies on the intertextual use of the Exodus imagery in Isaiah and then in the NT: Joel Marcus, *The Way of the Lord: Christological Exegesis of the Old Testament in the Gospel of Mark* (Studies of the New Testament and Its World; Edinburgh: T & T Clark, 1992), Chapter 2; Rikki E. Watts, *Isaiah's New Exodus in Mark* (Wissenschaftliche Untersuchungen zum Neuen Testament 2:88; Tübingen: Mohr-Siebeck, 1997); David W. Pao, *Acts and the Isaianic New Exodus* (Wissenschaftliche Untersuchungen zum Neuen Testament 2:130; Tübingen: Mohr-Siebeck, 2002).

[8] Indeed, Levenson argues that the first message of the Exodus is "a story of the enthronement of YHWH and the glad acceptance of his endless reign by his redeemed, the whole House of Israel" ("Exodus and Liberation," p. 142).

[9] For a classic instance, see Philo's comments in his *Vita Mos*, I.75.

[10] Childs argues that Rev. 1:8 moves as a natural development from Exod. 3 and Isa. 44:6 (*The Book of Exodus, p. 83*).

the God who provided for the patriarchs can supply the needs of enslaved Israelites a half millennium later, and the God who raised Jesus from the dead can ensure the future of his disciples struggling after his ascension.

Here we have an instance of background moving to foreground at the canonical and synthetic level. This means that we need to observe the distinction between exegesis and systematic theology, even as we maintain their organic unity. The immediate narrative focus of Exodus 3 is the call of Moses and its role in the redemption of Israel. The way this happens—the manner in which Moses is shown something new and powerful and by which his reputation is transformed from presumptive judge to authentic ruler—reveals great truths of God's character, and this proves to have enduring doctrinal implications. By seeing how Moses is called, we see much of the one who calls him.[11] Here we see a remarkable example of how revelation accomplishes things: growth in theological maturity seems to have a noticeable impact upon the character and comportment of Moses.

Intertextuality may run the other way also. The Jewish rabbi Rashi noted the similarity between Genesis 1:1-2 and Exodus 12:1-2.[12] He said that the latter was the real inception of what we call the Old Testament: the birth of Israel. While his focus on Exod. 12:2 may be a bit too narrow (though it is not without lexical links to Gen. 1:1-2), there are important conceptual ties to be seen between Exodus and Genesis. Genesis provides the wider angle lens to the focused concentration found in the rest of the Old Testament; whereas Genesis (especially chs 1–11) considers God's gracious gift of the whole world, this is but background to the later consideration of God's election of Israel. If Genesis 1:1 accentuates the transcendence of God over creation, forming and making it, then Exodus 3 functions within this later section to remind us of God's transcendence.

We can view this pictorially:

| God of the World | God of Israel |
| --- | --- |
| Genesis 1 | Exodus 3 |
| God creates and, thus, precedes creation. | God transcends both Israel and Egypt and, indeed, the whole world. |
| God dwells in creation, especially in Eden. | God identified in history, especially the history of Israel. |

[11] It would be well worth making a comparison between this call of Moses and the experience of Saul on the Damascus Road, inasmuch as both callings seem to involve new knowledge of God's identity and character. For helpful analysis of the latter event, see Seyoon Kim, *The Origin of Paul's Gospel* (Wissentschaftliche Untersuchungen zum Neuen Testament 2:4; Tübingen: Mohr Siebeck, 1984). In an excursus, Kim notes the antithetical link between the Damascus Road and the Sinai theophany (Exodus 19ff.), leaving examination of the earlier events at Horeb still to be considered.
[12] M. Rosenbaum and A. M. Silbermann (eds), *The Pentateuch with the Commentary of Rashi: Genesis* (Jerusalem: Silbermann, 1972), p. 2.

Both Genesis 1 and Exodus 3 reveal much about God, even as the narratives focus on others (creation *writ large* or Moses, respectively).[13] More pointedly, both reveal that God is other than and exceeds creation, even as God dwells within and can be known amid creation. To understand these two emphases, we must focus on the divine naming found in Exod. 3:13-15.

## II. The Naming

While the call of Moses is the immediate contextual point of Exodus 3, the naming of God is its wider doctrinal focus. This new knowledge tips the scales narratively, such that a story gone wrong is sharply reversed from this point onward. Because later canonical occurrences fix upon this aspect of Exodus 3, we have biblical reasons for focusing our commentary here as well.

> 13 Then Moses said to God, "If I come to the people of Israel and say to them, 'The God of your fathers has sent me to you,' and they ask me, 'What is his name?' what shall I say to them?" 14 God said to Moses, "I am who I am." And he said, "Say this to the people of Israel, 'I am has sent me to you.'" 15 God also said to Moses, "Say this to the people of Israel, 'The Lord, the God of your fathers, the God of Abraham, the God of Isaac, and the God of Jacob, has sent me to you.' This is my name forever, and thus I am to be remembered throughout all generations." (ESV).

Before investigating the naming, we must reflect on the question being asked. As mentioned earlier, Moses offers four questions in response to God's commission. The second question—"If I come to the people of Israel and say to them, 'The God of your fathers has sent me to you,' and they ask me, 'What is his name?' what shall I say to them?"—arises in v. 13. It is not obvious what Moses envisions here, and it seems that the Israelites never ask anything quite like this when he returns to them. What lies behind this question? Most likely, Moses is not asking for a new name. If so, and if he passed this new name along to the Israelites, how would they verify its rightful application to their God? More likely, Moses is asking about the meaning and significance of God's name or identity: what has God revealed to him that inspires such confidence in him amid this dreadful circumstance of slavery?[14] What has Moses learned

---

[13] For further reflection on debates regarding the theological link between Genesis and Exodus, how Genesis is the "Old Testament of the Old Testament," see R. W. L. Moberly, "On Reading Genesis 12–50," in *The Theology of the Book of Genesis* (Old Testament Theology; Cambridge: Cambridge University Press, 2009), pp. 121–140.

[14] The commentary offered by Exod. 6:2-9 upon the giving of the name in Exod. 3:13-15 suggests this, as God expounds the meaning of the name YHWH as his promised presence and their imminent deliverance, which ought to be trusted based on his prior faithfulness

of God that instills a new boldness and confidence, even leading him to return from the wilderness to the land of Egypt? Moses asks for a name—he seeks a character or an identity—ultimately, he wants reasons for hope of success.

We will consider the naming in two parts: the name of mystery and the name of mercy.

## II.a. The name of mystery

"I AM WHO I AM" (v. 14). Few statements have provided grist for the mill quite like this enigmatic name. First, we must note the translational difficulty. It might be rendered in past, present, or future tense: "I have been whom I have been," "I am who I am," or "I will be whom I will be." Exegetes have made much hay over the varying shades of meaning implicit in one or more of these renderings. Nonetheless, the basic import of the text is the same in any case, for all three translations maintain the self-referential nature of the name. Because of this self-referentiality, it makes sense to abbreviate the name (as is frequent in the Bible) to "I AM". That is the key: strictly speaking, God can only be understood by reference to God. Perhaps it is best to compare this situation to that of other beings. An interested observer could come to identify me by making comparisons and contrasts with other beings, be they human or animal. Look at a crowd, point out differences in various ways, and eventually you can identify me in that crowd. I am taller than some, shorter than others, and so on. Identification works by way of comparing those within a given species or group.

Yet Exodus 3:14 jolts us by saying that God is not grouped with others. God can only be known by comparison to himself. The name seems tautologous at first glance. It humbles the reader. Martin Noth even took Exodus 3:14 to be a delay of real naming.[15]

We must note, however, that this is a name given. The enigmatic is not altogether impenetrable. We must honor the *revealed* importance of the elusive.[16] I have elsewhere offered a historical analysis of Augustine's exegesis of this passage, and a few remarks made by the great Bishop of Hippo prove instructive at just this point.[17] Augustine notes various ways of explaining "I am who I am": "I

to their ancestors (6:3ff.). On the relationship of Exodus 3 and 6, see Moberly, *The Old Testament of the Old Testament*, pp. 5–35; Christopher R. Seitz, "The Call of Moses and the 'Revelation' of the Divine Name," in *Word Without End: The Old Testament as Abiding Theological Witness* (Grand Rapids, MI: Eerdmans, 1998), pp. 229–247.

[15] *Exodus: A Commentary* (Old Testament Library; trans. J. S. Bowden; Philadelphia, PA: Westminster, 1962), pp. 44–45.

[16] See the helpful reply to Noth by Dennis J. McCarthy, "Exod. 3:14: History, Philosophy, and Theology," *Catholic Biblical Quarterly* 40 (1978), pp. 311–322.

[17] The following material is drawn from Allen, "Exodus 3 after the Hellenization Thesis," pp. 179–196.

am eternal" or the one "who cannot change."[18] Augustine does not find this to provide information about God so much as to limit knowledge of God: "This is no creature—not sky, not earth, not angel, not power, not thrones, not dominions, not authorities." God's naming of himself provides an epistemic check on human efforts to know God—God is not an item in the universe (sky, earth, angel, etc.). Moses "believes this meant a lot for men" in that it showed our limitations. Again, images of distance and limitation are mentioned: "vast difference between this and men," "slightest ray of light," "how far, far below he is," "how far, far removed," and "ever so unlike it he is." Moses is driven to understand "that he was far, far from being equal to what was said to him, not to what he was shown, and practically incapable of attaining it on his own."[19] Our limits, however, are not naturally apparent but are revealed to us by God himself.

## II.b. The name of mercy

In the next verse, a second name is given: "THE LORD, the God of your fathers, the God of Abraham, the God of Isaac, and the God of Jacob, has sent me to you" (v. 15). God is identified within particular narratives, the stories of the Israelites and their God. Robert Jenson has heralded this emphasis: "Asked who God is, Israel's answer is, 'Whoever rescued us from Egypt.' Asked about her access to this God, Israel's answer is, 'We are permitted to call on him by name.' "[20] Of course, this is to skip ahead several steps, for God has not yet redeemed Israel. A broader point is pertinent, though, and deserves emphasis: God here says that he may be identified by giving attention to the stories of Israel. He specifically refers to the patriarchal narratives, but one can rightly infer Jenson's point as a logical and narratival corollary (the impending action of redeeming Israel also identifies God—eventually, the resurrection of Jesus fulfills a similar function).

The crucial issue is how the two names are to be related. Does the name of mystery minimize the import of the name of mercy? Conversely, does the name of mercy render the mystery null and void? Here exegesis and dogmatics converge.

First, we must see that they are distinct names. Some would demur. As Donald Gowan argues:

I see Ex. 3:14-16 to be the same kind of etymologizing wordplay. The name of the God of Israel was Yahweh. It had no definition, as the names of other

[18] Augustine, *Sermons*, Volume 1: *On the Old Testament* (The Works of Saint Augustine; ed. Edmund Hill; New York: New City, 1990), 7:7.
[19] Ibid., 7.7.
[20] Robert W. Jenson, *Systematic Theology*, Volume 1: *The Triune God* (New York: Oxford University Press, 1997), p. 44.

gods did . . . a way of expressing the freedom of the subject, in order to emphasize the human inability to know God's "being." What Israel could know about God follows immediately in verses 16b–22.[21]

Yet this is reductionistic, failing to see the repetition of verse 15 in verse 16b. Both speak of the historical availability of this YHWH, a point remarkably different from the initial naming of verse 14. As Augustine puts it, the two names can be distinguished by a contrast between "[t]hat name in himself, this one for us."[22] The first points to the fact that our knowledge will be limited, while the second offers a promise of adequate (if not perfect) naming.

Second, we must see that the second name comforts where the first name has challenged and perplexed. Just as law drives one to look for Gospel, so the name of mystery propels one to seek a name of mercy: in both cases, God provides. We do not comprehend God, but we do apprehend him in this redemptive history recorded in these biblical texts. So the two names exemplify a rhetorical and spiritual dynamic not to be missed: awe at God's vastness and transcendence, matched by assurance of God's nearness.

The exegetical task (and that of biblical dogmatics) is to affirm all that the canonical writings pressure us to affirm, even when our logical intuitions suggest that they may be contradictory. Here we must find ways to honor the integrity of both divine names. We thus honor revelation and locate mystery at the appropriate place in theological pursuit.

# III. The Implications

When the bush burnt, light was shed on many facets of biblical truth. While focusing on the doctrine of God, this concluding section ought to point at least to other areas of doctrinal concern that are elucidated or complexified by Exodus 3.

## III.a. Divine transcendence

The first divine name points to the otherness of God. Strictly speaking, God is simply himself. He is not a conflation or collection of parts. He is singular. He is simple. Theologians from Augustine to Thomas have argued that Exod. 3:14 teaches the simplicity of God, that is, the oneness and unity of God; for example, Thomas says that "Moses after then was more fully taught about the

---

[21] Gowan, *Theology in Exodus*, p. 85.
[22] Augustine, *Sermons*, 7:7; cf. F. Bourassa, "Theologie trinitaire chez saint Augustin," *Gregorianum* 58 (1977), pp. 675–725.

simplicity of the divine essence when he was told, *I am who I am.*"[23] Simplicity is contrasted with complexity here. It bears saying that God's simplicity is what makes human knowledge of God very complex. Humans are complex beings, made up of constituent parts from arms and legs to minds and spirits. We experience all of life amid complex beings and things, whether automobiles or corporations, that can be parceled out and pieced together again. We, therefore, have no comparison that fits God's being perfectly, because all our categories of thought are complex and finite. This is the point made by the first naming: God cannot be identified with anything else, however much he might identify himself amid the events of world history.

Is this metaphysical teaching? Étienne Gilson claimed: "Of course we do not maintain that the text of Exodus is a revealed metaphysical definition of God; but if there is no metaphysic *in* Exodus there is nevertheless a metaphysic *of* Exodus."[24] We do well to follow Matthew Levering in observing that metaphysics is not thought about abstract things; rather, metaphysics is abstract thought about very concrete things.[25] In this case, Exod. 3:14 identifies a particular character (YHWH) as a unique being in a class all by himself (sui generis). As Augustine says in *De Trinitate*, Exodus 3:14 makes God "difficult to contemplate."[26]

We can usefully link the doctrine of divine simplicity with the biblical nature of divine transcendence. Kathryn Tanner has served us well by clarifying the analytical difference between "quantitative" and "qualitative" forms of divine transcendence.[27] Whereas "quantitative" approaches assume a univocal relation between God's attributes and ours (with the difference being that God simply exemplifies them *more*), "qualitative" transcendence actually involves God's existence outside the very categories of creaturely life. God is not simply more loving in the same way that we are, or more good in the same manner that our friends are. Rather, God is good and loving in the way that God is; *he* is who *he* is. He exists on a wholly different plane of being— not a higher plane or a more fully realized plane, but a wholly distinct plane of being.

---

[23] Thomas, *Summa Theologiae*, 2a2ae.174:6, reply. A Christian version of divine simplicity was not only a Western fixation; it was also achieved in the theological work of the Cappadocian fathers, according to Andrew Radde-Gallwitz, *Basil of Caesarea, Gregory of Nyssa, and the Transformation of Divine Simplicity* (Oxford Early Christian Studies; Oxford: Oxford University Press, 2009).

[24] Étienne Gilson, *The Spirit of Medieval Philosophy* (New York: Charles Scribner's Sons, 1940), 433.

[25] Matthew Levering, *Scripture and Metaphysics: Aquinas and the Renewal of Trinitarian Theology* (Challenges in Contemporary Theology; Oxford: Blackwell, 2003).

[26] Augustine, *De Trinitate*, I:3.

[27] Kathryn Tanner, *God and Creation in Christian Theology: Tyranny or Empowerment?* (repr.; Minneapolis, MN: Fortress, 2004), chapters 2–3; cf. idem, *Jesus, Humanity, and the Trinity: A Brief Systematic Theology* (Minneapolis, MN: Fortress, 2001), pp. 1–14.

### III.b. Divine presence

The second divine name suggests the immanent presence of God in this world, more particularly, in the covenantal history of Israel.

According to Franz Rosenzweig, "all those who find here notions of 'being,' of 'the-one-who-is,' of 'the eternal,' are all Platonizing . . . God calls himself not 'the-one-who-is' but 'the one-who-is-there,' that is, there for you, there for you at this place, present to you, with you or rather coming toward you, toward you to help you."[28] Rosenzweig falsely construes transcendence and immanence as a zero-sum game, whereas the two namings here in Exodus 3 suggest that God's transcendence is what allows for his immanence. Indeed, the God who is thoroughly different from us is, nonetheless, "nearer to us than we are to ourselves."[29] As noted above, the canon pressures us to affirm both transcendence and presence; biblical exegesis and dogmatics will honor the breadth and coherence of the full canonical portrait even if it cannot fully explain how this is metaphysically compatible.

Again, Kathryn Tanner provides help: "What makes God different from creatures is also what enables God to be with what is not God rather than shut up in self-enclosed isolation . . . Immanence and transcendence, closeness and difference, are simply not at odds in God's relations with us."[30] Eventually, we will learn that a person is both divine and human: Jesus can have two natures, because the two natures are ontologically different or distinct. His divinity and transcendent glory is highlighted time and again by his identification with the divine name given in Exod. 3:14 (see Phil. 2:5-11; Heb. 1:1-4; the various "I AM" sayings of John's Gospel).[31] A noncompetitive relationship between the divine/transcendent and the human/immanent is essential as an ontological framework if the incarnation is to make any sense whatsoever.[32] Maintaining the truthfulness of both divine transcendence and presence allows us to maintain the full mystery of what the Bible pressures us to confess of God's economy

---

[28] Franz Rosenzweig, "A Letter to Martin Goldner," in Martin Buber and Franz Rosenzweig, *Scripture and Translation* (trans. Lawrence Rosenwald with Everett Fox; Bloomington, IN: Indiana University Press, 1994), p. 191.

[29] Karl Barth, *Church Dogmatics* II/1: *The Doctrine of God* (eds, T. F. Torrance and G. W. Bromiley; Edinburgh: T & T Clark, 1957), p. 314.

[30] Tanner, *Jesus, Humanity, and the Trinity*, pp. 12, 13.

[31] David S. Yeago, "The New Testament and the Nicene Dogma: A Contribution to the Recovery of Theological Exegesis," *Pro Ecclesia* 3 (1994), pp. 152–164; C. Kavin Rowe, "Romans 10:13. What is the Name of the Lord?," *Horizons in Biblical Theology* 22, no. 2 (2000), pp. 135–173; C. Kavin Rowe, "Biblical Pressure and Trinitarian Hermeneutics," *Pro Ecclesia* 11 (2002), pp. 295–312; Richard Bauckham, *God Crucified: Monotheism and Christology in the New Testament* (Grand Rapids: Eerdmans, 1998); Christopher R. Seitz, "Handing Over the Name: Christian Reflection on the Divine Name YHWH," in *Figured Out: Typology and Providence in Christian Scripture* (Louisville: Westminster John Knox, 2001), pp. 131–144.

[32] I have developed this argument in *The Christ's Faith: A Dogmatic Account* [T&T Clark Studies in Systematic Theology; London: T&T Clark, 2009], Chapter 4.

of salvation; it does not explain away the mystery, but it locates it properly. Unfortunately, many theologians in the modern period have domesticated the transcendence of God, rendering it less than qualitative and, thus, causing systematic problems in various doctrinal *loci* by jettisoning one of the names revealed here.[33]

## III.c. Mediation

Because the holy God is known amid the life of Israel, the creaturely realm is shown to have integrity and value. While God is different from creation and cannot be reduced to what is visible in the life of the covenant, covenant and creation do really witness to God's being. Exodus 3 manifests this mediation in two ways.

## III.d. Language: naming God

Karl Barth wisely affirmed that "as ministers we ought to speak of God. We are human, however, and so cannot speak of God. We ought therefore to recognize both our obligation and our inability and by that very recognition give God the glory."[34] Here we see that God continues to allow humans to name him, to address him, to pick him out of the heavenly crowd. Indeed, God responds to such prayer, as Exod. 2:23-25 makes very plain. "God heard their groaning," to be sure, but, more importantly, this led to deeper action: "God remembered his covenant with Abraham, with Isaac, and with Jacob." Then "God saw the people of Israel" and, therefore, "God knew." Because the language of prayer and divine address is valid and has real integrity, humans can summon God's engagement.

We need not engage in exegetical flights of fancy regarding where God might have been prior to this hearing and seeing Israel's groaning. For example, Donald Gowan thinks that Exodus 1–2 exemplify "the absence of God" (as does the book of Job).[35] Quite apart from the earlier mention of God's actions in blessing the faithful and daring Hebrew midwives (Exod. 1:20-21), the emphasis of these two chapters is clearly not on God's absence so much as the reality of Israel's plight in all its raw texture. Only after the reader sees the

[33] William C. Placher, *The Domestication of Transcendence: How Modern Thinking about God Went Wrong* (Louisville, KY: Westminster John Knox, 1996). Not all of Placher's historical work was equally shrewd (for example, chapter 9 is less than satisfactory), yet his overarching narrative is cogent, persuasive, and important.

[34] Karl Barth, "The Word of God and the Task of the Ministry," in *The Word of God and the Word of Man* (trans. Douglas Horton; London: Hodder and Stoughton, 1928), p. 186.

[35] Gowan, *Theology in Exodus*, pp. 1–24.

plight and the mire of slavery does groaning ensue and, then, God hears and
sees and knows. The point does not seem to be that God was absent or disinterested, but, rather, that human words have great importance in the divine
economy, whether they be prayerful groanings or prophetic witness.

So, as Christopher Seitz reminds us, "*[W]hat is at stake is whether we are entitled
to call God anything at all.* The proper question is whether we have any language that God will recognize as his own, such that he will know himself to be
called upon, and no other, and within his own counsel then be in a position
to respond, or to turn a deaf ear."[36] God does hand over a name, as Seitz says,
and so we can speak of and to God. Scholastic theologians employed a distinction between comprehensive and apprehensive knowledge of God, as well as a
distinction between *archetypal* and *ectypal* theology, to honor the nature of this
speech about God. We know God as finite humans can know an infinite and
transcendent LORD. While adequate and even good, such knowledge and talk
is neither divine nor perfect. Even when glorified, we shall still see the glory of
the LORD with creaturely, limited eyes. Yet we shall see, and we will praise. God
honors such language—so should we.

## III.e. Creaturely objects: the burning bush

If God's identification with a name is jarring, then God's appearance amid a
burning bush is downright scandalous. God is not only evident in the stories of
Israel, he is also dwelling in a particular plant at one point in time.

That words and objects can be employed for God's own purposes shows that
creation is not inherently flawed or unfit for God's presence. Of course, the
book of Exodus will later make much of the particular circumstances in which
God can dwell somewhere, namely, the Tabernacle. Yet our consideration of
such details must not trump the astonishing affirmation that nature can be
used for supernatural purposes. We may not have perfect linguistic capacity
for comprehensively defining God or concrete presences of God in every place
and time, but God does promise to be with us, to give us everything that we
need.[37]

Throughout the centuries that followed, Jews and Christians found themselves identified by that burning bush. Many Jews later interpreted their people
as burned yet not consumed, and eventually Protestants would see the church
as constantly suffering yet promised victory over the gates of hell.[38] In many

---

[36] Christopher R. Seitz, in *Word Without End*, p. 252 (emphasis in original).

[37] Stanley Hauerwas and Samuel Wells, "The Gift of the Church and the Gifts God Gives
It," in *The Blackwell Companion to Christian Ethics* (Blackwell Companions to Religion; eds,
Stanley Hauerwas and Samuel Wells; Oxford: Blackwell, 2004), pp. 13–27

[38] Liberation theologians have gone even further, identifying the bush with the marginalized, oppressed, and poor. Against such links, Jon D. Levenson has shown how the book of

ways, of course, this is to load the burning bush with meaning that it does not carry in its original context. Exodus 3 does not suggest that the burning of this plant is a bad or painful thing, rather it highlights the vivid and surprising nature of a burning bush that is still standing resolute. The symbol does not hint immediately at fortitude amid suffering (though that is surely a biblical emphasis) but about God's presence in the midst of creaturely life and human history. The bush must be interpreted by the naming: God can be named as the one involved with the patriarchs, and now as the God of enslaved Israel.

God comes near and works amid the physical. There are dangers in rewriting history and projecting oneself backward: as if this story is really about the presence of God with the poor. But there is reason to make good and reasonable inferences, bringing "the past, the story of Israel, to bear upon the present," as Jon Levenson says.[39] Eventually, this has implications for Christology, bibliology, and sacramentology. In every case, there is an identification of something creaturely with the presence of God. These creaturely objects are not themselves divine (even in Christ: while there is an hypostatic or personal union of the creaturely with the divine, nonetheless, the human nature does not itself become divine).[40] A salvation wrought "before the foundation of the world" (Eph. 1:4) unfolds by means of nails and blood and is passed along by water and wine as well as the feeble testimony of the saints through the ages. While gracious, the gospel involves the frame and fulfillment of nature.

## III.f. Holiness

Finally, we cannot comment on Exodus 3 and covenantal mediation without noting the theme of holiness. Moses is called to a particular bush to hear God's speech. There is a division of common and sacred, then, even in the setting. This distinction is clearly highlighted by God's warning: "Do not come near; take your sandals off your feet, for the place on which you are standing is holy ground" (v. 5).[41]

Holiness jolts Moses out of any sense of familiarity, and it does away with whatever privilege seems to flow from simple pedigree. When this fiery God reveals himself to Moses "I am the God of your father, the God of Abraham, the God of Isaac, and the God of Jacob" (v. 6), Moses does not reply with a

---

Exodus specifically deals with the liberation of a people promised blessing in covenantal form by their own God ("Exodus and Liberation," pp. 127–159.

[39] Ibid., pp. 156–157.

[40] John Owen exemplifies such an approach, as is well described by Alan Spence, *Incarnation and Inspiration: John Owen and the Coherence of Christology* (London: T & T Clark, 2007) and Kelly M. Kapic, *Communion with God: The Divine and the Human in the Theology of John Owen* (Grand Rapids, MI: Baker Academic, 2007).

[41] R. W. L. Moberly argues that holiness was not a category of patriarchal religion, and it was first introduced here in Exodus 3 (*The Theology of the Book of Genesis*, pp. 135–137).

relaxed or familiar tone. Instead, we are told that he "hid his face, for he was afraid to look at God" (v. 6). Reverence and awe are required from those who would encounter the living God of Israel. The Puritan John Owen, articulated what many have found here: "as Moses was then commanded to put off his shoes, the place whereon he stood being holy ground, so it will be the wisdom of him that writes, and of them that read, to divest themselves of all carnal affections and imaginations, that they may draw nigh unto this great object of faith with due reverence and fear."[42]

Thus, finally, Exodus 3 teaches about the special nature of God's presence—holiness and, as Leviticus will clarify soon, cleanness—and so we must conclude with words about worship. Indeed, Exodus 3 moves from knowledge of God to concern for Israel's welfare to preparations for worship, as the whole book of Exodus makes these very moves.[43] God reveals himself as transcendent and yet immanently present with Israel; thus, they can trust in his deliverance brought about through the ministry of Moses. Because they will be redeemed from bondage and brought back into the land from their exile, they will be able to serve the LORD rather than Pharaoh. Freedom and revelation lead to worship of the one true God (Exod. 3:12, 18; 4:31). The presence of the divine in the midst of history brings salvation, to be sure, but it also puts the redeemed in a position of awe and gives them a reverence for the holy.

---

[42] John Owen, "Christologia: Or a Declaration of the Glorious Mystery of the Person of Christ," in *Works of John Owen*, volume 1: *The Glory of Christ* (Edinburgh: The Banner of Truth Trust, 1965), p. 181.
[43] See the threefold structure argued by Levenson, "Exodus and Liberation," pp. 142–144.

# Chapter 4

# Psalm 22: Forsakenness and the God Who Sings

Kelly M. Kapic

## I. Introduction

"My God, my God, why have you forsaken me?" The opening words of Psalm 22 launch the worshiper into a painful tension, a tension that is as technically difficult as it is emotionally exhausting. But to choose between the emotions and the theology of this psalm is to miss both. A Christian handling of this psalm requires a canonical reading that examines the paradoxes of anguish and hope, promise and struggle, doubt and confidence. These paradoxes, it turns out, are the tensions of faith, and the wonder of God is that he solves these paradoxes by entering them—but we will need to wait until later in the chapter to explore that point.

First, we will briefly survey the basic movement and structure of the psalm, and observe some of the tensions contained therein. Second, we turn our attention to the historic debate about whom the psalm ultimately describes: David, Jesus, or us? This debate helps inform appropriate accommodation of the psalm for the church in our day. Third, we explore Jesus' relationship to this lament.

By hearing the cry, hope, and promise of the psalm and by watching the movement from the psalmist to Jesus to us, we internalize God's song and worship even as we follow the lead worshiper who remained faithful even amid the greatest divine silence and human violence. This psalm takes us to the heart of the gospel, not merely because it foretold future events, but because it tells us about the God who came in Jesus Christ, facing sin and death in order to bring the promise of life.

## II. The Movement of the Psalm

Three foundational points of theology come crashing together in Psalm 22: (1) the goodness of God's creation and covenant, (2) the anguish of a broken world filled with idolatry and violence, and (3) the struggle to lean on God's faithfulness amid the chaos. The psalmist struggles to display these factors realistically, not in terms of theological truisms, but as a song, a poem, a lament, and a praise.

Psalm 22[1] manifests the following general form and movement:

vv. 1–2: Sense of Forsakenness

vv. 3–5: The Holy God has been Trusted for Deliverance in the Past

vv. 6–8: Mockery about God's Absence Endured

vv. 9–11: Memory of God's Care from Birth

vv. 12–18: Mockery Continues as Languish Threatens

vv. 19–21: Prayer for Deliverance

vv. 22–26: Promise of Praise

vv. 27–31: Centrifugal Worship Extending out to Ends of the Earth

As is well known, the psalm begins with lament, with the cry of forsakenness.[2] But what is often forgotten is that to feel forsaken there had to be a time when you felt you belonged, you were secure. How can someone really consider himself forsaken without presupposing a real relationship or commitment? This cry of abandonment is so painful to hear partly because the psalmist and reader know that the crying heart aches for what is lost. For example, if, as some scholars argue, this is an exilic psalm, then the people have lost their promised land and the Temple.[3] In exile they struggled with their distance from the God of Israel—they were under the shadow of his judgment. But the

---

[1] For psalm numbering, keep in mind that the Septuagint (LXX) "makes Psalms 9 and 10 one psalm, so Psalm 11 MT then equals Psalm 10 LXX, and so on, until we reach Psalm 147 EVV, which the LXX divides into two. The Latin Bible follows this and so do some Roman Catholic English translations. So Psalm 51 MT is Psalm 50 LXX and Psalm 22 MT is Psalm 21 LXX." John Goldingay, *Psalms 1–41* (Grand Rapids, MI: Baker Academic, 2006), p. 26. To keep things simple, I use Psalm 22 as the number throughout, even though patristic authors, for example, often refer to this as the 21st psalm.

[2] For more on how this text fits into the larger theme of distress and lament, see Philip Johnston, "The Psalms and Distress," in *Interpreting the Psalms: Issues and Approaches* (eds, Philip Johnston and David G. Firth; Downers Grove, IL: InterVarsity Press, 2005), pp. 63–84; Claus Westermann, *Praise and Lament in the Psalms* (Atlanta, GA: John Knox Press, 1981).

[3] Moses Buttenwieser, *The Psalms; Chronologically Treated with a New Translation* (The Library of Biblical Studies; New York: Ktav Pub. House, 1969), pp. 588–603; Carroll Stuhlmueller, *Psalms 1: A Biblical-Theological Commentary* (Old Testament Message 21; Wilmington, DE: Michael Glazier, 1983), p. 147; C. Stuhlmueller, "Psalm 22: The Deaf and Silent God of Mysticism and Liturgy," *Biblical Theology Bulletin* 12 (1982), pp. 86–90. For an example of others still arguing for the probability of this Psalm read as Davidic, see Richard D. Patterson, "Psalm 22: From Trial to Triumph," *Journal of the Evangelical Theological Society* 47, no. 2 (2004), pp. 213–233.

psalmist steels himself to remember the history of divine provision and deliverance, the goodness of being created by Yahweh and standing in covenant with him: these memories make God's apparent absence intensely painful.

Harkening back to his own birth the psalmist claims that at the breasts of his mother Yahweh "made me trust [him]" (vv. 9–10). Even when we are weaned from breastfeeding, we never outgrow our dependence on the Creator; we are never outside his provision. The God who provides for his people through his good creation is also the only God who can deliver his people in their sufferings. Only the Creator can bring the psalmist back from "the dust of death" (v. 15) and quench his desperate thirst. Tension lingers in the song: despite belonging to God the psalmist suffers under the enemies, who like "dogs" surround him, not only mocking him, but taking what little he had, dividing it among themselves (vv. 17–18). Holding to the creation and covenant on the one hand, while not denying the tyranny and fear on the other, the psalmist wrestles through his lament.

God's promise of restoration remains, so the psalmist determines to praise God in the midst of the congregation (v. 22), and ends his song with hope rather than despair. This is not mere psychological trickery; he expects the future *shalom* to be actualized in history.[4] He anticipates standing in "the great assembly" (v. 25) again, where he will praise his God and pay his vows. The Lord will restore this lost *shalom*—harmony between God, his people, and the earth. No longer will the psalmist or his people contend with the bloody sword, a suffocating thirst, or the "ravening and roaring lion" (v. 13) seeking to devour.

Further, this new "great assembly" will include "all the families of the nations" (v. 27), some of which had actively persecuted Israel. Instead of threatening destruction for his adversaries he predicts a restoration, a *shalom* that includes "the ends of the earth" (v. 27). This is astonishing, since earlier these were his enemies, who acted like dogs, bulls, and wild beasts (vv. 20, 21), full of evil strength. The psalmist has returned to his robust creational theology: God is King of all the earth, not just Israel.[5] Israel brings God's promised blessing to the nations, drawing others to worship the Lord (Gen. 12:1-3).[6]

---

[4] Cf., "The transition from prayer to thanksgiving in certain psalms [e.g., Ps. 22] is to be explained, not by assuming an inward conviction on the worshiper's part, but by predicting the intervention of some objective sign from God," Roger Tomes, *"I Have Written to the King, My Lord": Secular Analogies for the Psalms* (Hebrew Bible Monographs; Sheffield: Sheffield Phoenix Press, 2006), p. 88.

[5] Hans-Joachim Kraus, *Psalms 1–59: A Continental Commentary* (1st Fortress Press ed.; Minneapolis, MN: Fortress Press, 1993), p. 300, cf. pp. 84–89.

[6] For a monumental attempt to unpack this theme as developed throughout the canon, with special attention given to the paradigmatic nature of Gen. 12:1-3, see Christopher J. H. Wright, *The Mission of God: Unlocking the Bible's Grand Narrative* (Downers Grove, IL: IVP Academic, 2006).

At the end of the psalm a figure stands in the midst of the congregation and sings God's praise, and then the song travels beyond the congregation to the ends of the earth. The promised declaration is almost unnerving, considering how the psalm began: the time is coming when all the nations "shall remember" and all "shall worship before you" (v. 27). What finally unites Israel and the nations is God's kingship, since his kingdom does not recognize any boundaries (v. 28). God's universal Kingship heals the animosity and division between Israel with the rest of the nations—all stand under Yahweh. One day this reestablishment (or, better, the re-creation) will end the despair and violence, bringing instead prosperity, worship, and life (v. 29). The despair of divine absence will be replaced by proclamation of his righteous presence: "He has done it" (v. 31).

# III. Voices, Echoes, and Identity:
# Who is Praying the Psalm?

Having quickly surveyed the rhythm and development within the psalm, we need now to ask who prays this lament? Is it "David,"[7] Messiah, or both? Since all four Gospel writers (Mt. 25:35, 39, 43, 46, Mk 15:24, 29, 34, Lk. 23:34, Jn. 19:24) tie this psalm to the crucifixion, we must examine how the history of redemption affects our interpretation of this text.

## III.a. David or Jesus?

From early on in the Church, Psalm 22 was read primarily in light of the Gospels, with less concern about its Old Testament setting. Part of the reason was that many did not think the psalm really matched David's life, while it perfectly fit with Jesus'. Lanctantius (240–320), Justin Martyr (100–165), Tertullian (160–220), and Eusebius of Caesarea (263–339) all deduce that this ancient song speaks of a suffering that is not true of David. The piercing of hands and feet, the division of garments, the numbering of his bones, and casting of lots: these were not the experiences of David, while they were

---

[7] Whether or not "David" himself was the author of the psalm is not really the point of this discussion. "David" here simply represents, for our purposes, the ancient author of the psalm, whoever that may have been. These questions are important, but we simply cannot address them here. On this theme of dealing with the antiquity, reliability, and relevance of such superscriptions, see Brevard S. Childs, "Psalm Titles and Midrashic Exegesis," *Journal of Semitic Studies* 16, no. 2 (1971), pp. 137–150; Bruce K. Waltke, "Superscripts, Postscripts, or Both," *Journal of Biblical Literature* 110, no. 4 (1991), pp. 583–596; Bruce K. Waltke and Charles Yu, *An Old Testament Theology: An Exegetical, Canonical, and Thematic Approach* (Grand Rapids, MI: Zondervan, 2007), pp. 872–874.

certainly the experiences of Messiah.[8] Working with similar assumptions, Augustine (354–430) observes that since the psalm was *originally* the words of Christ, he speaks "in the past sense" (e.g., pierced) though it had not yet been actualized.[9] In this way the voice carries content only possible in Christ, for they speak of the future as the past, and the present as the future. Leo the Great (d. 461) follows a comparable line of reasoning, with a slight twist: "David suffered in Christ, because Jesus was truly crucified in the flesh of David."[10] Leo and others assume some form of distinct union with Christ that makes such strong statements of identity possible.

Justin Martyr argues that here is "a parable of mystery," since the psalm requires a Christological reading, and to avoid it one must be "in all respects blind."[11] But this reading has its own kind of blindness, causing some to ignore the Old Testament context altogether. Over 1,700 years later, Charles Spurgeon (1834–1892), in the spirit of the patristic reading, writes that once Jesus is seen in this psalm, believers "will probably neither see nor care to see David."[12] It would be unfair to Spurgeon and to the early Fathers to say that they always viewed David and the psalm's original context as completely irrelevant. They do maintain, however, that the ancient context is not the main point of the story for those who hear these words this side of the cross. To follow Spurgeon's imagery, which only slightly modifies a common patristic symbol of light, even a brilliant star becomes "concealed by the light of the sun."

Resisting the tide of opinion in his day, Theodore of Mopsuestia (350–428) interpreted this psalm chiefly with reference to David, and this is one of the reasons for his condemnation at the Second Council of Constantinople.[13] Theodore warned against hasty Christological readings of the psalm. It was rash, he thought, to jump from the words of "forsakenness" to Christ so

---

[8] Lactantius, *The Divine Institutes,* in The Ante-Nicene Fathers, *Volume 7* (eds, Alexander Roberts and James Donaldson; Peabody, MA: Hendrickson, 1994), p. 121; Tertullian, *Answer to the Jews,* in The Ante-Nicene Fathers, *Volume 3* (eds, Alexander Roberts and James Donaldson; Peabody, MA: Hendrickson, 1994), pp. 166, 169; Justin Martyr, *Dialogue with Trypho,* in The Ante-Nicene Fathers, *Volume 1* (eds, Alexander Roberts and James Donaldson; Peabody, MA: Hendrickson, 1994), pp. 247–248; for Eusebius, see Craig A. Blaising and Carmen Hardin, *Psalms 1–50* (Ancient Christian Commentary on Scripture; Downers Grove, IL: InterVarsity Press, 2008), pp. 168, 169.

[9] See Augustine, "On the Gospel of John," in Nicene and Post-Nicene Fathers. First Series, *Volume 7* (ed. Philip Schaff; Peabody, MA: Hendrickson 1994), p. 397.

[10] Leo the Great, "Sermon 67:1-2." Blaising and Hardin, *Psalms 1–50,* p. 168.

[11] Martyr, *Dialogue,* pp. 247–248.

[12] C. H. Spurgeon, *The Treasury of David: An Expository and Devotional Commentary on the Psalms* (Grand Rapids, MI: Baker Book House, 1978), p. 365.

[13] His writings were condemned at the Second Council of Constantinople in 553. Aquinas observes that Theodore was condemned, among other reasons, for "explaining this psalm literally with respect to David . . . he ought to have explained it with respect to Christ." See Stephen Loughlin. "Thomas Aquinas: Psalm 21." Desales University. www4.desales. edu/~philtheo/loughlin/ATP/Psalm_21.html (accessed March 4, 2009).

quickly.[14] Although he did employ typology, Theodore viewed it as primarily working within the Old Testament itself and only rarely did he think those types extended into the New Testament.[15]

Although Theodore saw the significance of this psalm for the experience of Jesus on the cross, he read it not so much as a prophecy of the future, but rather as Jesus' application of the psalm to himself in his time of need. Jesus cries out in the words of this psalm on the cross, not using it as some oracle that had long ago been given about him, but rather to show that he was "never opposed to the paternal will," even as the Jews were claiming to crucify him for "undermining the law."[16] Using Psalm 22, Jesus both finds comfort for himself and clarifies the meaning of his crucifixion for his listeners, displaying how he followed the Old Testament pattern of suffering as God's servant. The stimulating part of Theodore's concerns is his effort to ground his Christology more deeply in its Jewish roots. This was an emphasis picked up again in the Reformation, as with Martin Bucer's handling of this psalm with his debt to Jewish commentators and with John Calvin's attempt at a restrained exegesis.

The Reformed theologian Martin Bucer (1491–1551) is a fascinating example of someone working through the theological, exegetical, and canonical challenges of this text. Aiming to preserve the original historical and literary context of the psalm, Bucer also did not want to shy away from its Christological import. Although he drew from Christian writings, the sources that he most explicitly engages and is shaped by are three medieval rabbis.[17] He appreciates the way these non-Christian readers value the "literal sense" of the psalm. These earlier Jewish commentators fall short, he judged, primarily because they refused to follow through and recognize the prophetic aspects of the text realized in Jesus the Messiah. But Bucer fully agreed with these Rabbis' quest to find the context of the psalm, and he worried about interpreters who thought David irrelevant to its meaning. To emphasize David does not mean to downplay the coming Messiah.

John Calvin (1509–1564) also moves between reading David as historically figured in the psalm and as serving as a type of Christ. Unlike many of the early Fathers, Calvin did not believe that just because the psalm spoke of Christ's sufferings these descriptions could not have also been David's afflictions in some

[14] Theodore, *Commentary on Psalms 1–81* (Writings from the Greco-Roman World; ed. Robert C. Hill; Atlanta, GA: Society of Biblical Literature, 2006), pp. 241, 243.

[15] S. E. Gillingham, *Psalms through the Centuries* (Blackwell Bible Commentaries; Oxford: Blackwell, 2008), p. 32.

[16] Theodore, *Psalms 1–81*, pp. 241–243.

[17] R. Gerald Hobbs, "Martin Bucer on Psalm 22: A Study in the Application of Rabbinic Exegesis by a Christian Hebraist," in *Histoire de l'exégèse Au Xvie siècle: Textes du colloque international tenu à Genève en 1976* (eds, Olivier Fatio and Pierre Fraenkel; Genève: Droz, 1978), p. 150. This paragraph is deeply shaped by Hobbs' article.

way.[18] Instead, the psalm applies to both David and Christ, and eventually its resonance penetrates our present struggles and temptations.[19]

Yet Calvin does not just jump straight from the psalm to the Gospels to make this point. Rather, he moves from the psalm to Isaiah 53 and then to the Gospels, believing that this ancient song explains Isaiah's words, and then they both help illumine what we discover in the Gospels.[20] Furthermore, Calvin does not just linger on the opening words, "My God My God," but carries through to the closing words of the psalm. While earlier in the psalm the words are easily applied both to David and prophetically to Christ, by the end of the psalm Calvin believes a corner has been turned. In his commentary on Hebrews, in which he refers to Psalm 22, he argues that this repeated language of "all" (e.g., all the families, all the ends of the world) turning to the Lord (v. 27) necessarily carries with it the promise of the coming future Messiah. "These things are found accomplished only in Christ, who enlarged the kingdom of God not over a small space, as David did, but extended it over the whole world."[21] While he believed David could have suffered the things described in the psalm, he didn't think David could properly be assigned the significance of the end of the song. Notice, this is not merely a historical but also a theological point. Consequently, Calvin deduces, there can be "no doubt but that his [Jesus'] voice is what is referred to in this passage."[22] Though Calvin reflects some of the concerns expressed by Theodore, his results differ because of his canonical approach. The psalm, which is David's song, is also clearly the voice of Jesus. Therefore, in his exegesis of the Gospels, Calvin concludes that David had spoken "metaphorically and figuratively" about experiencing these things himself; with Jesus they are seen "literally . . . and in reality" since the reality, and not just its shadow, was now present.[23]

The historic debate over the primary voice of the psalm continued in the sixteenth century as represented by differences between Lutherans and Calvinists. Those following Martin Luther (1483–1546) tended to interpret the speaker of the psalm as *Christ prophetically* speaking through David. On the other hand, according to the Calvinists, such as Theodore Beza (1519–1605), *the primary speaker is David*; Jesus then makes use of these words in his death on the cross.[24] Yet even for the Calvinists, these words still carry the Savior's voice.

---

[18] John Calvin, *Commentary on Isaiah* (Calvin's Commentaries; ed. Henry Beveridge; Grand Rapids, MI: Baker Books, 1996), p. 52.

[19] —, *Commentary on the Book of Psalms* (Calvin's Commentaries; ed. Henry Beveridge; Grand Rapids: Baker Books, 1996), pp. 303–304.

[20] Ibid., pp. 356, 356–390.

[21] —, *Epistle to the Hebrews* (Calvin's Commentaries; ed. John Owen; Grand Rapids, MI: Baker, 1996), p. 65.

[22] Ibid., p. 65.

[23] —, *Commentary on a Harmony of the Evangelists* (Calvin's Commentaries; ed. William Pringle; Grand Rapids, MI: Baker, 1996), vol. 3, p. 299.

[24] Here I draw heavily from Johann Anselm Steiger, "The Development of the Reformation Legacy: Hermeneutics and Interpretation of the Sacred Scripture in the Age of

Such a distinction can be helpful for highlighting differences in tradition, but this should not be overplayed, because it is more a difference of emphasis than of kind. Each Reformation tradition, in its own way, sought to avoid saying that only one voice is heard in this psalm. Why just one? Does a canonical reading of the text not require recognition of multiple attachments?[25] What was fairly agreed upon was the significant role of the Spirit guiding and illuminating David's words and giving them the prophetic Christological orientation in which they must be read by Christians.[26] Canonical assumptions make the differences between the various traditions less pronounced. Philipp Melanchthon (1497–1560), for example, always encouraged the readers of the psalms to remember "that often the voice of David is at the same time the voice of Christ, and conversely the voice is David's or our own."[27]

## III.b. Jesus or us?

Augustine addresses another interesting problem. When Jesus cries out, "My God, my God, why have you forsaken me?" on the cross (Mt. 27:46; Mk 15:34), citing Ps. 22:1, he sounds as if he is a sinner deserted by God because of his offenses.[28] But how can this be if he is the sinless Son of God (cf. Heb. 4:15; 2 Cor. 5:21: I Pet. 2:22)? Does this cry denote a sinner abandoned by a holy God? Why did Jesus take on this cry from the psalmist?

This tension helps this psalm work as a song of atonement, argues Augustine. While these are Christ's words, they are also the words of his people, with whom he completely identifies: "The body of Christ is speaking as one with its

Orthodoxy," in *Hebrew Bible, Old Testament: The History of Its Interpretation: From the Renaissance to the Enlightenment*, ed. Magne Sæbø (Göttingen: Vandenhoeck & Ruprecht, 1996), vol. 2, p. 720.

[25] Cf., "In this psalm painful reminiscences and prophetic foresight mix with free abandon," Stanley L. Jaki, *Praying the Psalms: A Commentary* (Grand Rapids, MI: W. B. Eerdmans Pub., 2001), p. 67.

[26] For example, Martin Luther, *Selected Psalms I* (Luther's Works 12; eds, Jaroslav Jan Pelikan and Helmut T. Lehmann; St. Louis, MO: Concordia Publishing House, 1955), p. 126. Calvin, *Commentary on the Book of Psalms*, vol. 1, p. 362. Cf., Tertullian, *Against Marcion*, in The Ante-Nicene Fathers, *Volume 3* (eds, Alexander Roberts and James Donaldson; Peabody, MA: Hendrickson, 1994), p. 341.

[27] From Melanchthon, CR 13, p. 1022, quoted in R. Gerlad Hobbs, "Pluriformity of Early Reformation Scriptural Interpretation," in *Hebrew Bible, Old Testament: The History of Its Interpretation: From the Renaissance to the Enlightenment*, ed. Magne Sæbø (Göttingen: Vandenhoeck & Ruprecht, 1996), vol. 2, p. 504. Melanchthon adds later: "Christ's passion and victories are described here, but David is not to be excluded."

[28] The launching point for Augustine's observation regarding indications of sin comes from Ps. 22:2b, which has a difficult history. Older texts [G] and translations rendered it, " 'the account of my transgressions is distant from my salvation,' apparently reading שִׁגְאָתִי ('transgressions') for MT's שַׁאֲגָתִי); but G was probably working from a different text, for it also contains an additional clause after 'My God,' namely: 'attend to me' (πρόσχες μοι)," Peter C. Craigie, *Psalms 1–50* (Word Biblical Commentary 19; Waco, TX: Word Books, 1983), p. 196.

Head."[29] Through our union with Christ these are the words of David, the words of Christ, and the words of his corporate body. "Let us hear them as one single organism, but let us listen to the Head as Head, and the body as body. The persons are not separated, but in dignity they are distinct, for the Head saves and the body is saved"; while the head and body are distinct, "the voice is one."[30] The one who identifies himself with the prisoner or desolate individual (Mt. 25:42-45) identifies here with his people in their sin. Based upon a theology of union with Christ, Augustine concludes: "Whenever you hear the voice of the body, do not separate it from the voice of the Head; and whenever you hear the voice of the Head, do not separate him from the body; they are two no longer, but one flesh."[31] Here is real identity, real union, and consequently real redemption. This leads us back to the issue about multiple attachments of this psalm. How can this be *our* song? What does it mean when we sing back to God not simply the words of David, but also the words Jesus uttered on the cross? Few understood this question or gave a richer response than Dietrich Bonhoeffer in his book on the Psalms.

> "How is it possible for a man and Jesus Christ to pray the Psalter together? It is the incarnate Son of God, who has borne every human weakness in his own flesh, who here pours out the heart of all humanity before God and who stands in our place and prays for us. He has known torment and pain, guilt and death more deeply than we. Therefore it is the prayer of the human nature assumed by him which comes here before God. It is really our prayer, but since he knows us better than we know ourselves and since he himself was true man for our sakes, it is also really his prayer, and it can become our prayer only because it was his prayer."[32]

The psalmist's lament is the lament of a wounded sinner, aching for the redemption that only the Creator can accomplish. In Jesus, the Creator has assumed the creation to himself, and so this lament becomes his lament in order that we might not remain forsaken.

## IV. Hearing the Song

"*Eli, Eli, lama sabachthani?*" Who was this man, this itinerant teacher brutally attached to a cross? Thieves were on his left and right; elders, scribes, and even

---

[29] Augustine, *Expositions of the Psalms* (The Works of Saint Augustine; ed. Maria Boulding and John E. Rotelle; Hyde Park, NY: New City Press, 2000), p. 151. Cf., Steiger, "Hermeneutics and Interpretation," pp. 713–714.

[30] Augustine, *Expositions of the Psalms*, p. 151.

[31] Ibid., pp. 151–152.

[32] Dietrich Bonhoeffer, *Psalms: The Prayer Book of the Bible* (Minneapolis, MN: Augsburg, 1970), p. 20–21. Cf., Dietrich Bonhoeffer, *Life Together* (New York,: Harper, 1954), pp. 44–50.

the chief priests surrounded and mocked him (Mt. 27:38-44). Open wounds baked in the sun, skin a mangled mess covered with dirt, blood, sweat, and spit. The scene projects despair, judgment, and abandonment. Jesus cries out the first verse of Psalm 22 in a loud voice, an earth-shattering lament: "My God, my God, why have you forsaken me?" How should we understand this scene?

The mockers, instead of casting stones, threw questions about his identity and about his God, questions that also function as accusations, especially voiced in the refrain: "Are you the King of the Jews?" (Mt. 27:11, 29, 37). The contempt of his tormentors becomes our perplexity at this mystery: How can God, the Son of God (cf. v. 43), hang helpless on a cross? "If you are the Son of God, come down from the cross" (v. 40). Yet there he hangs, powerless, vulnerable, and exposed. From this posture of humility, Jesus cries out the beginning of Israel's and David's psalm.

While Matthew and Mark both record that Jesus cited the first line of Psalm 22 (Mt. 27: 46; Mk 15:34), Luke's Gospel records the last words of Jesus on the cross as "into your hands I commit my spirit" (Lk. 23: 46). This language comes from Ps. 31:5, which more fully reads, "Into your hand I commit my spirit; you have redeemed me, O Lord, faithful God." A tradition in the early church arose in light of these quotes, that Jesus, while hanging on the cross, "silently recited all the lines of the Psalter that lie between these two verses."[33]

Whether or not the cultural background and the gospel testimony are too weak to support the idea that Jesus recited all that material on the cross, we do have these two extracts. What was Jesus doing with them? I believe that he was adopting them, proclaiming them, and transforming them.

## IV.a. Adopted

Jesus adopted the words by claiming them as his own material: he was living the psalm. Thus his cry is a real cry of dereliction. Not only is Jesus feeling a sense of abandonment, loneliness, and despair, but he is also carrying the reality of sin, death, and the curse of exile. No matter what else we say, let us not take away from the genuine struggle he faces as he bleeds and weeps amid the mockery and violence. These words mean *more*, but *never less* than a real cry of dereliction. Jesus is not acting here, he really knows the ache of forsakenness; this is his reality and nothing less. Patrick D. Miller has it right when he concludes, "Where in the Old Testament the human situation of degradation and desolation—a sense of abandonment by God, of being mocked and scorned

---

[33] Patrick Henry Reardon, *Christ in the Psalms* (Ben Lomond, CA: Conciliar Press, 2000), p. 41.

by everyone—is most strongly attested, the New Testament explicitly identifies that experience as Jesus'."[34] This observation helps expose further significance of Christ's death. Much of western orthodox Christianity has rightly focused on the way that Jesus' death is "God's way of dealing with the problem of human sin," as we find emphasized by the Apostle Paul. The Gospels also show, through this appropriation of Psalm 22, how the incarnation also displays "God's identification with all those who suffer and cry out to God." As Jesus adopts this painful human lament, he also points toward healing. His genuine solidarity with fallen humanity shows that he "died for human hurt as well as human sin."[35] Like the psalmist, however, Jesus does not leave those who hear his prayer in despair, for by quoting the beginning of the psalm he also points to the promised conclusion. Yet hope must be *believed* amid evidence to the contrary: here we encounter the Proclaimer not speaking forth from a forum in a powerful political capital, but wounded on a wooden and condemned cross.

## IV.b. Proclaimed

By proclaiming, I mean that he was directing his hearers where to look to understand this terrifying event.[36] If at a funeral in the American South one mourner begins to sing, "Amazing grace, how sweet the sound, that saved a wretch like me," then others will know to join in even before he gets to the word "sweet." Because of the culture, everyone knows that this is the right thing to do, and everyone knows the words. Everyone joins the song. Similarly, the idea that Jesus either does not or might not intend the whole psalm, that he might only be tearing the first verse out of context to apply to himself, ignores both the culture of his day and his own habit of directing exegetes (e.g., the Pharisees) to search the Scriptures.[37] Therefore this event points as much to the entire psalm, and not just to its first verse, as the psalm points to the event. Jesus here is living the whole content of Psalm 22, which is why some

---

[34] Patrick D. Miller, *Interpreting the Psalms* (Philadelphia, PA: Fortress Press, 1986), p. 109.

[35] Ibid., pp. 109–110. The above quotes also come from Miller.

[36] Cf., Ellen F. Davis, "Exploding the Limits: Form and Function in Psalm 22," *Journal for the Study of the Old Testament* 53(1992): pp. 103–104; James L. Mays, "Prayer and Christology: Psalm 22 as Perspective on the Passion," *Theology Today* 42 (1985), pp. 322–331.

[37] Cf., Holly J. Carey, *Jesus' Cry from the Cross: Toward a First-Century Understanding of the Intertextual Relationship between Psalm 22 and the Narrative of Mark's Gospel* (Library of New Testament Studies; London ; New York, NY: T & T Clark, 2009); C. H. Dodd, *According to the Scriptures* (New York: Scribner, 1953), pp. 57–59, 96–98; Naomi Koltun-Fromm, "Psalm 22's Christological Interpretive Tradition in Light of Christian Anti-Jewish Polemic," *Journal of Early Christian Studies* 6, no. 1 (1998), pp. 51–52; Barnabas Lindars, *New Testament Apologetic: The Doctrinal Significance of the Old Testament Quotations* (Study ed.; London: S. C. M. Press, 1973), pp. 89–93.

of the early church Fathers called this psalm, the "'fifth Gospel' account of the crucifixion."[38]

Nearing the end of the psalm we hear this proclamation: "The afflicted shall eat and be satisfied; those who seek him shall praise the Lord! May your hearts live forever!" (v. 26); "All the ends of the earth shall remember and turn to the Lord" (v. 27). Finally, the closing verses of the psalm are, "Posterity shall serve him; it shall be told of the Lord to the coming generation; they shall come and proclaim his righteousness to a people yet unborn, that he has done it" (vv. 30–31). The last words of the psalm, "He has done it," naturally remind Christian readers of John's Gospel, where Jesus' final words on the cross are: "It is finished" (Jn 19: 30). Whereas the original psalmist wrote of his lament, his prayer, and his hope, Jesus embodies the lament, prays the prayer, and becomes the hope.

In explaining what the crucifixion means, Psalm 22 also explains its own use of the word "forsaken." Verse 24 obviously excludes the widespread and oft-repeated idea that the Father turned his back on Jesus during the crucifixion. But if the forsakenness was more than mere feeling, what could this mean? The Hebrew (עָזַב □*azab*) and Greek (ἐγκαταλείπω *egkataleipo⁻* and σαβαχθανι *sabachthani*—Greek translation of the Aramaic) words for "forsaken," like the English word "leave," can bear the sense of "to withhold one's hand from." The opposite of forsaken can mean "to deliver"; this helps explain why language of forsakenness often has one wondering why one's plea (to God, one's neighbor, etc.) goes unanswered.[39] Paradoxically, deliverance is withheld because only in this way can lasting deliverance be achieved.

God withheld his hand from rescuing Jesus from the cross, "leaving" him there but without departing from him. Jesus *is* the action and Word of God in this event. God neither abandons his Son nor does the Trinity dissolve, but God enters into the affliction of his people through his Son. This awful silence and inaction constitutes the forsakenness—this is the only way to penetrate the gates of hell (cf., Mt. 26:36-46). There had always been the promise that, even if the people forsook God, if they then cried out to him, he would hear their cry and bring renewal (e.g., Deut. 31:8; Josh. 1:5; Ruth 2:20; 1 Sam. 12: 10–11, 1 Kgs 6:12–13, etc.).[40] But their cries had always

---

[38] Craigie, *Psalms 1–50*, p. 202.

[39] Cf., Willem VanGemeren, *New International Dictionary of Old Testament Theology & Exegesis* (Grand Rapids, MI: Zondervan, 1997), vol. 3, pp.364–365; J. P. Louw and Eugene Albert Nida, *Lexical Semantics of the Greek New Testament : A Supplement to the Greek-English Lexicon of the New Testament Based on Semantic Domains* (Resources for Biblical Study; Atlanta, GA: Scholars Press, 1992), vol. 1, p. 465. Louw and Nida explain: "Languages differ appreciably in expressions meaning 'to forsake, to abandon.' For example, the most appropriate equivalent in some instances is 'to leave alone' or 'to leave behind.' In other instances one may employ a phrase such as 'to leave without help' or 'to leave and refuse to care for.'"

[40] Cf., Ps. 9:10; 16:10; 27:10; 37:28, 33; 94:14, where the psalmists consistently cling to the truth that God had never left or forsaken his people. The aim was then to remain

proven unstable, untrustworthy, and imperfect. They had so often forsaken God, and thus experienced the reality of eventually being forsaken by him, facing his judgment (e.g., Deut. 28:20; 29: 25–28; 31:16-17; Josh. 24:20; Judg. 2:12-13; 1 Sam. 8:7-9; 1 Kgs 9:9, etc.). A true and perfect Israel, a new Adam, was needed. Just as Jesus' life recapitulated the story of Adam and Israel, showing faithfulness where they had shown unfaithfulness (e.g., temptation in the wilderness), so here Jesus likewise embodies the exile and forsakenness of Israel and the world in order to bring them back to God forever. Only the faithful Messiah who alone perfectly kept the commandments, fulfilled the law, and became the culmination of the covenants, could accomplish this reconciliation.

According to the biblical story of redemption, all of humanity, including God's representative Israel, has forsaken and abandoned God. God deals with the dereliction, not by ignoring it, but by entering into it and exhausting it through the Messiah. Jesus does not cease to be God in this moment. Instead, the eternal, holy, righteous God who cannot be manipulated or beaten, answers the damning cry of humanity in their sin. God in the incarnate Son never ceases to be divine in this great condescension, and therefore he exerts his holy power in redemptive action by entering into the judgment himself. God's Spirit sustains and does not leave him, and by God's Spirit he will return from the depths of hell, bringing the newness of life (Acts 2:24; Heb. 9:14).[41] This Spirit he then gives to his people who can know that no matter the circumstances and "evidence," God never abandons them, for they will be raised with Christ (Rom. 8:11; 1 Pet. 1:21). In other words, the cross does not represent a rupture in the Trinity, but the greatest expression of the Triune God's holy love and purpose.

## IV.c. Transformed

So we discover that the psalm is transformed because of him who sings it. Whereas the psalmist trusts God to deliver him *from* death, Jesus trusts the Father to deliver him *through* death. Jesus assumes and conquers our sin, death, and forsakenness. The Father sends his Son, and the Son comes in humility, weakness, and pain. And Jesus, who is truly God and truly man, cries out with and for us, "My God my God, why have you forsaken me?" According to Saint Paul, in Jesus, "He who knew no sin became sin, that we might become the

---

faithful in light of God's mercy. But Israel was not always faithful, and this instability is felt throughout the Psalms. A lasting peace was needed to overcome the danger of forsakenness, and this would only be established through David's offspring (Ps. 89: esp. vv. 19–37).

[41] Cf., Gerald F. Hawthorne, *The Presence & the Power* (Dallas, TX: Word, 1991), pp. 179–198.

righteousness of God" (2 Cor. 5:21). Martin Luther described this solidarity displayed on the cross as follows:

> "And all the prophets saw this, that Christ was to become the greatest thief, murderer, adulterer, robber, desecrator, blasphemer, etc., there has ever been anywhere in the world. He is not acting in His own Person now. Now He is not the Son of God, born of the Virgin. But He is a sinner, who has and bears the sin of Paul . . . of Peter . . . of David . . . . In short, He has and bears all the sins of all men in His body—not in the sense that He has committed them but in the sense that He took these sins, committed by us, upon His own body, in order to make satisfaction for them with His own blood."[42]

The author of Hebrews makes this further connection. In Heb. 2:12, he quotes Ps. 22:22, "I will tell of your name to my brothers; in the midst of the congregation I will praise you." Beautifully, the author attributes these words directly to Jesus, who is not ashamed to call believers his brothers and sisters (Heb. 2:11). Our brother Jesus sings in the midst of the congregation.[43] He is the "sweet singer of Israel" who comes as the "bridegroom singing over his bride (Zeph. 3:17)," displaying God's holy love through the song of his death that points to his unquenchable life.[44] At the center of our congregation he sings the praise of the Father, and we as brothers and sisters of Jesus, enter into the song of redemption. Jesus has followed us into exile and brought us back with him. Jesus has been forsaken so that we might be welcomed. God did not stand off in the distance, but he entered our peril through Jesus Christ our Lord. When a congregation lifts the praises of God in song, singers also need to listen so that we might hear Jesus, for he sings in our midst. Is this not the fulfillment of the hope that God will "inhabit our praises?" (Ps 22:3). He is not only worshiped, but he is the lead worshiper.

On Christmas Eve of 1914, the story is told of German and British troops in their respective trenches facing each other, leaving a quiet no-man's-land

[42] Martin Luther, *Lectures on Galatians 1535 chapters 1–4* (Luther's Works 26; trans. and ed. Jaroslav Pelikan; Saint Louis, MO: Concordia Publishing House, 1999), p. 277.

[43] The connection of Psalm 22 with song has historical precedent in the Targum on v. 9, which reads, "I sang before the LORD, and he rescued me" (David M. Stec, *The Targum of Psalms. Translated, with a Critical Introduction, Apparatus, and Notes* [ArBib 16; eds, K. Cathcart et al.; Collegeville, MN: Liturgical, 2004], p. 58). Though it is doubtful that this reflects an original Hebrew text with the same meaning, it nonetheless witnesses to an interpretation of this psalm in connection with singing by the early Medieval period. Thanks to Scott Jones for this historical note.

[44] Edmund P. Clowney, *The Church* (Contours of Christian Theology; Downers Grove, IL: InterVarsity Press, 1995), pp. 134–135. For more on this motif, see Reggie M. Kidd, *With One Voice: Discovering Christ's Song in Our Worship* (Grand Rapids, MI: Baker Books, 2005).

between them.[45] Apparently some Germans began to decorate their trenches in memory of the day, and some of them sang a carol loud enough for their enemies to hear. The British responded with a carol of their own. Eventually the singing brought them out of the trenches and toward one another, with some reports of gifts exchanged and laughter heard. In some spots the informal truce lasted until New Year's Day. It was a taste of peace brought on by singing. But it was not long before the shooting and death returned. How different it could have been, however, if the leaders of those nations had been the ones singing, for then true peace could have begun.

The Gospels show us that Jesus is the great King, not only of Israel, but of all the nations. When the mockers reject Jesus' claim to be King they show they have missed the point. "He saved others; he cannot save himself" (Mt. 27:42). The only way he saves others is by not saving himself, not holding back, but going all in. God manifests his sovereign Lordship through his sacrificial gift. He alone has sung the lament of forsakenness that we might sing of hope and healing. We sing because Jesus sings. This is why we need to know more than the first line of the song, because Jesus uses it to point us to our hope. He alone is in the position to declare, "It is finished."

# V. Conclusion

Charles Spurgeon argued that the order of the Psalter is no accident. It is only after we have read, "My God, my God, why have you forsaken me?" (Psalm 22), that we can truly say, "The Lord is my shepherd" (Psalm 23).[46] More recently, John Eaton similarly concluded that for us "to enter fully into the peace of [Psalm] 23, the pilgrim must first make the daunting journey through 22, through that place where the lonely representative suffers to the uttermost, holds true, and obtains victory; having stood with him in that awesome place, the pilgrim will know the joy of the homecoming."[47]

For the Psalmist the sense of forsakenness was not the final reality, and thus he clung to the God of Abraham, Isaac, and Jacob—this is the God of the living and not the dead. So Jesus, as he prays these words, clings to life amid the black hole of hell that he is experiencing. Adopting these words and taking

---

[45] The "Christmas True of 1914" is an oft-repeated story, reported in history in various forms and versions. For example, hear the song "Christmas in the Trenches" by John McCutcheon or Christian Clarion's "Joyeux Noel" (France: Sony Picture Classics, 2005), DVD.

[46] For a more academic argument, see J. H. Eaton, *Kingship and the Psalms* (Studies in Biblical Theology 2d Ser. 32; London: S. C. M. Press, 1976).

[47] J. H. Eaton, *The Psalms: A Historical and Spiritual Commentary with an Introduction and New Translation* (London: Continuum, 2005), p. 124.

them to himself, Jesus enters the savagery of human anguish, sin, and death; he enters as a divine warrior goes into battle knowing that blood will be spilled, but also knowing the purpose is to restore life and *shalom*. The new life he achieves comes in the most paradoxical way; Jesus actualizes the psalmist's hope and healing, not by avoiding death, but *through* death which then gives way to the power of his resurrection.[48]

---

[48] Thanks in particular to Samuel Belz, John Yates, and Scott Jones who offered valuable insights and feedback in the process of writing this chapter.

# Chapter 5

# Proverbs 8: Hearing Lady Wisdom's Offer Again

## Daniel J. Treier

In Proverbs 8 Lady Wisdom, like Dame Folly, cries out very publicly. She seeks to be winsome but her appeal has its limits, trying to gain a suitor's long-term attraction rather than practicing Dame Folly's short-term aggression. Lady Wisdom cries out but does not kiss the young man impudently. She desires to persuade with the truthful content of her speech. Verses 1–3 present her return to the stage, and vv. 4–11 offer her initial appeal in a new act of the unfolding drama. This addresses everyone (8:4), with particular reference to the simple who need to start paying attention (8:5). The basis for this initial aspect of the appeal concerns the truth of her words: they not merely convey mental knowledge, but more profoundly are righteous, straightforward rather than devious and deceptive (8:6-9). Hence they have greater value than the choicest metals and jewels (8:10-11). This claim is not modest; the extent of the comparison is such that Wisdom should be chosen "rather than," not simply in addition to or before, the alternatives.

The next ten verses, 8:12-21, unfold Wisdom's value even further. The section ends with a series of claims about Lady Wisdom's bestowal of riches and honor, again comparing her favorably to gold and silver (8:18-21). Verses 12–13 begin the section similarly to the previous one, connecting Wisdom with prudence and distancing her from perverted speech. In the middle, 8:14-17 relate Wisdom to kingship, as the principle by which rulers govern rightly. In this way the rule of God is reflected: "With God are wisdom and strength; he has counsel and understanding" (Job 12:13). It is important for "the spirit of wisdom and understanding" to rest upon the shoot of Jesse that will someday rule Israel and the nations for God (Isa. 11:2). Joshua presaged this, "full of the spirit of wisdom" (Deut. 34:9), as did Solomon in his initial request to the Lord (1 Kings 3). Likewise, after the exile and in anticipation of the Messiah, Ezra employed wisdom in efforts to organize and instruct the people (Ezra 7:25). God's design is for leaders to mediate divine rule by way of Wisdom. The translation of צֶדֶק in Prov. 8:18 is usefully ambiguous, regarding whether it designates righteousness or "prosperity," as in the NRSV. Either way, these go together, not in the seeking of prosperity itself but rather in its attainment

by seeking first God's Wisdom. "But seek first His kingdom and His righteousness; and all these things shall be added to you" (Mt. 6:33 NASB).

The end of Proverbs 8, in vv. 32–36, contains the expected conclusion; Lady
Wisdom offers blessing to those who listen—carefully and constantly—in
order to keep her ways. This blessing consists in life and, more profoundly
than purely physical existence, favor from the Lord. Alternatively, those who
spurn Wisdom love death—which, by implication, is not solely physical. Notice
the parallel with the end of Proverbs 7: both chapters end with the starkness
of death as the result of spurning Lady Wisdom. The rabbis took references
to gates and doors in 8:34—vis-à-vis the synagogue, in their case—as enjoin-
ing prayer along with the study involved in pursuing Wisdom.[1] In light of the
temple allusions soon to follow and the vocabulary of "watching," this seems
appropriate. We should not simply listen to Wisdom by studying, but more
holistically pursue her via personal relationship; study must therefore be
prayerful, pursuing covenant fellowship with God. The metaphorical—and
literal—importance of marriage registers in a parallel between Prov. 8:35 and
18:22. In the former, finding Wisdom obtains favor from the LORD; in the latter, finding a good wife does so. The relational context of pursuing Wisdom is
frequent and consistent.

In this way Proverbs 8 serves as the apex of a background argument supporting Lady Wisdom's climactic invitation in Proverbs 9. The name "Lady
Wisdom" pertains, like the contrastive "Dame Folly," because the preface
"Woman" would be too generic and vague. "Dame Folly" is indeed dubious in
character, a connotation that "Dame" begins to convey. And "Lady Wisdom,"
while not aristocratic in an obnoxious sense, is regal in bearing, as references
to jewels and kings in Proverbs 8, along with her house and sumptuous feast
in Proverbs 9, connote. Choosing Lady Wisdom over Dame Folly opts for long-
term, dare we say sophisticated, flourishing over short-term pleasures.

The apex of Proverbs 8, vv. 22–31, strengthens Lady Wisdom's case by tying
her *comprehensively* to God's rule of the cosmos, not just in the present but also
in the remotest past—its creation—and (by implication) future. The passage is
famously disputed at several points regarding Christology—or whether it even
has Christological implications in the first place. Wisdom's claim that "[t]he
LORD created me at the beginning of his work, the first of his acts of long ago;
ages ago I was set up, at the first, before the beginning of the earth" (8:22-23)
juxtaposes intriguingly but awkwardly with "[i]n the beginning was the Word,
and the Word was with God, and the Word was God; he was in the beginning with God; all things came into being through him" (John 1:1-3a). The
matched "beginnings" tempt Christian readers to equate Wisdom with Jesus
Christ, God's Son, through whom God created; yet heretical Arian Christology

---

[1]  See *Proverbs Rabbah* on this verse in *The Midrash on Proverbs* (trans. Burton L. Visotzky; Yale
     Judaica, vol. 27; New Haven & London: Yale University Press, 1992), p. 47.

could treat this Logos as the mediator of creation while playing up the language of Proverbs 8 to suggest that the Son remained a creature—not the one, self-existent Creator. For both historical–critical and doctrinal reasons, then, many scholars downplay or outright deny the Christological overtones of our text.

Yet one should not get the idea that Proverbs 8 would be simple if we kept Jesus out of it; problems of translation and interpretation abound in any case. Among these are (1) the meaning of the verbs in 8:22-26; (2) the meaning of אמון, translated "master worker" by the NRSV, in 8:30; (3) the timing of various acts; and (4) the literary function and identity of Wisdom. Building upon these considerations we can finally return to addressing (5) the Christological relevance of the passage.

## I. The Meaning of the Verbs in 8:22-26

The first of the debated verbs is קנה in 8:22. Its normal usage in the Old Testament involves acquiring or possessing, and this is frequently the case elsewhere in Proverbs. Aquila, Symmachus, and Theodotion, followed by the Vulgate, took this line. However, in some passages "create" seems better; the LXX, Targum, and Peshitta take this route in Prov. 8:22. A third option involves procreation, as in Gen. 4:1, which best fits parallels in Prov. 8:23-25. A contemporary parallel to the range of this term would be the pair "get" and "beget."[2] Here the mode of acquisition appears to be specific, in terms of "bringing forth." This begetting of Wisdom transpired at the beginning of the Lord's way, onto which the audience is invited. Following that way would align the wise person with God's design from the outset. There are clearly temporal markers in 8:22 such as "beginning," but it will be important to note their points of comparison ("first" of what?) as we proceed, instead of quickly assuming that they depict Wisdom as a creature.

The second of the verbs, נסכתי in 8:23, is unclear regarding its root. The concept is either "formed" or "shaped" if the root is סכך, or else "installed" or "set up" if the root is נסך. Ps. 2:6 offers a possible parallel, in which the same consonants are used to say, "I have set my king on Zion, my holy hill," thus leading scholars to see Wisdom receiving royal investiture in Prov. 8:23. However, others see "to weave" as a possible translation for either root, with the metaphor involving gestation: this would follow nicely from 8:22 and lead into the repetition of origination metaphors in 8:24-25. Though the latter view seems more likely given the nearest context, either way there is again a temporal marker for the activity. So far, then, 8:22-23 have Lady Wisdom claiming, "The

[2] Tremper Longman III, *Proverbs* (Baker Commentary on the Old Testament Wisdom and Psalms; Grand Rapids, MI: Baker Academic, 2006), p. 204.

LORD acquired/possessed me by bringing me forth at the beginning of his way (which you can follow), before his other earliest works. From everlasting I was woven together, from the very beginning, from the earliest times of the earth."

As if that were not enough emphasis, 8:24 chimes in, attaching a series of states (currently in place) and events (subsequent) to the bringing forth (חוללתי) of Wisdom. This verb is passive to highlight divine agency, unquestionably introducing a birth metaphor, repeated at the end of 8:25. The pattern of 8:24-26 on the whole moves from down to up, and from waters and mountains toward what is for human habitation.[3] The text places the waters, a source of potential chaos, firmly in hand under God's Wisdom so that they can be a source of life and blessing instead. This anticipates the movement of 8:29-31, which mirrors the water elsewhere in Proverbs profiling the dangers and delights of sexuality: within divinely set, wise limits, there is profound joy, but outside those limits lies destruction.

## II. The Meaning of אמון in 8:30

The pattern of 8:27-29 moves in the opposite direction of 8:24-26, from up to down. The reason is similar, though: God wisely makes the cosmos fit for human habitation. The chaos associated with water, so feared by the ancients, cannot escape the boundaries marked out by the same Lord whose commands in the Torah also set boundaries for human life. Rabbinic exegesis, almost ubiquitously, equates Wisdom with Torah.[4] Once this entered the tradition it could be assumed, rather than proven, in particular places. But the vocabulary of divine command does appear in Prov. 8:29. Parallels for not violating the word from God's mouth, such as Balaam (Num. 22:18, 24:13),[5] reinforce the personal, active dimension of divine law for both the sea and the sage. The limits for the sea are not merely the chance result of evolutionary processes (however much these may have been involved); they stem ultimately from the divine decree.

Temporal clauses lead up to Wisdom's claim that "I was beside" the LORD who created, "like a master worker; and I was daily his delight . . . " in 8.30. Translating this proves to be very difficult. Among the possibilities for אמון would be "artisan," as in "master worker" from the NRSV, but this rests on such a meaning in Jer. 52:15, itself disputable. Proverbs 3:19 might offer support by suggesting that Wisdom was God's agent in creation; however, it could also

---

[3] Bruce K. Waltke, *The Book of Proverbs Chapters 1–15* (New International Commentary on the Old Testament; Grand Rapids, MI: Eerdmans, 2004), p. 411.

[4] See, for example, Lev. Rab. 35:4.

[5] Raymond C. Van Leeuwen, "Liminality and Worldview in Proverbs 1–9," *Semeia* 50 (1990), pp. 111–44 (124).

entail no more than wisdom serving as God's instrument. Plus other contextual reasons make this first possible meaning unlikely. The dominant alternative to "artisan" until recently was "nursling'" or "child," usually based on emending the (Hebrew) Masoretic Text, following Aquila. Some opt for this second possibility because they view the first ("artisan") interpretation to be theologically troubling—introducing a second Creator, so to speak. However, lack of an expected feminine form (to cohere with the *Lady* Wisdom motif) is problematic at a more basic level—as are other grammatical routes for getting to this interpretation. Moreover, contextually this is not a snug fit. Despite the apparent progression from preoccupation with birth earlier in the section, the playful delight of a little child is not the best case Proverbs could make for Wisdom having *gravitas* due to involvement with creation.

Recently a more promising possibility surfaced. Waltke translates the first phrase of 8:30, "And I was beside him constantly," taking the root of אמן) as "to be firm, faithful."[6] Stuart Weeks similarly highlights this lexical background, translating the term as "faithfully," according to which "Wisdom is either existing '(as) a faithful one' or '(in) faithfulness.'"[7] The fidelity involved may transcend merely temporal presence to connote religious piety as well.[8] In that case the possible allusion to Prov. 8:30 in Rev. 3:14 makes more sense: "The words of the Amen, the faithful and true witness, the origin of God's creation." There is no need to make ἀρχή, "origin" in Rev. 3:14, which is complex enough in its own right, correspond directly to אמון in Prov. 8:30. Rather, there is an allusion that stays both closer to the "Amen" and within the overall unfolding of the entire phrase. Therefore it seems that interpreting Prov. 8:30 in relation to constancy or faithfulness was not unknown in early Christianity.[9]

## III. The Timing of Various Acts

If we opt for this interpretation of Prov. 8:30, then the verse raises new questions about the timing of the states and events described. According to the usual understanding, Prov. 8:30 places Wisdom beside God during creation, with the delight of Prov. 8:31 presumably being subsequent to this act or process of creation itself. However, against such an interpretation, (1) the "when" clauses introduced by both in 8:27-29 could already go with "I was there" in 8:27 rather than "I was beside him" in 8:30, and (2) there are catchwords linking 8:30-31 together, which renders a temporal shift therein less likely.[10]

---

[6] Waltke, *The Book of Proverbs*, pp. 391, 420.
[7] Stuart Weeks, "The Context and Meaning of Proverbs 8:30a," *Journal of Biblical Literature* 125 (2006), pp. 433–42 (440).
[8] Ibid., p. 441.
[9] Ibid., p. 439n24.
[10] Ibid., p. 437.

The day-by-day dimension of delight in 8:30b more naturally fits with 8:31, subsequent to creation. It is preferable, therefore, to view 8:27-29 as depicting Wisdom's presence during creation, with 8:30-31 depicting her delight in the divine presence ever since. The passage "is not merely a statement that Wisdom was with God early on, but a declaration that she has been with God throughout the history of the world, and still is."[11] This qualifies her all the more to be the principle by which kings rule and humans find *shalom*.

It remains to work backward, addressing the manner in which Wisdom precedes the cosmos (8:22-26). There is repeated verbal emphasis on her being begotten, in 8:22, 23, 24, and 25. Each of the latter three verses makes clear that prior to Wisdom some feature of the cosmos did not exist or had not yet transpired. This is perfectly compatible with the claims of John's Gospel, and Nicene Christology, about the Logos through whom all things were made. The most challenging question appears in 8:22. Wisdom is not necessarily a creature according to the first clause. The verb, as we saw above, probably means either less ("acquired") or, most likely, more ("begot") than "created." Furthermore, as Athanasius points out, "the Lord created me" would not be automatically equivalent to "I am a creature" in the sense of passing from nonexistence into existence.[12] Metaphorical uses are frequent for the concept of creation in Scripture, and after all this text is poetry. Nevertheless, creation aside, begetting is probably the issue, and what we must address theologically concerns its nature and timing. A non-literal understanding of begetting is entirely consistent with the poetic nature of the passage and the symbolic force of household imagery throughout Proverbs. Classic Christian theology rightly highlights the text's metaphorical establishment of Wisdom's divine pedigree.

In some respects, then, the more challenging clause in 8:22 is the second one. Does "the first of his acts of long ago" place Wisdom's begetting at the beginning of a series of cosmic, temporal works? Not necessarily. The term rendered "first," קֶדֶם, conveys remoteness in time, yet can further point to the divine sphere, as in Hab. 1:12: "Are you not from of old, O LORD my God, my Holy One? You shall not die." The addition of מֵאָז, "of long ago," at the end of Prov. 8:22 is significant. Not only does this emphasize Wisdom's ancient character; it also calls to mind Ps. 93:2: "your [the LORD's] throne is established from of old; you are from everlasting." The phrasing gives every appearance of trying to convey Wisdom's distinctiveness, not her fit within creaturely patterns. To be sure, the vocabulary is not precise enough to rule by itself on technical theological questions that arose later in a Christian context. When

---

[11] Ibid., p. 438.
[12] Athanasius, *Four Discourses Against the Arians* in Nicene and Post-Nicene Fathers Second Series, *Volume Four* (hereafter *Or. Ar.*), II.19.44.

we now pose such questions to the text, though, our options are limited and canonically guided, as shall become clear.

## IV. The Literary Function and Identity of Wisdom

To begin with the obvious, when seeking to identify Lady Wisdom with some theological referent: Her personification is a literary motif in the midst of a passage that takes poetic license. Of course no claim is directly made regarding a *hypostasis* named Wisdom, divine or otherwise. The parallel with Dame Folly makes this clear.

Yet Wisdom cannot refer simply to a divine attribute. It would make no sense, even metaphorically, to claim that God gave birth to his own character or could act in such a way before (and therefore without) wisdom. Proverbs 8 is not suggesting that there was a time when divine wisdom was not. By definition a divine attribute is not subsequently created or begotten. Nor can we settle for Wisdom personifying the book of Proverbs itself, treated as a solely creaturely reality. Whatever may be the case regarding Proverbs 8–9 as preparation for Proverbs 10–31, such teaching provides revelation via strikingly personal divine condescension. It cannot be merely human wisdom writ large, for that would be inconsistent with the extent of Wisdom's divine association in this passage.

The text associates its personal invitation to receive divine self-revelation with mysterious origins connected to God's life—from the very beginning, as it were. It is not appropriate for Christian theologians to tell Jewish readers how they ought to read Old Testament texts as *their* Scriptures, but it is understandable how readings by the early (Jewish) Christians would naturally involve the messianic hopes, connected to future divine self-revelation, that were now thought to reach fulfillment. "Then they will know that I am the Lord," Isaiah and Ezekiel declare over and over again. Such a work of God would have to fulfill expectations about fuller knowledge of Yhwh accompanying Israel's redemption, without altering commitment to practical monotheism.[13] The hope would be that the mysterious relationality of the divine life, at which Old Testament texts occasionally hint, might come to fuller light with God's new activity in redemptive history. The resulting quandaries of interpretation for Christians naturally concern the Creator–creature dynamic, since Wisdom

---

[13] On the special implications of Isaiah in this connection see, for example, Richard Bauckham, *God Crucified: Monotheism and Christology in the New Testament* (Grand Rapids, MI: Eerdmans, 1999); David S. Yeago, "The New Testament and the Nicene Dogma: A Contribution to the Recovery of Theological Exegesis," in *The Theological Interpretation of Scripture: Classic and Contemporary Readings* (Blackwell Readings in Modern Theology; ed. Stephen E. Fowl; Oxford: Blackwell, 1997), pp. 87–100. This point holds regardless of the checkered nature and history of "monotheism" as a technical concept.

clearly is beyond just another created reality (on the one hand) while not solely identifiable with God either (on the other hand). Hence the eventual debate between Athanasius and the Arians is perfectly appropriate to the subject matter of Proverbs 8 even though Jesus Christ is not present directly on the text's surface. Although on some technical matters today we may reach different conclusions than earlier Christian interpreters, almost certainly incorporating other forms of reasoning, still the classic theologians teach us to address the revelatory and redemptive logic of the text.[14]

If Wisdom here cannot be solely a feature of creation or a divine attribute, then its mysterious origination from within the divine life begs for exploration. Wisdom has a mediating role between God and the world, particularly God and humanity: Yhwh is the first word in this text, and Adam (or son of *adam*, man) is the last. In the original context of Proverbs 8, part of the emphasis lies on the fact that "Wisdom, not simply the monarchy or the temple, serves as the link between heaven and earth."[15] For Wisdom is God present, teaching and ruling through not only kings and priests but also parents and nonhuman creatures. The resulting challenge lies in discerning the nature of this mediation—whether Wisdom is quasi-divine but ultimately a creature of some kind, as the Arians held, or indeed fully divine in some form of condescension, as the orthodox came to hold. Such an interpretive challenge takes particular shape in light of Jesus Christ claiming to be the Son of God, yet stems from a mystery already latent in the text itself. If Wisdom has some kind of creaturely connection but is chronologically and otherwise distinct from everything else in the cosmos, what are we to make of its identity? The begetting metaphor, far from subordinating the Son to the Father as creature to Creator, actually indicates continuity of divine life and character.

Philippians 2:5 states the goal of wisdom, "Let the same mind be in you that was in Christ Jesus," even using the terminology of *phronesis* (the impossible to translate "Let the same mind . . . "): Wisdom is the way God has made for humans to walk. Philippians 2:6-11 points to the divine source of Wisdom by

---

[14]  So it is disappointing to find a brilliant contemporary commentary repeat the older cheap shot of R. P. C. Hanson, in which he dubbed the patristic conflict "two blindfolded men trying to hit each other" (cited in Waltke, *Proverbs 1–15*, p. 128). Of course modern commentators treat particular grammatical and historical details with sophisticated new resources, but the reduction of "exegesis" to those details—as implied by Hanson-like comments—results in theologically impoverished analysis. Neglecting classic Christian theological exegesis helps to produce and circulate problematic views such as wisdom being merely a divine attribute. Moreover, given the numerous speculative and conflicting hypotheses in modern, critical literature on Proverbs 8, contemporary scholars appear to be just as vulnerable as Hanson's targets to swinging wildly without landing many punches. Theological exegetes should read both classic and contemporary critical scholarship with grateful yet cautious attention, open to the respective contributions of each.

[15]  Leo G. Perdue, *Proverbs* (Interpretation, Louisville, MO: Westminster John Knox, 2000), p. 140.

narrating its vocational shape in Jesus Christ: first descent, then ascent; humiliation before exaltation. Humans softly echo the crescendo of divine condescension, but Paul's appeal in Philippians works precisely because in Jesus we see *divine* condescension. The exaltation of Phil. 2:9-11 returns Christ to the enjoyment of equality with God that he let go in 2:6-8; the exaltation involves not a new status (divinity he never had) but a new identity with which to enjoy that status (the Lord is now the God-*man*). Only on this basis do humans have the possibility of imitating the mindset of Christ Jesus: our exaltation is securely rooted as participation in exaltation already begun and sure to be completed; and our sinful self-exaltation is decisively interrupted by divine, redemptive condescension. Philippians 2 narrates the incarnation; Proverbs 8 does not. Yet Philippians 2 has parallel logic, insofar as wisdom requires *both* divine condescension *and* human form for us to attain. And Proverbs 8 poetically establishes Wisdom's divine pedigree presumed in Philippians 2, while presuming throughout that her invitation takes a form people can accept. This satisfies the conceptual challenge of human finitude, but there remains the historical challenge of human fallenness. According to Philippians 2, in fulfilling Israel's redemptive hope for final revelation of YHWH, Jesus Christ provides the theological resolution of both.

## V. Christological Relevance

Jesus Christ therefore does not finally complicate the interpretation of Proverbs 8 but presents instead the resolution of a mystery latent in the text, though not always clearly recognized. The Arian solution lay in treating the Son of God as a creature, albeit an eminently unique one. In this way, some thought, the monotheistic commitment of biblical faith could be protected. The LORD alone is Creator, whose greatness is preserved by keeping an arm's length from creation. The mediator of the process, whose timeless begetting began it all, is Jesus Christ, God's Son. Even so, for the Arians "there was a time when he was not"; his is not the eternity of the uncreated God and Father of all, but rather the derivative being of a mediating creature through whom all others receive existence.

Athanasius correctly recognized the problematic character of such a mediator. If creation required mediation because direct contact with the divine was unendurable, then what would that entail for the Word as a creature through whom this mediation transpired?

> [I]t follows either that, if He could endure it [direct contact], all could endure it, or, it being endurable by none, it was not endurable by the Word, for you say that He is one of originate things. And again, if because originate nature could not endure to be God's own handywork, there arose need

of a mediator, it must follow, that, the Word being originate and a creature, there is need of medium [sic] in His framing also, since He too is of
that originate nature which endures not to be made of God, but needs a
medium. (*Or. Ar.* II.17:26)

In other words, without a mediator who originates from the divine life, we are
stuck with infinite regress—always dealing with creatures that need a mediator through which to endure divine contact. Sooner or later there must be a
form of mediation that is itself divine.

What if "Arians" attempt to respond by making wisdom "a constituent or
complement of His [God's] Essence, unoriginate as well as Himself, which
moreover they pretend to be the framer of the world, that so they may deprive
the Son of the framing of it" (*Or. Ar.* II.18:38)? Then God's simplicity would
be threatened.[16] In that case it would appear as if God were a compound
being, composed of parts or aspects, including wisdom. In the end this would
threaten the practical monotheism to which Proverbs 8 doubtless remains
true. Wisdom cannot be merely an attribute that God creates (poetically or
not), or through which God creates. God's perfections are neither divine components nor instruments doing the divine bidding while keeping creation at
arm's length from the divine being. Rather, God's perfections denote human
ways of speaking analogically about the mystery of the sole Creator acting to
reveal himself and to redeem us.

As a mediator the Son is guarded from being imprisoned in temporality by
the titles of Word and Wisdom, which are associated with the divine means
behind the speech-act of creation. Unless these titles imply eternity of the Son,
they recoil upon the work of the Father, as if God had to "devise for Himself"
the offspring by which to create (*Or. Ar.* I.7:25). As already noted, this creates
the absurdity of God (unwisely?) creating wisdom in order to act wisely—in
the future, as it were. And it presumes what Proverbs 8 counteracts, namely
the idea that God cannot be directly engaged with the cosmos but must create
through an intermediary to avoid getting his own hands dirty. But Proverbs
8 has Wisdom rejoicing *with* God in creation as *God's* work, not serving as a
quasi-divine pinch hitter. Nor, according to Athanasius, could there be a separation of Word and Son, so as to associate the divine act of creation with the
former but not the latter. The Word is from God, *the speaker*, so he must be the
Son, a chip off the old speaking block as it were; the Son is from everlasting,
so he must be the Word, spoken right from the beginning (*Or. Ar.* IV.15–24).

---

[16] For a demonstration that this appeal to divine simplicity was pervasive throughout pro-
Nicene early Christian theology, and did not owe distinctively to Neo-Platonic influence,
see Lewis Ayres, " 'Remember That You Are Catholic' (*serm.* 52:2): Augustine on the Unity
of the Triune God," *Journal of Early Christian Studies* 8 (2000), pp. 39–82 (especially
pp. 69–80).

Accordingly the Father is the Father of the Son, in a distinctive sense, as compared to being the Father of the many children whom the Son brings to glory (Heb. 2:10).

God is the Father of the eternally begotten Son by nature, yet the Father of humanity by grace (*Or. Ar.* II.21:59). Athanasius correctly teaches that titles stemming from Proverbs 8 in the New Testament, "only begotten" and "firstborn of all creation," conflict unless they respectively concern these different relations. The Son is "only begotten" with respect to the Father, by nature, as just noted. The Son is "firstborn," implying the Father's begetting others, by grace, with respect to both creation and redemption. The former deals with the Son's existence, while the latter pertains to the Son's economic activity (*Or. Ar.* II.20:51–II.21:62).

At this juncture, however, some of Athanasius's exegetical conclusions are doubtful. He parallels Marcellus of Ancyra by referring the begetting of Prov. 8:22 to the Incarnation, to the humanity of the Son in Jesus Christ (see, e.g., *Statement of Faith* 3–4, in *NPNF²* 4:85). Yet the begetting of Prov. 8:25 is the eternal begetting of the Son by the Father.[17] Thus Proverbs 8 would reverse the sequence of existence and economy, introducing the earthly economy of the Son first in 8:22 before moving backward to the Son's (pre)existence in 8:25. But it seems quite unlikely that these verses would have different events in view, or that God would have Proverbs 8 foresee the Incarnation with this much specificity. A narrative beginning with the Incarnation—with the begetting of the Son's humanity in Jesus Christ—then flashing back to his preexistent divine sonship, is not impossible, but should contain textual signals to that effect. Instead the clues point the other way, as shown earlier: the verbs of 8:22-25 are repetitive and linked together, as are the (pre)temporal markers. All the material prior to 8:26 concerns Wisdom's precedence before any of the cosmos; 8:27-29 proceed to Wisdom's presence at the creation of the cosmos; 8:30-31 finally affirm Wisdom's present rejoicing in the cosmos God has made, so as to call for our embrace of this mediator in 8:32–36. Athanasius' interpretation at this point is an unnecessary expedient if we dismiss "created" from our translation of 8:22a, or even simply accept that such poetic license would not entail an Arian ontology in any case. Here is an instance in which the LXX, rendering 8:22 with ἔκτισεν ("created"), creates an avoidable problem.[18] It is no wonder that Arians pounced on this as perhaps their primary

---

[17] See not only *Or. Ar.* II.21:59, but also Origen, *Homiliae in Ieremiam*, in *Homilies on Jeremiah and 1 Kings 8* (Fathers of the Church 97; trans. John C. Smith; Washington, DC: Catholic University of America Press, 1998), p. 93 (X.5).

[18] And Aloys Grillmeier suggests that the essential, defining characteristic of Arianism is treating the Son in relation to the term kti/sma, creature (*Christ in Christian Tradition*, vol. 1, *From the Apostolic Age to Chalcedon* [2nd revised edition; Atlanta, GA: John Knox, 1975], p. 246).

proof-text. But Athanasius' solution, however much a theological improve-
ment over the alternatives, was not radical enough.

Nevertheless, Athanasius points toward the fundamental issue that determines how to read this text: is Wisdom the divine presence, outgoing in
creation; or is Wisdom some kind of super- or supra-creature? Generally, structural analysis highlights Wisdom's uniqueness while relegating claims about
the created cosmos to subordinate temporal clauses.[19] More specifically, as
early as Prov. 8:10-11, Wisdom's value is not just quantitatively but qualitatively
unique in comparison with creation. "Again it is written: *And* all things desirable *are not to be compared unto* Her, [which means] that even things that are
of Heaven's desire are not comparable to Her?"[20] Reflecting on these verses,
Athanasius asks, "is there any similarity between things eternal and spiritual,
and things temporal and mortal?" (*Or. Ar.* III.13:55) The exhortation to choose
Wisdom "instead of," not just as "better than," such creaturely treasures, hints
at a qualitative distinction according to which Wisdom is divinely valuable,
associated first with the Creator rather than just the creature. The claim in
Prov. 8:15-16 that Wisdom enables kings to rule suggests her divine identity,
since elsewhere in Proverbs and the Old Testament as a whole this is the prov-
enance of the LORD. Likewise, claims such as Prov. 8:17 ("I love those who love
me . . . ") make the most sense by relating Wisdom to the identity of the LORD
who makes similar claims elsewhere: "When you search for me, you will find
me, if you seek me with all your heart" (Jer. 29:13); "If any of you is lacking
wisdom, ask God . . . " (Jas 1.5; see also Mt. 7:7-8).[21] Even Sirach 24, which
speaks of Wisdom's "creation" (24:9), lauds her in this extraordinary language
of divine identity: "Those who eat of me will hunger for more, and those who
drink of me will thirst for more. Whoever obeys me will not be put to shame,
and those who work with me will not sin" (24:21-22). Christian readers soon
realize that this language ultimately points to One who creates more hunger
and thirst by satisfying all other hunger and thirst (Jn 4:13-15, 31–34; 7:37-39).
And that is because this Word who gives us God's Spirit "came forth from the
mouth of the Most High" (Sir. 24:3). Precise speech about eternal begetting
rather than creation may have taken considerable time and debate for the
tradition to discern, but the necessity of the mediator's divine origin is latent
in the foundational texts.

Later, in Prov. 8:30-31, the mention of rejoicing further contributes to a
cumulative case for Wisdom's eternity, since God has never not rejoiced (*Or.
Ar.* II.22:82). The catalog of creaturely realities preceding these verses is

---

[19] Jean-Noel Aletti, "Proverbes 8, 22–31. Etude de Structure," *Biblica* 57 (1976), pp.
25–37 (35).

[20] *B. Mo'ed Qat.* 9b.

[21] So Tewoldemedhin Habtu, "Proverbs," in *Africa Bible Commentary* (ed. Tokunboh Adeyemo;
Grand Rapids, MI: Zondervan 2006), pp. 747–786 (758).

deliberately comprehensive, a merism communicating that Wisdom is uncreated because it is "before" everything God made. If by contrast the Son only excels other creatures on a relative basis, as one star differs from another, then Wisdom cannot be a cause or power to frame others but is itself caused (*Or. Ar.* II.16:21)—with all the attendant problems noted earlier of treating Wisdom as either fundamentally a creature or else merely a divine attribute. The Bible knows of only two categories, Creator and creature, not three—there are no quasi-divine mediating creatures. Even if neither Jewish nor Christian traditions are entirely uniform in discerning this fundamental implication of biblical teaching, still it bolsters the basic Athanasian logic by which to make sense of the mysteries of Proverbs 8.

At the same time, Athanasius does not provide the only manner of identifying Wisdom according to patristic orthodoxy. In fact, Theophilus of Antioch and Irenaeus actually identified this Wisdom with not the second, but the third, Person of the Trinity—the Holy Spirit.[22] Although the images of sonship are dominant enough to preclude this identification and favor a Christological one, this example prompts us to recognize significant parallels between Prov. 8:22-31 and Genesis 1: the distinction of works of creation from one another; the heavens being created first, with the setting apart of the waters; ראשית at the beginning of both texts; and so forth.[23] In a broader context Wisdom points to a theology of Word and Spirit: while order, distinction, and cohesion are appropriated to the Logos who prevents cosmic chaos, the vitality and delights of communion involve the divine presence of the Spirit as well.[24]

Among those who treat Wisdom Christologically yet differently from Athanasius, Basil of Caesarea correctly acknowledges that Prov. 8:22 refers to the preexistent Son. Yet he recognizes that this does not entail the Son being only a creature, since (1) this position would have to overcome the weight of scriptural evidence on the other side, (2) proverbs as a genre are complex and demand interpretation that goes beyond a simplistic literal sense, and (3) one could translate "acquired" instead of "created."[25] Whatever one makes of this rationale, Basil illustrates the breadth of options and debates within the classic tradition. Nor is that tradition frozen in time. The proposal adopted in the present commentary fits its revelatory and soteriological substructure while updating some of the lexical and grammatical reference points.

---

[22] Henri Cazelles, "La Sagesse de Proverbes 8:22 Peut-elle Être Considérée comme une Hypostase," in *Trinité et Liturgie* (eds, Achille M. Triacca and Alessandro Pistoia; Rome: CLV Edizioni Liturgiche, 1984), pp. 51–57 (51).

[23] Michaela Bauks and Gerluch Baumann, "Im Anfang war . . . ? Gen 1,1ff und Prov 8:22-31 im Vergleich," *Biblische Notizen* 71 (1994), pp. 24–52.

[24] Henri Blocher, *La Doctrine du Péché et de la Rédemption* (Vaux-sur-Seine, France: Edifac, 2001), p. 221.

[25] Mark DelCogliano, "Basil of Caesarea on Proverbs 8:22 and the Sources of Pro-Nicene Theology," *Journal of Theological Studies* 59 (2008), pp. 183–90.

Christian orthodoxy freely appealed to New Testament texts for understanding Prov. 8:22-31. John 1 offers an aforementioned parallel, since the
Logos has overtones of Old Testament Wisdom in the background. This Word
was "with God" yet also the Word "was God," through whom "all things came
into being" (Jn 1:1, 3). The passage goes on to call this Son μονογενής(Jn
1:18), designating the favorite or privileged son, the unique heir. Regardless
of one's text-critical decision, the surrounding context of Jn 1:18 makes a
strong claim for the divinity of this Son. Incidentally, Wisdom makes several "I am" claims in Proverbs 8, and is God's "way" (8:12, 13, 22, 32), the
truth (8:7), and the life (8:35), thereby fitting the pattern elsewhere in John's
Gospel, notably in 14:6.

The terminology of divine "fullness" (Jn 1:16) also appears in Col. 1:19 as
dwelling in the Son. Colossians 1:15 famously speaks too of the Son as the "firstborn [πρωτότοκος] of all creation." When interpreting this statement, again
we find distinction between the Son and the invisible One now understood
as God the Father ("He is the image of the invisible God;" Col. 1:15), along
with strong statements of divine identity for the Son ("He himself is before all
things, and in him all things hold together;" Col. 1:17 and so forth). It is difficult to put the Son solely or primarily on the side of creatures when the emphasis of Col. 1:16 goes on all creation—even of the great powers that transcend
this earthly cosmos—occurring in and through and for him. Proverbs 8:22b,
placing Wisdom at the beginning of God's way, makes this begotten One the
model point of reference for the work of creation. Orthodox creedal formulae
set forth the grammar by which to make sense of these various statements.

Matthew 11:25-30 and like passages unfold the logic of revelation through
which to understand Wisdom's divine self-giving in Proverbs 8. The Father ini-
tiates the divine condescension—and remarkable condescension it is, bypass-
ing any qualifications of human wisdom and addressing relative infants. Even
so, the Son by whom we receive this revelation is fit to share all things with the
Father. Thus the Son's knowledge of the Father is self-knowledge. Athanasius
puts the claim in terms of the Son being able to call him both "Father" and
"Lord" (*Or. Ar.* II.19:50): this is the form of mediation that sets the pieces of
Prov. 8:22-31 into place.

After citing Mt. 11:27, Augustine explicates the necessary distinctions for
situating Jesus Christ as Wisdom within a theology of the Holy Trinity.[26] Some
terms, such as Word, are relational and pertain to particular persons. Other
terms, such as wisdom, are substantial, pertaining to the divine nature of all
three persons. That said, it is appropriate for some of these substantial terms,
such as Wisdom, to be associated especially with one of the three divine persons
on account of salvation history; often theologians call this "appropriation."

---

[26] See especially Augustine, *The Trinity* (The Works of Saint Augustine; ed. Edmund Hill, O.
P.; New York: New City, 1991), pp. 217–224 (VII.1–6).

The Nicene Creed exemplifies appropriation in the realm of action, associating creation especially with the Father, redemption with the Son, and the perfection of all things with the Spirit. Thus, pertaining to divine attributes, "it is not surprising that scripture should be speaking about the Son when it speaks about wisdom, on account of the model which the image who is equal to the Father provides us with that we may be refashioned to the image of God; for we follow the Son by living wisely."[27] This is not to deny that the Father is wise or that the Spirit is strongly connected with our attainment of wisdom in the Son. Even so, the Bible particularly associates wisdom with Christ, the crucified One who *is* Wisdom for us.

Speaking of "Wisdom Christology" has currently become popular, treating wisdom as a crucial category for understanding the identity of Jesus Christ. For some this is a historical claim about the influence of Old Testament or intertestamental Jewish texts upon New Testament or early Christian understandings. For others, such historical influences are more Greco-Roman, whether in terms of Jesus' self-presentation as a wandering sage or in regard to philosophical motifs. For still others, "Sophia" presents feminist possibilities for reinterpreting traditional theological categories or the male Jesus in woman-friendlier ways. Some of these claims are not mutually exclusive, but other scholars caution against inflated Wisdom Christologies, sensing that various agendas spawn the myriad historical hypotheses. Though certain historical cautions are warranted, and in this case feminist theological claims are overblown, we should not overreact. It will not do to minimize Pauline and other New Testament Wisdom vocabulary entirely, as if it were only and always minimal and polemical. To take one example, polemical or not, the hymn in Colossians 1 reflects a positive, even glorious pattern of appropriating the Christological implications of Proverbs 8.

Interpreting Proverbs 8 as having Christological relevance helps to hold together creation and redemption rather than prioritizing either in lopsided fashion. Even if we assume with Athanasius and most traditional theologians that the Incarnation only occurred due to God's redemptive plan for counteracting the effects of our fall into sin, still the Redeemer is the Logos by whom the world came into being. On the other hand, lest wisdom devolve into mere common sense immanent to creation—a matter of opinion polling among sinful humans taking their own looks at a created order that is actually under a curse—in Christ God confronts us with true Wisdom that is personal and redemptive, entailing response to divine initiative. Covenant life means the renewal of creation, while creaturely life is ultimately designed for covenant fellowship with God. In *On the Incarnation* Athanasius once again strikes the proper balance: "Creation was there all the time, but it did not prevent men

---

[27] *De Trinitate* VII.5 (p. 223 in Hill, *The Trinity*).

from wallowing in error,"[28] yet "*the renewal of creation has been wrought by the Self-same Word Who made it in the beginning.*"[29]

Thus Prov. 8:31 comes alive in light of Jesus Christ. The verse identifies humanity as integral to God's delight. As already noted, יהוה (YHWH) is the first word in 8:22, and ארם) (humanity) the last in 8:31; at the end of the first eleven stichs and before the second eleven stichs, Wisdom—the Mediator—says, "I was there" (8:27).[30]

> The LORD, your God, is in your midst,
> a warrior who gives victory;
> he will rejoice over you with gladness,
> he will renew you in his love;
> he will exult over you with loud singing as on a day of festival. (Zeph. 3:17)

Jesus Christ endured the cross for the joy set before him (Heb. 12:1-2), because of God's commitment to creation and particularly humans who bear the divine image. This Son shares the Father's character, so that by grace we might do so in turn.[31]

---

[28] *De Incarnatione* I.14 (p. 42 in *On the Incarnation* [trans. a religious of C. S. M. V.; Crestwood, NY: St. Vladimir's Seminary Press, 2002]).

[29] Ibid., I.1 (p. 26 in *On the Incarnation* [translator's emphasis]).

[30] See Aletti, "Proverbes 8:22-31. Etude de Structure," p. 28.

[31] With the kind permission of the publisher, this chapter is largely excerpted from Daniel J. Treier, *Proverbs and Ecclesiastes* (Brazos Theological Commentary on the Bible, Grand Rapids, MI: Brazos, 2011). It is a great privilege to honor Henri Blocher, first my teacher in print and in person, and later a senior colleague as well—while always a godly example and a deeply biblical theologian.

Chapter 6

# Ezekiel 14: "I, the Lord, Have Deceived That Prophet": Divine Deception, Inception, and Communicative Action

Kevin J. Vanhoozer

*Everything recorded about God, even if it may be immediately unsuitable, must be understood worthy of a good God.*

(*Origen, Homilies on Jeremiah*)[1]

## I. Introduction: An Exegetical Stress Fracture in the Hip of Dogmatic Theology? Divine Deception in Ezekiel 14:9

The Bible's depictions of God as complicit in deceiving others, infrequent though they are, nevertheless pose for the theological interpreter of Scripture a problem than which nothing greater can be conceived. Among these passages, Ezekiel 14:9 is a particularly painful thorn in the theological interpreter's flesh given its portrayal of God as the ultimate if not proximate cause of a prophet's deception. Most systematic theologians who presuppose divine perfection (and hence truthfulness) typically tend not to linger over this verse. It falls to the biblical exegete (or pastor!) to wrestle with the particulars of the text, and to do this high-wire interpretive work without a net (i.e., the traditional doctrine of God and the divine attributes). To the extent that it represents a further complication in the already strained relationship between biblical studies and theology, then, our passage serves as an excellent case study in the theological interpretation of Scripture.

Ezekiel's message to his fellow exiles in Babylon concerns the rightness of Yahweh's judgment on Judah and Jerusalem. The destruction of Jerusalem was not a contradiction but rather a fulfillment of the covenant and its sanctions

[1] Origen, *Homilies on Jeremiah. Homily on 1 Kings 28* (The Fathers of the Church; trans. John Clark Smith; Washington: Catholic University of America Press, 1998), p. 221.

for disobedience and unfaithfulness to God's Word (Ezek. 5:5-17). However, Yahweh has not finished with Israel: he continues to speak and act (Ezek. 11:14-21). The future of the covenant people depends entirely on their response to the Word of God. It is therefore of the utmost importance that the exiles continue with all their hearts to heed God's Word, and its servants the prophets. This explains both Ezekiel's diatribe against false prophets (ch.13) and his critique of those who seek to abuse the prophetic institution itself by inquiring unworthily (14:1-11).

Ezekiel's account of the elders of Israel seeking a prophetic word provides a fascinating lesson in divine communicative action. On the face of it, the request is unobjectionable. Yet the word Ezekiel hears from the Lord reveals that the elders "have taken their idols into their hearts" (v. 3). It is as if their very hearts had become idolatrous "high places" replacing love of Yahweh with love of something else.[2] Their very attempt to "divine" God's will by approaching Ezekiel as if he were a fortune-teller is evidence that the elders were not truly interested in communication—hence Yahweh's rhetorical question indicating that the elders are not fit dialogue partners: "Should I indeed let myself be consulted by them?" (v. 3).

The inquiring elders get more than they bargained for: Yahweh instructs Ezekiel to say that the Lord will indeed answer such men so that he may lay hold of their idolatrous hearts (v. 5) and to instruct the people to repent and turn away from idols (v. 6). Or else what? The twofold quasi-legal answer follows: first, any idolatrous inquirer will have to answer to Yahweh himself rather than the prophet (v. 7). The Lord will respond by making that idolater a "sign" of his displeasure by banishing him from his covenant presence—call it communication by excommunication (v. 8).[3] Second, any prophet who aids and abets an idolatrous inquirer by speaking a word allegedly from God will be deceived by God himself, and then destroyed (v. 9). The inquirer and the prophet both suffer the same fate, so that Israel will learn how rightly to engage the divine economy of covenantal communication (vv. 10–11).

Of particular interest is the meaning of v. 9a: "And if the prophet is deceived and speaks a word, I, the Lord, have deceived that prophet." In addition to standing under the same threat as the idolatrous inquirer, the prophet tempted to communicate in Yahweh's name is susceptible to a strange communicative work of God whereby God as it were speaks nothing out of the

---

[2]  Cf. Calvin: "For God has erected the seat of his empire in our hearts: but when we set up idols, we necessarily endeavor to overthrow God's throne" (*Commentaries on the Prophet Ezekiel* [Eerdmans: Grand Rapids, 1948], vol. 2, p. 45).

[3]  Robert Jenson notes that the Lord does not give Ezekiel a new second-person word for the elders but rather has him recite a third-person command (*Ezekiel* [Brazos Theological Commentary on the Bible; Grand Rapids: Brazos, 2009], p. 117). Interestingly, Jenson dubs his section on Ezek. 14:1-11 "The Sign of Jonah" (p. 116).

left side of his mouth.[4] Only here and in two other passages (1 Kgs 22:1-38; Jer. 20:7-13) is the Hebrew term *pth* used in the Piel stem (indicating an intensive type of action in the active voice) with Yahweh as the subject and a prophet as the object: "And if the prophet is deceived [*pth* in the Pual] . . . I, the Lord, have deceived [*pth* in the Piel] that prophet" (Ezek. 14:9). The verb *pth* appears twenty-seven times in the OT, most often in the Piel stem. The verb in the Qal means "to be gullible or foolish" (Deut. 11:16; Job 5:2; Prov. 20:19) and in the Piel "to fool, mislead" in the sexual, legal, and religious realms: "In particular, however, the term refers to God's compelling persuasion."[5] The various English translations of this crucial verb anticipate the differing interpretations: "have deceived" (ASV, KJV, ESV, NRSV); "have enticed" (NIV); "have prevailed upon" (NASB). Zimmerli provides his own translation: "have befooled."[6] In any case, there is clearly a negative connotation to the verb, either because the act itself is wrong or because its effect is harmful.

Henri Blocher has written article and book-length studies of the most intractable theological interpretive conundrums: the days of creation; the origin of evil; the problem of original sin; the unity and diversity of metaphorical views of the atonement; the meaning and fittingness of hell as eternal conscious punishment. For many, these issues represent an offense to reason, scandalous interpretation-stoppers that inhibit a fruitful reading of the Bible. Like his erstwhile compatriot John Calvin, Henri is the best kind of exegete: one who ministers understanding, holding a high view of the text but lifting the name of God even higher. His interpretive solutions are far from contrived or speculative. On the contrary, he is able to combine a rigorous adherence to what the text says with a fresh appreciation for what it could mean, always within the context of theological orthodoxy and the absolute authority of Scripture. That is the goal here too: to read Scripture in such a way that we come to have a better understanding not only of the text but of the God who authored and fills it. Emboldened by Henri's courage and instructed by his

---

[4] "Nothing is that from which God separates himself and in face of which he asserts himself and exerts his positive will . . . . As God is Lord on the left-hand as well, He is the basis and Lord of nothingness too" (Karl Barth, *Church Dogmatics* III/3 [ed. G. W. Bromiley and T. F. Torrance; trans. G. W. Bromiley and R. J. Ehrlich; London: T&T Clark, 1960], p. 351).

[5] Ernst Jenni and Claus Westermann, eds, *Theological Lexicon of the Old Testament* (Hendrickson, 1997) vol. 2, p. 1038. According to the *Theological Wordbook of the Old Testament*, the "basic verb idea" is "be open, spacious, wide," suggesting a certain gullibility. See also Daniel Block, who notes that occurrences of *pth* in the Piel and Pual stems "are used of persuasion, seduction, and deception" (*The Book of Ezekiel Chapters 1–24* [New International Commentary on the Old Testament; Grand Rapids, MI: Eerdmans, 1997], p. 434).

[6] Walther Zimmerli, *Ezekiel I: A Commentary on the Book of the Prophet Ezekiel, Chapters 1–24* (Hermeneia Philadelphia, PA: Fortress, 1979), p. 306.

example, the present essay tackles a similarly difficult issue, though without Henri's exegetical panache.

## II. Divine Sovereignty and Human Responsibility: Ezekiel 14:1-11 in Doctrinal Context

What precisely is doctrinally at stake in suggesting that God deceives? Four distinct though related issues which, taken together, represent a veritable high-light reel of evangelical and Reformed theology: divine trustworthiness, the problem of evil, human responsibility, and the nature of divine action.

### II.a. Divine trustworthiness

To affirm the trustworthiness of God is to affirm that God is as good as his Word. Trustworthiness is first cousin to truthfulness: in both cases, it is a matter of God's utterly reliable word. At stake in the idea that God might sometimes deceive, then, is the truthfulness both of God and Scripture (God's Word). Indeed, we might even say that it is God's *godness* that is ultimately at stake, so much does Scripture emphasize divine faithfulness—God's being true to his Word. Stated differently, divine deception is a matter of first theology, of establishing the proper relationship between who God is (theology proper) and what God says/does (the doctrine of Scripture).[7]

There is both clear biblical testimony and a widespread consensus of Christian tradition to the effect that God does not lie: "God is not man, that he should lie" (Num. 23:19); "The glory of Israel will not lie" (1 Sam. 15:29); "God, who never lies" (Tit. 1:2); "it is impossible for God to lie [*pseudomai*]" (Heb. 6:18). St. Hippolytus speaks for most church fathers when he writes: "Scripture utters absolutely (*holôs*) no falsehood, and the Holy Spirit does not mislead his servants the prophets, through whom he was pleased to announce God's counsel to human beings."[8] Stated more positively: "God is true" (Jn. 3:33; cf. Rom. 3:4) and his word truth (Jn 17:17; cf. Jn 14:6). The truthfulness of God is so taken for granted that James Barr is able to formulate what he calls the Liar Argument: "The Liar Argument is any argument that criticizes

---

[7] "There is an unbreakable connection with our doctrine of God, the words of God as presented in the biblical text, and the actions of God to which the text bears witness" J. Gary Millar, "'A Faithful God Who Does No Wrong': History, Theology, and Reliability in Deuteronomy," in *The Trustworthiness of God: Perspectives on the Nature of Scripture* (eds, Paul Helm and Carl R. Trueman; Grand Rapids, MI: Eerdmans, 2002), p. 5.

[8] *In Danielem* 4, 6.

a biblical interpretation on the ground that it implies that God, in uttering or supporting some biblical utterance, was lying."[9]

According to Barr, to lie is to make a false statement with an intent to deceive.[10] The lie is a speech act that uses words to misrepresent the past, present, or future of the world. For Augustine, lying is an inherently disordered speech act, "a fissure between thought and utterance."[11] The liar says to be true what he knows to be false. This duplicity is, for Augustine, the evil proper to lying.[12] The lie is essentially a disordered communicative act that breaks the covenant between word, thought, and world that is of the essence of truth.[13]

To succeed in understanding how a God who cannot lie can nevertheless be said to deceive, one must ask the right preliminary questions, chief among which is that of definition: what does "deceiving" mean? A biblical commentator would do well to consult the philosopher at this point in order to appreciate the fine conceptual distinctions between lying and deceiving. For example, "to lie is to break an implicit promise to tell the truth that one makes whenever one uses language to make statements."[14] However, not all lies deceive; some are patently obvious: "An act must actually cause someone to have false beliefs in order to count as a case of deception."[15]

Of course, one can deceive without making a false statement or any statement at all. Moreover, true statements can sometimes be deceptive. For a speech act to be deceptive, it must meet the following conditions: the speech agent must *intend* the communicative patient to hold a false belief (e.g., by asserting something false), must *know* the belief to be false, and must successfully *cause* the victim to hold the false proposition. Let me therefore propose the following definition: *"x deceives y" means that x intentionally causes y to believe p, where p is false and x knows it to be so.* In brief: *deceive* "is a success or achievement verb, and deceiving is a perlocutionary act."[16]

Philosophers often have more scruples about affirming the possibility of divine deception than did some church fathers. Gregory of Nyssa, for example, claims that God deceived Satan by hiding Christ's deity under the veil of

[9] James Barr, "Is God a Liar? (Genesis 2–3)—and Related Matters," *Journal of Theological Studies* 57 (2006), p. 1.

[10] Ibid., p. 6.

[11] Paul J. Griffiths, *Lying: An Augustinian Theology of Duplicity* (Grand Rapids, MI: Brazos, 2004), p. 25.

[12] Ibid., p. 29.

[13] I shall return to Augustine's assumption that thought is "the word conceived in the heart" (Griffiths, *Lying*, p. 76) in my constructive remarks below.

[14] Thomas Carson, "Lying, Deception, and Related Concepts," in *The Philosophy of Deception* (ed. Clancy Martin; Oxford: Oxford University Press, 2009), p. 163.

[15] Ibid., p. 153.

[16] James Edwin Majon, "A Definition of Deceiving," *International Journal of Applied Philosophy* 21 (2007), p. 181. The "illocutionary" act describes what the speaker is doing in speaking (e.g., asserting; promising); the "perlocutionary" act pertains to the effect of one's utterance upon another (i.e., what one brings about *by* speaking).

his flesh. That Satan took the bait is only poetic justice, for Satan originally gained power over men and women by deceiving them.[17] Conversely, Plato argued from the moral goodness of God against God's having anthropomorphic appearances, on the grounds that such phenomena would be deceptive. Medieval reflections about certitude and divine deception represent an important footnote to this Platonic idea. Several fourteenth-century thinkers debated Ockham's claim that God can deceive us by causing us to perceive things that do not exist.[18] This would be an instance of deception by *inception*, namely, the planting in the mind of an idea or intuition.[19] While divine omnipotence entails that God could work such inception, the consequence is that we can never be sure that our perceptions correspond to what is really there, and thus that our conceptions are true.[20]

Perhaps no philosopher has thought more about the possibility of divine deception and its disastrous epistemological consequences than René Descartes.[21] How, he wonders in his "Second Meditation," can we be sure that God is not deceiving us all the time?[22] Descartes ultimately has to appeal to divine perfection: "it is impossible for God ever to deceive me, for trickery or deception is always indicative of some imperfection. And although the ability to deceive seems to be an indication of cleverness or power, the will to deceive undoubtedly attests maliciousness or weakness. Accordingly, deception is incompatible with God."[23] In response to the objection by Thomas Hobbes that God might deceive us for good reason, Descartes makes a concession, and seems to have our very passage in mind in doing so: "Nevertheless, I would not want to criticize those who allow that through the mouths of the prophets God can produce verbal untruths which, like the lies of doctors who deceive their patients in order to cure them,

[17] Gregory of Nyssa, *Oratio Catechetic*, p. 23. See also Darby Kathleen Ray, *Deceiving the Devil: Atonement, Abuse, and Ransom* (Cleveland, OH: Pilgrim Press, 1998) and Nicholas P. Constas, "The Last Temptation of Satan: Divine Deception in Greek Patristic Interpretation of the Passion Narratives," *Harvard Theological Review* 97 (2004), 139–163.

[18] See the various essays in Henrik Lagerlund (ed.), *Rethinking the History of Skepticism: The Missing Medieval Background* (Studien Und Texte Zur Geistesgeschichte Des Mittelalters; Leiden: E. J. Brill, 2010).

[19] Cf. the 2010 science fiction film "Inception," in which implantation of ideas figures as an important plot device.

[20] Thomas Aquinas, in the context of discussing the body and blood of Christ in the bread and wine, claims that God makes us see things that do not exist not to deceive us but to enable us to have deeper insights into reality, that is, beyond the surface "accidents" (*Summa theologiae* III, q. 76, art. 8).

[21] See Paul Sperring, "Descartes, Doubt, and Divine Deception," *Richmond Journal of Philosophy* 17 (2008): www.richmond-philosophy.net/rjp/rjp17_sperring.php.

[22] *Meditations on First Philosophy*, in *The Philosophical Writings of Descartes* (tr. John Cottingham, Robert Stoothoff, and Dugald Murdoch; Cambridge: Cambridge University Press, 1985), vol. 2, p. 17.

[23] Ibid., p. 37.

are free of any malicious intent to deceive."[24] It is an open question, then, whether Descartes actually succeeds in avoiding skepticism if indeed God could be justified in deceiving me with regard to any given proposition I believe.[25]

Paul Helm appeals to the nature of divine perfection as the sufficient ground for both divine trustworthiness and the truthfulness of Scripture: "the trustworthiness of God is . . . an essential part of his nature because it is entailed by such features of his nature as his knowledge, power, and goodness."[26] It is God's nature to be "omnitrustworthy"—*perfectly* trustworthy. Unlike the other "omni's," however, divine trustworthiness is a relational property, though it is one that God has in every possible world in which he exists, hence it is necessary. The point is that philosophers and not a few theologians approach the biblical text, including Ezekiel 14:9, with an idea of what an infinitely perfect being must be like. The problem arises when biblical scholars confront this concept of perfect being with stubborn particulars of the text: "What makes the Bible so problematic for theology is the representation in some of its narratives of Yahweh as a being who uses lies or encourages deception in order to get his own way."[27] Walter Brueggemann champions what he calls Israel's "countertestimony": biblical texts that depict Yahweh as "on occasion devious, ambiguous, irascible, and unstable"[28]—the very opposite of divine trustworthiness! Brueggemann notes that *pth* is "an extraordinary term to use with reference to Yahweh," and goes on to imply that divine deception bears certain similarities with violent abuse, even rape.[29]

## II.b. Problem of evil: the argument from communicative neglect

It is the very perfection of God, in particular the combination of sovereignty and goodness, which generates our second issue: a communicative variation on the problem of evil. The traditional formulation of the problem asks how to explain the continuing existence of evil in light of God's being all-good,

---

[24] Ibid., p. 102. Origen too appeals to the analogy with the physician as part of his argument that divine deception is always beneficial. See Joseph W. Trigg, "Divine Deception and the Truthfulness of Scripture," in *Origen of Alexandria: His World and His Legacy* (ed. Charles Kannengiesser and William L. Petersen; Notre Dame: University of Notre Dame Press, 1988), pp. 147–164.

[25] See Joshua Seigal, "Skeptical Theism, Moral Skepticism, and Divine Deception," *International Journal for Philosophy* 15 (2010), 251–274.

[26] Paul Helm, "The Perfect Trustworthiness of God," in *The Trustworthiness of God*, p. 239.

[27] Robert Carroll, *Wolf in the Sheepfold: The Bible as a Problem for Christianity* (London: SPCK, 1991), p. 43.

[28] *Theology of the Old Testament: Testimony, Dispute, Advocacy* (Minneapolis, MN: Fortress, 1997), p. 359.

[29] Ibid., p. 360. See also Nancy Ruth Bower, "The role of YHWH as Deceiver in True and False Prophecy" (Ph.D. diss., Princeton Theological Seminary, 1994).

all-powerful, and all-knowing. The so-called argument from neglect depicts God as a neglectful parent who either fails or is unable to intervene to protect his children. Philip Clayton and Steven Knapp work a communicative varia-tion on the argument: if God were to give *some* people thoughts or feelings that would prevent them from making mistakes or keep them from harm, God would then incur an obligation not to neglect doing so for *all*.[30] Stated differently: if God speaks the truth here and there, then God is obligated to speak truthfully to everyone everywhere at all times. Note that this argument too works from an a priori assumption of what a perfect being "must" do, an assumption that Ezekiel 14:9 puts into question. Calvin does not lessen the problem when he observes that God decrees destruction on the wicked for his glory "even though the Lord could have softened their hearts."[31] In neglecting to communicate light and truth to an errant prophet, is God neglecting his own nature, failing to be himself?

## II.c. Human responsibility: between regeneration and reprobation

The third issue follows from the preceding: How can human beings be held responsible for not knowing the truth if God has kept it from them? How can God hold people responsible for the very ignorance of which he is the ultimate cause? In German criminal law, one who deliberately induces another to com-mit a crime incurs the same punishment as the actual doer (English law would consider that person an "accessory before the fact").[32] Stated baldly: what room is there for human responsibility if human willing is merely the effect of divine instrumental or strategic action (i.e., predestination)? Exegetes cannot interpret Ezekiel 14:9 without taking a position on one of the most intractable doctrinal issues of all: the relationship of sovereign grace and free will.

## II.d. Divine action

Ezekiel 14:1-11 raises, finally, the question of the nature of divine action, spe-cifically as this concerns the means and ends of God's communicative inter-action with human covenant partners. Elsewhere I have appealed to Jürgen Habermas's distinction between "communicative" and "strategic" action in

---

[30] Clayton and Knapp, "Divine Action and the 'Argument from Neglect," in *Physics and Cosmology: Scientific Perspectives on the Problem of Natural Evil* (eds Nancey Murphy, Robert John Russell, and William R. Stoeger; Berkeley, CA and Vatican City State: Center for Theology and the Natural Sciences and Vatican Observatory, 2007), pp. 179–194.

[31] *Inst.*, III. 24.14.

[32] See David Daube, *The Deed & the Doer in the Bible. David Daube's Gifford Lectures* (West Conshohocken, PA: Templeton Foundation Press, 2008), p. 131.

order to highlight the form of God's verbal interaction with human persons and to clarify the nature of his effectual calling of the elect.[33] God deals with us according to our natures, I suggested, communicating intelligibly ("Come now, let us reason together"—Isa. 1:18) and efficaciously ("unless the Father . . . draws him"—Jn 6:44) in order to bring about understanding (the result of communicative action). By contrast, "strategic" action achieves its results through coercive or manipulative means more appropriate to "I-it" (subject–object) rather than "I-thou" (subject–subject) relations.[34] In strategic action, one uses language to get one's way other than by securing agreement, thus instrumentalizing the listener (e.g., "Get out or else!").[35]

Habermas believes that social justice requires communicative action—action oriented toward bringing about understanding—and that reaching understanding is "the inherent telos of human speech."[36] How much more is this the case in a covenantal relationship where the parties coordinate their actions by way of agreement. To engage in communicative action is to imply that what one is saying is not only intelligible but also true, truthful, and right.[37] Conversely, "If the actors are interested solely in the *success*, i.e., the *consequences* or *outcomes* of their action, they will try to reach their objective . . . through external means by using weapons or goods, threats or enticements. Such actors treat each other *strategically*."[38] Lying, bullying, and deceiving are part of the arsenal of such strategic speech acts.

If these are the only options—communicative (i.e., rational) vs. strategic (i.e., utilitarian) discourse—where should we locate divine deception? Habermas' analysis prompts the question: what kind of speech act is *deceiving*? Is it indeed a type of coercion or, as Brueggemann suggests, verbal *abuse*? Is divine deception a kind of violence, the communicative form that God's displeasure takes

---

[33] See my *Remythologizing Theology: Divine Action, Passion, and Authorship* (Cambridge Studies in Christian Doctrine; Cambridge: Cambridge University Press, 2010), pp. 316–317.

[34] See Habermas, *the Theory of Communicative Action vol. 1: Reason and the Rationalization of Society* (trans. Thomas McCarthy; Boston, MA: Beacon Press, 1981), pp. 285–295. Note that Habermas here develops his distinction between communicative and strategic action on the basis of J. L. Austin's distinction between illocutions and perlocutions respectively (cf. Austin, *How to Do Things with Words* [Oxford: Oxford University Press, 1962]).

[35] Habermas believes the two forms of action are mutually exclusive: "Speech acts cannot be carried out with the simultaneous intentions of reaching an agreement with an addressee with regard to something and of exercising a causal influence on him" (*On the Pragmatics of Communication* [Cambridge, MA: MIT Press, 1998], p. 222). We shall see, however, that unlike human speakers, God is both true and lord of the perlocution.

[36] Ibid., p. 287.

[37] Habermas is continuing the Enlightenment project by spelling out the universal validity conditions implied in all communicative acts, namely, that what is said corresponds to the real, expresses one's subjective state, and is contextually appropriate or fitting. See his "What is Universal Pragmatics," in *Communication and the Evolution of Society* (Boston, MA: Beacon Press, 1979), pp. 1–68.

[38] Habermas, *Moral Consciousness and Communicative Action* (Cambridge, MA: MIT Press, 1999), p. 133.

toward sinners? Might there be a distinct form of communicative action under God's left hand?

Perhaps the key theological question concerns the nature of divine causality. How are we to understand the "deed and doer" of deception? If God causes the inception of a misleading idea, does he then become the intellectual author of error?[39] How can God bring about misunderstanding without becoming "a God of confusion" (1 Cor. 14:33)? More pointedly: how can the God who is light, and in whom there is no darkness (1 Jn 1:5), cause darkness? The challenge, in brief, will be to specify both the locus and the nature of divine deceiving. The way forward will be to suggest that all God's communicative acts (illocutions) are true, truthful, and right in and of themselves, even when they bring about effects (perlocutions) other than understanding.

# III. Does God Deceive? Ezekiel 14:1-11 in Canonical Context

No one questions Israel's "core" testimony to Yahweh's faithfulness and reliability (i.e., truth). Yet Ezekiel 14:1-11 is not the only text that ascribes to God what at first glance strongly resembles deception.[40]

## III.a. Divine deceit in OT theology

Perhaps the first instance of a strategic deception is Yahweh's plan for Moses to ask Pharaoh to let the people go on a three-day trip into the wilderness to worship (Exod. 3:18; 5:1, 3) when in fact the plan was to deliver them permanently.[41] Samuel employs a similar ruse, again at the behest of Yahweh, in order to anoint David king without arousing Saul's suspicion (1. Sam. 16:1-5).[42]

Two other passages (Jer. 20:7-13; 1 Kgs 22:1–38) provide closer parallels to Ezekiel 14, however, in using the verb *pth* with Yahweh as the subject and a

---

[39] See Daube, *The Deed & the Doer*, vol. 1, chapter 6: "Intellectual Authorship."

[40] The closest parallels to Ezekiel 14 are narrative passages where Yahweh commissions another agent to deceive (Exod. 3:16-18; 1 Sam. 16:1-5; 1 Kgs 22:19–23) and passages in which Yahweh is said to deceive a prophet (Jer. 20:7-13).

[41] I pass over Barr's overly literalistic suggestion that God intended to deceive Adam and Eve by saying that they would die the day they ate the forbidden fruit (Gen. 2:17), as well as the claim that Yahweh was complicit in Jacob's deceit of Isaac (Gen. 27). For the latter, see John Anderson, *Jacob and the Divine Trickster: A Theology of Deception and YHWH's Fidelity to the Ancestral Promise in the Jacob Cycle* (Winona Lake, IN: Eisenbrauns, 2011).

[42] Strictly speaking, what God says to Pharaoh and Saul respectively was the truth, but not the whole truth: "There is a vast difference between telling a lie and concealing information that others have forfeited a right to know because of their hostile attitude toward God" (Walter C. Kaiser, Peter H. Davids, F. F. Bruce, Manfred Brauch, *Hard Sayings of the Bible* [Downers Grove, IL: IVP, 1996], p. 138).

prophet or prophets as the recipient of Yahweh's action. First, Jeremiah 20:7: "O Lord, you have deceived me, and I was deceived." According to Origen, divine deception, unlike its Satanic counterpart, is beneficial: God deceives Jeremiah for good reason, similar to a father's teaching a child to be good by threatening a spanking.[43] Calvin, for his part, says that Jeremiah is not complaining but rather speaking ironically, implying that if he, Jeremiah, had been deceived (but he has not), he would be an object of derision and God would be a liar.[44] Walter Kaiser proposes his own solution: "The strong statements of Jeremiah in 4.10 and 20.7 are merely complaints of the prophet who had mistaken the promise of God's presence for the insurance that no evil or derision would come on him or his ministry."[45] By contrast, Brueggemann interprets Jeremiah as saying that Yahweh has "abused" or "violated" him for commissioning him to speak but then abandoning him.[46]

1 Kings 22:1-38 (cf. 2 Chron. 18) depicts Yahweh sending a "lying spirit" into the mouths of Ahab's 400 prophets to entice him into attacking Ramoth Gilead (and dying there). It provides a far closer parallel to our passage, not least in its focus on Israel's leaders (kings rather than elders) inquiring of prophets for the Word of the Lord, its concern for the distinction between true and false prophecy, and its status as "one of the most puzzling passages in the Bible."[47] Brueggemann's gloss is positively irreverent: Yahweh's political strategizing to overthrow Omri's dynasty is "as cynical and ignoble as anything the 'plumbers' in Richard Nixon's White House might have devised."[48] Some commentators agree with Brueggemann in seeing divinely ordained deception[49]; others do not.[50] Moreover, some of the solutions for absolving God from the charge of deception in this passage are not applicable in Ezekiel 14. For example, some commentators contend that Micaiah delivered his false prophecy promising victory for Ahab (1 Kgs 22:15) in falsetto (i.e., sarcastically), thus communicating by the mode of his discourse that its con-

---

[43] Origen, *Homilies on Jeremiah*, 20.4.4.

[44] Calvin, *Commentaries on the Book of the Prophet Jeremiah and the Lamentations* (Grand Rapids, MI: Baker, 2005), vol. 2, pp. 26–28. The translator adds an intriguing note: "I find none agreeing with Calvin in his view of this verse" (p. 29 n. 1).

[45] Walter C. Kaiser, *Hard Sayings in the Old Testament* (Downers Grove, IL: InterVarsity, 1988), p. 121.

[46] Brueggemann, *A Commentary on Jeremiah: Exile and Homecoming* (Grand Rapids, MI: Eerdmans, 1998), pp. 181–182. Similarly, Bowen claims that Yahweh's deception arises from his inability to make good his promise to protect Jeremiah ("The Role of YHWH as Deceiver in True and False Prophecy," ch. 4).

[47] Peter Leithart, *1 & 2 Kings* (Brazos Theological Commentary on the Bible; Grand Rapids, MI: Brazos, 2006) p. 217.

[48] Brueggemann, *Old Testament Theology*, p. 361.

[49] Bowen, "The Role of YHWH as Deceiver," p. 50; Chisholm, "Does God Deceive?" p. 13; Robert, "Does God Lie?" p. 217.

[50] Richard Mayhue, for example, attributes the deceiving agency to Satan ("False Prophets and the Deceiving Spirit," *The Masters Seminary Journal* 4, no. 2 [1993], 135–163).

tent was not to be trusted. Micaiah then gives the true prophecy concerning Ahab's defeat (1 Kgs 22:17), so it is not as if God has not spoken truth into the situation.[51] This still leaves unexplained, however, the statement about God sending a lying spirit to entice or deceive Ahab (1 Kgs 22:21-23).

The best treatments of the conundrum of divine deception in 1 Kgs 22 (and elsewhere, for that matter) are those that attend not only to the lexical evidence (e.g., *pth*) but also to the broader literary context and to what the biblical authors are really doing in ascribing "deceit" to Yahweh. Walter Moberly insists that the story is in the canon because its author recognizes Micaiah as a truth-teller and understands what is going on: Micaiah's problem is knowing how to get through to someone who does not want to hear the truth.[52] Considered rhetorically, his message about the heavenly commissioning of a lying spirit that would deceive Ahab is actually a warning intended to provoke Ahab to repent: Micaiah is telling Ahab to his face that he is being duped by the 400 prophets. What motivates Yahweh's announcement of disaster is not deception but compassion (i.e., an intention to provoke Ahab to repent). Daniel Block provides a somewhat different "close reading" by calling attention to the ambiguity of the prophetic oracle: "Go up, for the Lord will give it into the hand of the king" (1 Kgs 22:6). The statement leaves unclear who will be delivered into whose hand. Block suggests that the spirit sent by Yahweh does not "lie" but "persuades" Ahab to construe the prophecy in a way that, while favorable to him, is false. The spirit sent from Yahweh's heavenly council inspires an utterance that is capable of more than one interpretation and then persuades (causes?) Ahab to opt for the wrong one.[53]

Both Moberly and Block demonstrate the importance of attending not only to the syntactic and semantic but also to the pragmatic dimension of the biblical text. What is of theological significance is not simply the meaning of individual terms like *pth* but also, and perhaps more importantly, the covenantal circumstances of their use. Discourse is a matter of someone saying something about something in some way to someone for some purpose. Hence what matters is not simply what is said but also *the spiritual condition of those to whom it is being said*. It follows that one must not read all statements in these passages as if they were timeless truths or abstract theological propositions, but rather as a series of dialogical moves in a high stakes sacred contest fraught with covenantal significance.

---

[51] A point that P. J. Williams underlines in his "Lying Spirits Sent by God? The Case of Micaiah's Prophecy," in *The Trustworthiness of God*, pp. 62–63.

[52] R. W. L Moberly, "Does God Lie to His Prophets? The Story of Micaiah ben Imlas as a Test Case," *Harvard Theological Review* 96 (2003), 1–23, esp. p. 15.

[53] Daniel I. Block, "What has Delphi to do with Samaria? Ambiguity and Delusion in Israelite Prophecy," in *Writing and Ancient Near Eastern Society: Papers in Honour of Alan R. Millard* (eds, P. Bienkowski, C. Mee, and E. Slater; New York/London: T & T Clark, 2005), pp. 189–216, esp. p. 207. See also Leithart, *1 & 2 Kings*, p. 161.

Only God knows what is in the human heart and what effect his word will have upon it: "The king's heart is like a stream of water in the hands of the Lord; he turns it wherever he will" (Prov. 21:1). The image here is that of a farmer who is able to divert water to an irrigation ditch by digging in the right place. This seems closer to strategic than communicative action, as does Isaiah's account of his prophetic commissioning where God instructs him to say to the people: "Keep on hearing, but do not understand; keep on seeing, but do not perceive" (Isa. 6:9). Isaiah's commission is to minister something other than understanding: "Make the heart of this people dull, and their ears heavy, and blind their eyes; lest they see with their eyes, and hear with their ears, and understand with their hearts" (Isa. 6:10). Again, it is important to understand this dark saying in the broader context of redemptive-history. As God explains later to Isaiah, those who honor him with their lips while their hearts are far from him will lose the ability to discern truth (Isa. 29:13-14). This is a key point for, as we shall see, divine deceiving is wholly other than lying, being rather a peculiar communicative act that effects a culpable *misunderstanding*.

## III.b. Divine deceit in NT theology

False prophecy is an important theme in the New Testament as well (Mt. 7:15-20; 1 Jn 4:1). Jesus uses the LXX term for "deceived" in Ezekiel 14:9 (*planao*) to refer to false prophets who will lead many astray (Mt. 24:11, 24). Satan is the father of lies (Jn 8:44) and deceiver of nations (Rev. 20:3). By contrast, Jesus is the truth (Jn. 14:6), the one to whom the Spirit of truth points (Jn 15:26). It is too easy, however, simply to identify Jesus as the "true" revelation of God in light of which the disturbing Old Testament images of God fade away.[54] For Jesus too, the definitive prophet greater than Moses (cf. Heb. 3:1-6), spoke in parables designed in part to *conceal* (Mt. 11:25). The reasons Jesus gives for speaking in parables make for a distinctly curious list of educational aims and objectives: "lest they should see with their eyes and hear with their ears and understand with their heart" (Mt. 13:15). Upon closer inspection, however, there is wise method in this apparent pedagogical madness. It is difficult to instruct those whose eyes, minds, and hearts are closed, resolutely opposed to the Word of God. In cases where a heart is set against God, more divine words lead to further hardening. Indeed, Jesus cites Isa. 6:9 as a gloss on his own prophetic ministry: "[God] has blinded [LXX *ekammusan* "closed"] their eyes and hardened their hearts" (Jn 12:40). These verbs (closing, hardening) seem on

---

[54] See, for example, Eric A. Seibert's claim that "the general portrait of Jesus that emerges [from the Gospels] is reliable enough to serve as a standard by which to evaluate portrayals of God in the Old Testament and elsewhere" (*Disturbing Divine Behavior: Troubling Old Testament Images of God* [Minneapolis, MN: Fortress, 2009], pp. 187–188).

one level more conducive to strategic than communicative action. Again they force the question: does God coerce someone to believe what is false?

The most important New Testament clue to the phenomenon of divine deception in Ezekiel 14:9 is undoubtedly 2 Thess. 2:11: "Therefore God sends them a strong delusion [*energeian planes*], so that they may believe what is false [*pseudei*]." The man of lawlessness or Antichrist is the epitome of the false prophet and the culmination of the anti-redemptive history that began in the Garden of Eden with the first deception of Adam and Eve by the serpent.[55] Note that Satan's work is always counterfeit, parasitic on the truth. It is a history of falsehood oriented toward idolatry, which is to say *nothingness*. For to speak what is *false* is to speak what is *not* (cf. Isa. 41:22-29). Here in 2 Thessalonians, Paul is concerned to expose the counterfeit parousia of the man of lawlessness.[56] Significantly, the Lord Jesus will defeat this last false prophet "with the breath of his mouth" (one word!) and thus "bring [him] to nothing" [Gk. *katargesei* = "nullify"] (2 Thess. 2:11), a fitting fate.

Who is it that God deludes? Only those who refuse to "love the truth" (2 Thess. 2:10), an expression found only here in the New Testament. Loving the truth is not a matter of being an intellectual: Paul has in mind not truth in general but the particular truth of the gospel, the proclamation of the word made flesh and poured out on the cross. To love this truth is to be personally and passionately committed to the God who is faithful. That one must love the truth reminds us that it is ultimately a matter of the disposition of our hearts, and ultimately a matter of communing with him who is the truth.

It is to those who refuse to love the truth that God then sends (not "permits") "a powerful delusion" (NIV; NRSV) or "working of error" (ASV) [Gk. *energeian planes*] (2 Thess. 2:11). How are we to make theological sense of this divine act, this closest of New Testament analogues to Ezekiel's claim that God himself deceives the prophet? In both cases, the mistake in question is thoroughly theological: a matter of a counterfeit *Word* of God in the one and a counterfeit *god*, and gospel, in the other. The persistent question is how God can cause people to believe what is false—work error—without fathering a lie. God seems to "energize" Satan's deception by speeding the lie on its nefarious mission: the utter undoing of the unrighteous. Many commentators, noting the judicial nature of God's act ("in order that all [i.e., those who refused to

---

[55] Cf. Leithart's observation that "the crux of Israel's history is not its political fortunes or the various battles that the kings fight, but the contest of true and false prophecy" (*1 & 2 Kings*, p. 158).

[56] "The Rebel is in some respects the mirror image of the Lord; so he also has a parousia" (Ernest Best, *A Commentary on the First and Second Epistles to the Thessalonians* [London: A. & C. Black, 1979], p. 305). Leon Morris suggests that the "coming of the lawless one" (2 Thess. 2:9) is "a parody of the incarnation" (*The First and Second Epistles to the Thessalonians: The English Text with Introduction, Exposition, and Notes* (New International Commentary on the New Testament; Grand Rapids, MI: Eerdmans, 1959], p. 231).

love the truth] may be condemned"—2 Thess. 2:12), suggest that God uses the evil men as instruments of his righteous judgment. Hence the divine delusion is God's judgment on prior error (unrighteousness) more than it is a cause of some new falsehood: "this is not a matter of God deceiving but rather of God using the lie the followers of the Antichrist have already chosen."[57]

# IV. God in the Dock:
## Six Interpretations (of Divine Deceit) in Search of an Explanation

To this point we have examined Ezek. 14:1-11 in doctrinal and canonical context. Before presenting my own reading of this passage, it will be useful to review the major interpretive options for the phenomenon of divine deception in general.

## IV.a. God speaks only truth

At one end of the spectrum is the claim that God speaks truth and truth only. Divine deception on this view resembles an anthropomorphism or figure of speech in which the appearance belies the reality.[58] God's own law condemns anyone who misleads the blind (Deut. 27:18). "Concealing" truth is not the same as lying. Furthermore, in the case of 1 Kings 22 and Ezekiel 14, Yahweh announces in advance his intent to deceive.

## IV.b. God literally deceives

At the other end of the spectrum is the claim that God literally deceives (i.e., intentionally causes people to believe something known to be false), either because he is not altogether trustworthy or because his victim deserves it.[59] Deceiving—a clear case of a strategic speech act—is Satan's signature move, however, not God's. The following four positions are thus all located in the

---

[57] Gregory H. Harris, "Does God Deceive? The 'Deluding Influence' of Second Thessalonians 2:11," *The Masters Seminary Journal* 16 (2005), 91.

[58] F. W. Farrar describes the language of 1 Kgs 22 as "daringly anthropomorphic" (*The First Book of Kings*, in *The Expositor's Bible* [ed. W. R. Nicoll; New York: A. C. Armstrong and Son, 1903], p. 492).

[59] So Brueggemann, *Theology of the Old Testament*, pp. 360–362. Bowen suggests that YHWH deceives in times of political transition, as part of a strategy for changing the status quo ("The Role of YHWH as Deceiver," p. 134).

middle of the spectrum, acknowledging divine deception but then going on to soften it somewhat with various qualifications.

## IV.c. God permits deception

Several commentators see a parallel between 1 Kgs 22:19–23 and the heavenly council scene in Job 1 and go on to suggest that God does not himself deceive but permits Satan to do so.[60] However, no such intermediary lying spirit is mentioned in Ezekiel 14. On the contrary, v. 9 goes out of its way to block that particular escape route: "I, the Lord, have deceived that prophet." Still, some commentators maintain that the overarching theme of God's truthfulness "is not felt to be compromised in any way by his sovereign control over spirits of deceit."[61]

## IV.d. God works deception via secondary causes

The peculiar difficulty of Ezekiel 14:9 resides in the absence of any intermediary figures, spiritual or otherwise, on which to pin the blame: "I, the Lord, have deceived . . . ." At least one exegete finds a theological (i.e., Thomistic) distinction helpful at this point: "Such a statement is only intelligible when we remember that ancient habits of thought overlooked secondary causes, and attributed events directly to the action of God."[62]

## IV.e. All's fair in holy war

Whereas the previous two interpretations seek to distance the divine agent from the act of deceiving, the present interpretation and the next emphasize the *rightness* of divine deceit. Ken Esau argues, in connection with Yahweh's deception of Pharaoh, that various strategies of deception (e.g., camouflage, diversions) are legitimate in wartime.[63] It is even more warranted when one's cause is just and one is combating evil powers and principalities. Yahweh is a divine warrior, "and deception is part of his art of holy war."[64]

---

[60] See, for example, Richard Mayhue, "False Prophets and the Deceiving Spirit," *The Masters Seminary Journal* 4, no. 2 (1993), 135–163.

[61] Williams, "Lying Spirits Sent by God?" p. 66.

[62] G. A. Cooke, *A Critical and Exegetical Commentary on the Book of Ezekiel* [International Critical Commentary; Edinburgh: T & T Clark, 1936], p. 151.

[63] "Divine Deception in the Exodus Event?" *Direction* 35 (Spring 2006) 4–17.

[64] Leithart, *1 & 2 Kings*, p. 164.

## IV.f. God deceives only those who deserve it

A number of commentators treat Ezek. 14:9 under the rubric not of truth but justice. In Walter Eichrodt's words: "The only explanation is that it is a blindness caused by God himself, as he punishes sin by sin."[65] Only this last explanation of divine deceit—that it is a just punishment, a form of God's communicative wrath—responds to the problem of divine trustworthiness. The basic idea is that, while God keeps his Word to covenant keepers, unrepentant sinners and idolaters have forfeited the right to truth.[66] Those who refuse to love the truth must suffer the consequences, namely, blindness: the loss of the capacity to see (or hear) the truth. We could here speak not of the teleological suspension of the ethical (Kierkegaard) but rather of the eschatological hastening of the judicial. Robert Jenson reads Ezekiel 14:9 as an "if-then" pronouncement of law, with a crucial difference: "He leaves no room for priestly judicial process, instead announcing: I, the Lord, will in this case act as myself both judge and executioner."[67]

Augustine got there first: "This ought to be the fixed and immobile conviction of your heart, that there is no unrighteousness with God. Therefore, whenever you read in the Scriptures of Truth, that men are led aside, or that their hearts are blunted and hardened by God, never doubt that some ill deserts of their own have first occurred, so that they justly suffer these things."[68] Calvin concurs: God is willing to deceive the prophet "because [his] impiety deserves it."[69] He says something similar in the *Institutes*: God does not delight in deception but nevertheless exercises "just judgment" in deceiving hypocrites.[70] Indeed, God wills "to make those believe lies who refuse to obey the truth."[71] Hence God is "the chief author of his own just vengeance, while Satan is but the minister of it."[72] A final quote: "That the Lord sends his Word to many whose blindness he intends to increase cannot indeed be called into question."[73]

In my opinion, this latter view is the best of the traditional explanations. The Bible depicts both YHWH and Jesus occasionally speaking words intended not to bring about understanding but, on the contrary, to make people, in

---

[65]  *Ezekiel* (Old Testament Library; Philadelphia, PA: Westminster Pres, 1970), p. 183.
[66]  So Block, *The Book of Ezekiel Chapters 1–24*, p. 435. Chisholm comments: "While this use of deception may seem contrary to God's truthful character, it is actually consistent with His justice" ("Does God Deceive?" p. 28).
[67]  Jenson, *Ezekiel*, p. 118.
[68]  *On Grace and Free Will*, ch. 43.
[69]  *Commentaries on the Prophet Ezekiel*, vol. 2 p. 56.
[70]  *Inst.*, I.18.2.
[71]  Ibid., I.18.2.
[72]  Ibid., I.18.2.
[73]  Ibid., III.24.13.

Calvin's words, "grow even more stupid."[74] However, while we cannot question that God's Words sometimes have this effect, we can, in faith, seek greater understanding of this phenomenon. I therefore propose to dig deeper and inquire into the "ontology" as it were of deceiving as a divine action: is it possible to construe this peculiar communicative act so as to reconcile it with the truthfulness and goodness of the divine communicative agent? I shall argue that divine deception (if indeed that is still the best term) is something quite distinct from its human (and satanic) analogue.

## V. Dialoguing with the Dark-Minded: A Constructive Proposal

We now return to Ezekiel 14:1-11, a passage made up almost entirely of dialogue or reports of dialogue: between Ezekiel and the elders of Israel, Ezekiel and God, God and the house of Israel, Israel and a hypothetical false prophet and, finally, God and that hypothetical false prophet. The prophet in question is hypothetical in the sense that v. 9 records God supposing what could be the case ("*if* the prophet is deceived and speaks a word . . . ").

### V.a. Restating the problem: divine inception

The main theological issue at stake is how to account for God's deceiving the prophet, and thus being complicit in false prophecy. The most plausible explanation, we suggested above, is that God deceives only those who forfeited their right to truth. Both the idolater who consults a prophet and the prophet who collaborates in what is ultimately a deception or hoax are deserving of divine judgment, in this case, being cut off from Israel—excommunicated: "the punishment of the prophet and the punishment of the inquirer shall be alike" (v. 10).

The difficulty arises because God himself claims to have a hand in the deception. Who, then, is the agent of false prophecy: the inquirer, the prophet, or God? Who is the "intellectual author" of the deceit?[75] This is where the biblical thorn presses most painfully into the interpreter's flesh: can God be the author—the speaker or doer—of what is false? Stated differently: is there something defective about God's illocutions that renders them "infelicitous?"[76]

---

[74] Ibid., III.24.13.

[75] According to Daube, the intellectual author is the instigator or "first cause" of the event in question (*The Deed & the Doer*, pp. 131–139).

[76] According to John Searle, a well-structured illocutionary act must satisfy certain preparatory, sincerity, and essential conditions in order to be "felicitous" (*Speech Acts: An Essay in the Philosophy of Language* [Cambridge: Cambridge University Press, 1969], pp. 64–71).

There is good biblical attestation for what I am here calling divine inception. The effectual call is a good positive example of an internally persuasive divine communicative act.[77] Through the preaching of the word and the work of the Spirit, God causes us to hear, understand, and respond to the gospel, and this not by violating but regenerating our natures as communicative agents in covenantal relation (i.e., persons). Both Jews and Gentiles heard the same words in Paul's sermon at the synagogue in Antioch, but only "as many as were appointed [Gk. *tetagmenoi* = "ordained"; "destined"] to eternal life believed" (Acts 13:48).

Evangelical Reformed theologians have no difficulty affirming God's gracious intellectual authorship, as it were, of faith. Jesus says "no one can [from Gk. *dynumai* = "to be able"] come to me unless the Father . . . draws [Gk. *elko* = "attract; drag"] him" (Jn 6:44).[78] He goes on to say that those who have thus been taught—who have heard and learned from God—will indeed come to him [Jesus] (Jn 6:45). Calvin agrees with Augustine's exposition of this verse: the effect of the action (i.e., learning) is the affect of the will (i.e., coming).[79] In speech act terms: the perlocution follows from an effective understanding of the illocution. Elsewhere Augustine says: "If God wills to have mercy on men, he can call them in a way that is suited to them, so that they will be moved to understand and to follow."[80] The effectual call is thus a distinctly communicative causal effect.

Can the same be said, however, for the divine *pth* of Ezekiel 14:9? Even when it is deserved, can God be the intellectual author of deception? Block provides a helpful clue to the way forward: "The delusion is not the result of a divine lie, but the effect of the work of Yahweh on his ear and his mind."[81] The theological challenge is to specify the nature of this strange, yet entirely righteous, communicative work. As we suggested above, word studies alone will not yield understanding of this matter. We must attend as well to the pragmatics of the discourse in its redemptive-historical context.[82]

---

[77] See the extended discussion in my *Remythologizing Theology*, pp. 370–375.

[78] This verb is interesting inasmuch as it is susceptible of both a communicative and a strategic interpretation. On the one hand, "attract," like "entice," suggests that it is the content of the communication that has drawing force; by contrast, "drag" is a strategic action in which the ministry of understanding—the aim of properly communicative action—apparently has no place.

[79] *Inst.*, 3.24.1.

[80] *To Simplician*, 1.2.13.

[81] Block, "What has Delphi to do with Samaria?" p. 211. In context, Block is referring to 1 Kings 22, but something similar pertains to Ezekiel 14:9.

[82] I am assuming that we cannot rightly understand the semantics of biblical language (the "what" in "what is said") without also attending to the pragmatics of biblical language (the "who," "why," "where," and "when" of language in use, i.e., discourse).

## V.b. Hard-heartedness and/as self-deception

God sends a spirit of delusion only to those who have already shown themselves to be lovers of the lie rather than the truth. There is no more fundamental lie than idolatry: the implicit or explicit affirmation that what is not God is God.[83] The problem with those who come to inquire of the prophet is that they have taken idols into their hearts (Ezek. 14:4, 7). Eichrodt's comment is apt: "They had thus allowed another into the place which belonged to Yahweh alone."[84] How dare they make a pretense of communicating with the one from whom they have excommunicated themselves!

### *V.b.1. Hardening: toward a possible solution?*

The Lord himself will "answer" hypocritical inquirers by "laying hold of" [Heb. *tfs* = "seize"] their hearts (v. 5). At first blush, the verb seems to signal a strategic rather than a communicative action. What exactly is God doing to human hearts? Augustine answers: "God works in the hearts of men to incline their wills wherever He wills."[85] There is ample biblical warrant: "For it was the Lord's doing to harden [the Hivites'] hearts that they should come against Israel in battle" (Josh. 11:20). The question this raises, however, is whether God really moves persons according to their natures or whether such an operation on the heart counts as an instance of not merely strategic but coercive, even violent, action.[86] Here Calvin may be closer to the mark, when he suggests that God's "laying hold of" is actually a matter of "[extracting] from them what was formerly hidden in their own hearts."[87]

In describing what God does in closing, hardening, seizing, enticing, and deceiving hearts, then, much depends on the redemptive-historical context. As we have seen, the objects of hardening and deception are those who have failed to love the truth, those who "by their unrighteousness suppress the truth" (Rom. 1:18), exchanging the truth for a lie (Rom. 1:25). What is truly horrendous about false prophets is not that they get one prediction wrong or cause people to commit a crime. It is rather that the false prophet induces one into a union or relationship of love with something other than the one true God, thus corrupting all desiring, thinking, and doing at the core. This something other, the idol, is in fact *no thing* at all: false gods neither initiate nor respond to communication (Ps. 115:3-7; Isa. 45:5-7). The idol has no positive

---

[83] D. A. Carson rightly speaks of idolatry as the "grotesque de-godding" of God (*Scandalous: The Cross and Resurrection of Jesus* [Re:Lit; Wheaton, IL: Crossway, 2010], p. 44).

[84] *Ezekiel*, p. 180.

[85] *On Grace and Free Will*, ch. 43.

[86] I am assuming, first, the persons are capable of causing their own motions (i.e., by willing) and, second, that motion that is contrary to a thing's nature may be said to be violent.

[87] *Commentaries on the Prophet Ezekiel*, vol. 2 p. 48.

reality whatsoever, and the only thing they have to communicate or "make common" is the nothingness that seizes the idolater's heart.

Here we might speak of "universal *fallen* pragmatics": it is of the nature of sin always and everywhere to distort the truth. Among the felicity conditions for understanding, then, are certain prerequisites in the hearers.[88] How then does one speak the Word of God to people whose communication is so perverted that they call evil good and good evil (Isa. 5:20)? Both Isaiah (Isa. 6:9-10) and Jesus (Mt. 13:14-15) faced this challenge and, as we have seen, the effect of their words was to intensify rather than correct the misunderstanding. Their prophetic communicative action served either to provoke the people to repentance (cf. Ezek. 14:5) or to confirm their heart condition: "hardening is the judgment specifically with respect to the lack of righteousness in the area of communication."[89] The hardening of the heart is thus a kind of rigor mortis, the progressive immobility or stiffening of the soul that has exchanged the truth for a lie. This, I submit, is how God's communicative action "causes" idolatrous hearts to further harden. It is also how God's Word can "cause" sinners to "grow more stupid."

## V.b.2. Darkening: the "logic" of self-deception

According to Calvin, there are some events in which God, man, and Satan alike are active, though not all on the same level or with the same purpose.[90] Scripture clearly states that God hardens Pharaoh's heart (Ex. 4:21; cf. 7:3; 9:12; 10:1, 20, 27; 11:10; 14:4, 6, 17) and that Pharaoh hardens his own heart (Ex. 8:15, 32; 9:34). In Calvin's words: "man, while he is acted upon by God, yet at the same time himself acts."[91] To be sure, there is a great mystery here. Yet, considering what happens when God "deceives" may make the mystery less dark (i.e., unintelligible) than deep.

God is always himself in all that he does, including speaking. It is precisely this divine simplicity that makes our passage so problematic: "deceiving" does not typically figure among the divine perfections. What, then, is God doing

---

[88] Given what I am calling universal fallen pragmatics (cf. Rom. 3:23), the question naturally arises: how does one come to have a receptive heart? If we are all idol mongers, why does God not justly deceive all? The answer, for Israel and us, is divine election: God has chosen efficaciously to communicate his light, life, and love to the children of the Abrahamic promise (Rom. 9:6-18). The focus of the present chapter, however, is on the mode of God's communicative action toward the hard-hearted rather than the question of why God leaves them in that condition.

[89] Torsten Uhlig, "Too Hard to Understand? The motif of hardening in Isaiah," in *Interpreting Isaiah: Issues and Approaches* (eds David G. Firth and H. G. M. Williamson; Downers Grove, IL: InterVarsity Press, 2009), p. 71.

[90] *Inst.*, II.4.2.

[91] Ibid., I.18.2.

in "deceiving" the prophet? I submit that *God is being entirely true to himself, and hence speaking only truth, which is precisely why his communicative action has such a peculiar effect on hard-hearted and dark-minded idolaters.* As the law increases sin (Rom. 5:20; 7:8), so truth increases dark-minded error because sinners suppress truth in unrighteousness.

God hardens/deceives those who have already/not-yet hardened and deceived themselves. "Already": the inquirers who come to the false prophet are hypocrites, unwilling to be rightly answerable to God; "not yet": the full extent of their blindness has yet to be reached. What occasions this further hardening and darkening is the Word of God—not lying but lordly discourse. God's commanding, truth-telling word acts as a catalyst in the idolaters' own undoing. It is, after all, *truth* that occasions sinners to suppress and idolaters to invert it.

2 Sam. 22:26–27 formulates the general principle: "You prove to be loyal to one who is faithful; . . . but you prove to be deceptive to one who is perverse" (NET). Far from being out of character, then, God is being fully himself in declaring that he will entice (i.e., internally persuade) the hypothetical false prophet. God "causes" the prophet to be deceived by speaking truth in a situation where the prophet's heart and mind are unable rightly to receive it. What God is doing on the illocutionary level is communicative: truth-telling. The perlocutionary effect—misunderstanding—is nevertheless inevitable given the infelicity condition of hard hearts and dark minds (and the absence of the enlivening Spirit of truth). This is especially clear in 1 Kings 22:19–23, where Micaiah tells Ahab to his face that he is being duped but he still fails to discern the truth, even though it is staring him in the face, or rather, *stating* itself in his face.

God does not lie. Nor does he deceive the way humans do, with illocutionary acts that assert or imply falsehood. On the contrary, God's speech compels hard-hearted, dark-minded interlocutors to harden and darken themselves against God even further. Why should this be? Because the one thing that those whose hearts are disposed to believe lies must resist is the truth. God deceives in the sense that his utterance is a contributing cause (i.e., occasion and catalyst) to a king's, prophet's, or people's *self-deception*.

Self-deception is perhaps as perplexing an anthropological phenomenon as divine deception is a theological one. There must be knowledge of the truth before there can be deception: how can one and the same person both know something and then act as if it were not true? Philosophers have sought to explain this paradox, but theologians need not look far for the answer: sin. People tell lies to themselves in order to hide from themselves the knowledge of God and especially the knowledge of themselves as sinners before God (Rom. 1:18-23). Recent work on self-deception by philosophers may nevertheless help us come to a better understanding of our passage.[92]

---

[92] For an overview of the epistemological, psychological, social, and moral issues involved in analyzing and explaining self-deception, see Brian P. McLaughlin and Amélie Oksenberg

First, self-deception is "almost always a matter of coping rather than a celebration of falsehood as such."[93] According to Robert Solomon, we deceive ourselves "to protect . . . our emotional attachments."[94] It follows, second, that self-deception is a matter of managing our beliefs for the sake of some goal other than truth.[95] In Augustine's words: "It is one thing to be ignorant, and another thing to be unwilling to know. For the will is at fault in the case of the man of whom it is said, 'He is not inclined to understand.' "[96] Third, self-deceivers are motivated by anxious desires that "cause them to be biased in favor of beliefs that reduce their anxiety."[97] Fourth, self-deception is typically not a one-time event but a general policy commitment, a disposition to avoid spelling out or "avowing" some aspect of one's engagement in the world as one's own.[98] It is not only a denial of some proposition that one knows at some level to be true but also an evasion of responsibility for what one is doing, for what one *is* or has *become*.

The paradox of self-deception helps us better to understand how God could be said to deceive or entice the prophet *and* the prophet be said to deceive himself: (1) the idolatrous inquirers are not seeking truth but trying to maintain the semblance of covenant fidelity; (2) they are trying to maintain their religion on their own terms (cf. Jas 1:26; 1 Cor. 3:18); (3) they are misled by their anxious desire to acknowledge neither the one true God and his claim on their lives on the one hand nor their covenant infidelity and thus the rightness of divine judgment on the other; there is no greater emotional attachment than an idolater's devotion to her idol, which is to say, her *illusion* (i.e., her construal of nothingness); (4) their anxious desire is not a one-time event but a general disposition—the *wrong kind* of "fear of the Lord." Self-deception—the inability to acknowledge the true God and themselves before him—thus becomes a way of life, characterized by hardheartedness and dark-mindedness. In sum: the divine address both exposes and exacerbates the stupidity (i.e., self-deception) of the idolater.[99]

Rorty, eds, *Perspectives on Self-Deception* (Berkeley, CA: University of California Press, 1988).

[93] Robert C. Solomon, "What a Tangled Web: Deception and Self-Deception in Philosophy," in *Lying and Deception in Everyday Life* (ed. Michael Lewis and Carolyn Saarni; New York and London: Guilford Press, 1993), p. 43.

[94] Ibid., p. 51.

[95] See Gregg A. Ten Elshof, *I Told Me So: Self-Deception and the Christian Life* (Grand Rapids, MI: Eerdmans, 2009), pp. xiv, 25.

[96] *On Grace and Free Will*, ch. 5.

[97] Annette Barnes, *Seeing Through Self-Deception* (Cambridge: Cambridge University Press, 2007), p. 59. Cf. the similar analysis by Alfred R. Mele, *Self-Deception Unmasked* (Princeton, NJ: Princeton University Press, 2001), pp. 54–56.

[98] So Herbert Fingarette, *Self-Deception* (Berkeley, CA: University of California Press, 2000), p. 66.

[99] A full-orbed analysis of deception must include a violation of the deceived's right not to have his or her trust violated (Barnes, *Seeing Through Self-Deception*, p. 159). However, in the case of Ezek. 14:1-11, neither the people of Israel nor the hypothetical false prophet

# VI. Conclusion: Divine Authorial Consummation

*In dialogue a person not only shows himself outwardly, but he becomes for the first time that which he is.*[100]

It only remains to bring our proposed interpretation to bear on the doctrinal issues we discussed at the outset. However we construe the answer God gives to the idolatrous inquirers and their collaborating prophet, we must insist that the God presented in Scripture remains radically sovereign and radically good (i.e., trustworthy), and that evil remains radically evil.[101] It follows that whatever God is doing in "deceiving," it must ultimately be deemed good. The best of the traditional interpretations—that God deceives those only that deserve it—is fully in line with this requirement. At the same time, we have seen that deceiving is not an illocutionary but a perlocutionary act, or rather, a peculiar strategic effect of a properly communicative act. We must therefore conclude that God's "deceiving" is "wholly other than another."[102] Divine judicial hardening, that is, has nothing to do with human lying and deceit.

Calvin says that the preaching of God's Word is sometimes the means of closing ears, hardening hearts, and darkening minds: "to those whom he pleases not to illumine, God transmits his doctrine wrapped in enigmas in order that they may not profit by it except to be cast into greater stupidity."[103] God is lord of his perlocutionary effects. Yet Calvin also insists that God does not deal with us impersonally, pulling our strings to make our puppet limbs move and our puppet mouths open and close: "Who is such a fool as to assert that God moves man just as we throw a stone?"[104] We need a term other than "deceiving" to describe how God prevents enemies of the truth from learning the truth. Perhaps the best English equivalent is "keeping in the dark."[105] Keeping hard-hearted, dark-minded idolaters in the dark is a peculiar kind of communicative act. It is not a lie but, on the contrary, *an expression of communicative righteousness toward those who refuse sincerely to address or be addressed by God.* It is an

---

trusts Yahweh to begin with. Strictly speaking, then, God is not a deceiver, for there was no genuine trust on the part of the deceived.

[100] Mikhail Bakhtin, *Problems of Dostoevsky's Poetics* (Minneapolis, MN: University of Minnesota Press, 1984), p. 252.

[101] I am here following Blocher's excellent discussion, in *Evil and the Cross: An Analytical Look at the Problem of Pain* (Grand Rapids, MI: Kregel, 1994), ch. 4.

[102] I am here borrowing a phrase from Jules Monchanin, as cited in Blocher, *Evil and the Cross*, p. 93.

[103] *Inst.*, III.24.13.

[104] Ibid., II.5.14.

[105] So Carson, "Lying, Deception, and Related Concepts," p. 180.

instance not of communicative neglect but communicative wrath.[106] Wrath is the fitting form that divine righteousness takes in a communicative encounter with people of unclean lips (Isa. 6:5).

How, finally, might God's keeping (and confirming) idolaters and false prophets in the dark throw light on the question of divine sovereignty and human responsibility? Our analysis of what happens in Ezekiel 14 is an example of what I have elsewhere called divine authorial consummation: God "authors" human characters through communicative action and dialogical interaction.[107] God is the author of our being; his word both constitutes and "consummates" us, engages and completes us, by searching out and penetrating us as deep as soul and spirit, joints and marrow (Heb. 4:12). Here we may speak not of Socratic but "soteric" dialogues whereby God efficaciously leads his human interlocutors to the desired dialogical end: God's Word—God's presence in communicative activity—is one and the same, but it is "to one a fragrance from death to death, to the other a fragrance from life to life" (2 Cor. 2:16). It is through dialogical interaction that God completes his work of authoring our own chosen identities, identities that come into focus, and being, in the characteristic style of our relating to God. Dialoguing with the living God constitutes and consummates both saints (by bringing about further understanding) and scoffers (by leading to further confusion).

Must not God communicate truth? God must be himself to everyone, everywhere, and at all times. And so he is. Ezekiel 14:1-11 shows us not a God who lies but a God who exhibits communicative righteousness to those who have refused to heed his prior communications. God is under no obligation to give his Spirit to and so enlighten anyone (otherwise it would not be a gift).[108] Blocher rightly speaks of divine causality with respect to evil as "deficient," in the sense that God is content not to act, or communicate.[109] Instead, God "gives them over" [Gk. *paradidomai*] to the error of their ways (Rom. 1:24, 26) and, in so doing, brings truth to light.

Consider the following noncanonical example of divine dialogical consummation.[110] In the final chapter of C. S. Lewis' *The Horse and His Boy*, "Rabadash the Ridiculous," Aslan approaches the defeated Prince Rabadash, the antago-

[106] On the general theme of divine wrath, see Jeremy Wynne, *Wrath Among the Perfections of God's Life* (T & T Clark Studies in Systematic Theology; London and New York: T & T Clark International, 2010).
[107] For a further development of this Bakhtinian theme, see my *Remythologizing Theology*, pp. 231–237.
[108] It is precisely the gift of the Spirit that creates the necessary condition (i.e., faith) for felicitous reception and understanding of God's word. The reason why the Spirit is not given to all belongs to the deep things of God (i.e., "the counsel of his will"—Eph. 1:11). The present chapter focuses on understanding how to parse the problem of divine sovereignty and human responsibility in terms of communicative and strategic action.
[109] *Evil and the Cross*, p. 99.
[110] I owe this illustration to my wife, Sylvie, who first suggested it.

nist of the story, and encourages him to accept the terms of surrender: "Take heed. Your doom is very near, but you may still avoid it. Forget your pride . . . and your anger . . . and accept the mercy of these good kings."[111] Rabadash ignores the offer and instead accuses Aslan of being a demon and fiend—an enemy of the gods—to which Aslan replies: "Have a care, Rabadash. The doom is nearer now; it is at the door: it has lifted the latch." Rabadash continues in his delusion, however, until Aslan declares judgment—"The hour is struck"— whereupon Rabadash transforms into a donkey.[112] His misbegotten dialogue with Aslan makes him into what he essentially already was: an uncomprehending ass.

The NET translates Ezekiel 14:9 "I, the Lord, *have made a fool of* that prophet," and this captures the gist of the present argument. God makes or causes a prophet to be a fool by demonstrating the prophet's own foolishness, namely, the hard-heartedness that hinders wisdom. He does so through a strange act that still counts as communicative: even though it brings about misunderstanding (on the part of the prophet), it is ultimately oriented toward truth (i.e., exposing self-deception). God is never truer, or trustworthier, than in sovereignly proving a false person false.

---

[111] (New York: Puffin, 1954), p. 182.
[112] Ibid., p. 183.

Chapter 7

# Mark 12: God's Lordly Son and Trinitarian Christology

Scott R. Swain

## I. Introduction

The purpose of the present chapter is to reflect theologically upon the riddle posed by Jesus in Mark 12:35-37, the so-called *Davidssohnfrage*. The goal is to demonstrate the way in which this text contributes to Mark's trinitarian Christology, that is, his claim that the Messiah is *unus ex Trinitate*, God's lordly Son. Before discussing this passage, however, a few words regarding the nature of theological commentary in general, and regarding the theological interpretation of the Gospels in particular, are in order.

Theological commentary is a human activity ordered by and to the knowledge of the triune God. As such, it is bound and shaped by realities common to every dimension of the *scientia Dei*.[1] The possibility of theological knowledge is grounded ontologically in the intratrinitarian knowledge and love of God himself. "No one knows the Son except the Father, and no one knows the Father except the Son" (Mt. 11:27). The possibility of theological knowledge is grounded epistemologically in the fact that God, in his sovereign good pleasure, has condescended to reveal himself to babes (Mt. 11:25-26). "No one knows the Father except the Son and anyone to whom the Son chooses to reveal him" (Mt. 11:27).[2] To know and adore the blessed Trinity is not our possession by natural right. Here we are dealing with a knowledge that is natural only to God, a knowledge that is ours therefore only because God has freely "granted" us to know "the mystery of the kingdom of God" (Mark 4:11). In acquiring this knowledge, we are like the one in Mt. 13:44 who stumbles upon a treasure hidden in a field. We did not mean to find it. Our possession of this treasure is not the conclusion to our skillful quest. Nevertheless, though the

---

[1] Geerhardus Vos, "The Idea of Biblical Theology as a Science and as a Theological Discipline," in *Redemptive History and Biblical Interpretation* (ed. Richard B. Gaffin, Jr.; Phillipsburg, NJ: Presbyterian & Reformed, 1980), p. 4.

[2] For a recent reflection on theology's twin *principia*, see John Webster, "Principles of Systematic Theology," *IJST* 11 (2009), pp. 56–71.

finding of this treasure does not result from our intelligent action, its finding
does result in manifold forms of intelligent activity. The lucky day laborer of
Mt. 13:44 becomes the skillful scribe and wise householder of Mt. 13:52. The
gift of theological knowledge awakens and energizes the work of theological reason. This work of theological reason, like all regenerated energies, is
in turn a work characterized by mortification and vivification. In terms of
mortification: There is a selling of all that we have to lay hold of this hidden
treasure—a kind of intellectual and affective divestment, an ascesis, that follows from our finding this gift. We do not know God. But, in God's kindness,
we have come to know him. And therefore we forsake all that we think we
know in order more fully to know him. In terms of vivification: There is a new
manner of "mindfulness" (William Desmond) that corresponds to the riches
freely received. This new mindfulness is characterized by confidence, corresponding to the promise of divine assistance which accompanies our study:
"Consider what I say, for the Lord will give you understanding in everything"
(2 Tim 2:7 NAS). It is also characterized by a holy diligence, corresponding to
the gravitas of our study's object and end.[3] Moreover, as is the case with every
labor carried out under the banner of the risen Christ (cf. 1 Cor. 15:58), this
work is characterized by *hilaritas*: "I rejoice at your word like one who finds
great spoil" (Ps. 119:162).[4]

As a mode of theological reasoning, theological commentary concerns
itself directly and specifically with the textual mediation of God's self-revelation
in the sacred writings of his authorized emissaries, the prophets and apostles. The concern here is not simply the sacred writings taken as a whole,
as in dogmatics, but the sacred writings in their distinctive portions and
places (cf. Heb. 1:1). Theological commentary is that branch of theological reasoning which attends to the *specific* words of Isaiah, Mark, or Paul.
Holy Scripture affords us with an embarrassment of riches, and we are
concerned to identify and appreciate each treasure of Holy Scripture in
its distinctive beauty and worth. Theological commentary thus devotes its
attention to the particular words of a particular scriptural text or book in
its particular historical and literary setting in order to provide a faithful
representation of its particular message. This attentiveness to particularity is preserved from myopia and atomism because it attends to the
various *words* of Holy Scripture under the promise of finding *the Word
made flesh* therein. "If any one . . . reads the Scriptures with attention,"
Irenaeus assures us, "he will find in them an account of Christ, and a
foreshadowing of the new calling. For Christ is the treasure which was

---

[3] John Chrysostom, *Homilies on Matthew* 1:17.
[4] Karl Barth, *Evangelical Theology: An Introduction* (trans. Grover Foley; Grand Rapids, MI:
    Eerdmans, 1963), pp. 155–156.

hid in the field."[5] Here we must emphasize that the principle of scriptural unity is not simply a literary hypothesis that the commentator, as rational subject, brings to the text, which is his object. The Word made flesh is the lively subject of scriptural revelation[6] who communicates himself in and through the words of his Spirit-inspired ambassadors, thus enabling us to appreciate their fundamental unity and coherence in him (Lk. 24:44-47; 1 Pet. 1:11; Rom. 10:17). Reading is therefore a living *conversation* between an eloquent Lord and his attentive servants, a conversation in which the reader is summoned to hear what the Spirit of Christ *says* to the churches (Rev. 2:7). Answering this summons, theological commentary is the work of scribes "trained for the kingdom of heaven" (Mt. 13:52), who labor diligently in the field of the Word's self-communication and who, like wise householders, freely distribute the fruits of their labors, "both enriching the understanding of men, and showing forth the wisdom of God."[7] Such labor is both pleasing to God (2 Tim. 2:15) and (quite literally) salutary in its ends (1 Tim. 4:13-16). Such labor therefore requires no further warrant.

The four Gospels play a distinctive role in the unfolding economy of God's self-revelation and we must be aware of this role if we are to read them responsibly. The Gospels announce the historical realization and revelation of "the mystery of the kingdom of God" (Mk 4:11). According to the four evangelists, God has exercised his "kingly self-assertion"[8] in accomplishing the salvation long promised in Israel's Scriptures. In doing so, he has unveiled secrets "hidden from the foundation of the world" (Mt. 13:35). Central to these accounts of the kingdom's realization and revelation is the figure of Jesus, God's anointed Son. The unveiling of God's saving kingship thus comes in and through the unveiling of Jesus' identity and mission. And so, while the Gospels include instruction about eschatology, the church, salvation, politics, and discipleship, they are primarily "*about Christ*, telling who he is, what he did, said, and suffered."[9] The chief aim of the evangelists, says Calvin, is to "place before our eyes" the "Christ who has been sent by the Father, that our faith may acknowledge him to be the Author of a blessed life."[10]

---

[5] Irenaeus, *Against Heresies* 4:26.1.

[6] Cf. Vos, "Idea," pp. 4–5.

[7] Irenaeus, *Against Heresies* 4:26,1.

[8] Herman Ridderbos, *The Coming of the Kingdom* (trans. H. de Jongste; Philadelphia, PA: Presbyterian and Reformed, 1962), p. 19.

[9] Martin Luther, "A Brief Instruction on What to Look for and Expect in the Gospels," in *Martin Luther's Basic Theological Writings* (ed. Timothy F. Lull; Minneapolis, MN: Fortress, 1989), p. 105 (emphasis mine).

[10] John Calvin, *Commentary on a Harmony of the Evangelists, Matthew, Mark, and Luke* (Calvin's Commentaries 16; trans. William Pringle; repr. Grand Rapids, MI: Baker, 1998), p. xxxvii.

The literary form of the Gospels corresponds to the historical form of the kingdom's fulfillment in Jesus. Because the Gospels intend to tell us who Jesus is, what he did, said, and suffered, their message is rendered in the form of "a chronicle, a story, a narrative."[11] The Gospels are narrative Christologies. As is characteristic of their narrative form, the Gospels' material claims are more often rendered indirectly than directly. Like their Old Testament narrative counterparts, the Gospel narratives do not "sermonize."[12] They prefer to "show" their doctrine rather than to "tell" it.[13] Moreover, because these Messianic narratives concern the historical realization and revelation of a *mystery*, we find ourselves confronted with parables, riddles, and enigmas on almost every page. The enigmatic forms of these writings repeatedly threaten to confound us even as they promise to communicate and to console. This feature of the evangelical histories should not be taken as evidence of Christological ambiguity on the part of the evangelists, however. The Gospels are *revelations*, not perpetuations of the mystery. Consequently, they intend to evoke a quite definite confession on the part of the reader (cf. Mk 15:39; Jn 20:28, 31). Nor is the more reticent form of the evangelists' claims evidence of an early stage in the evolution of Christological reflection. The Ritschlian–Harnackian narrative of dogmatic development long ago outwore its promise as a hermeneutical lens for interpreting these texts. (Let the reader understand!) The indirect nature of the evangelists' *modus loquendi* is a sign neither of theological ambiguity nor of theological primitiveness. Rather, the literary form of the Gospel records corresponds to their appointment to serve the mystery of God's kingship, which is realized *sub contrario*. God's revelation is realized through his hiddenness, God's salvation through his judgment, God's kingly reign through his humble service (cf. Mk 10:45).[14] Accordingly, it belongs to the reader of the Gospels not only to follow them *to the place* they wish to lead us—to the knowledge of the triune God and to eternal life (Jn 17:3), but also to follow them *on the path* they wish to lead us if we are to receive their gift and understand their message.

As stated at the outset, the focus of the present study is Jesus' question regarding the Messiah's filial descent in Mk 12:35-37. The exegesis will proceed in the following order:

II: Translation, Setting, and Structure; III: Commentary; IV: Exegetical and Theological Synthesis.

[11] Luther, "Brief Instruction," p. 105.
[12] J. P. Fokkelman. *Reading Biblical Narrative: An Introductory Guide* (Louisville, KY: Westminster John Knox, 1999), p. 149.
[13] Mark Allan Powell, *What is Narrative Criticism?* (Minneapolis, MN: Augsburg Fortress, 1990), p. 52.
[14] Compare with Ridderbos, who speaks of "the specific modality of the revelation of the kingdom of heaven" (*Coming*, pp. 123–129).

# II. Translation, Setting, and Structure

## II.a. Translation

*And while he was teaching in the temple, Jesus answered[15] and said, "How can the scribes say that the Messiah is the son of David? David himself declared in the Holy Spirit, 'The Lord said to my Lord, Sit at my right hand, until I put your enemies under your feet.' David himself calls him Lord; so how is he his son?" And the great crowd heard him gladly.*

## II.b. Setting

Our text appears in the middle of the last major section of Mark's Gospel (11:1-13:37) before the Passion Narrative (14:1-15:47).[16] The events of 12:35-37 transpire on the last day of Jesus' three-day sojourn in the temple and its environs, on Tuesday of Mark's "holy week."[17] Verse 35 relates the immediate setting of these events as occurring διδάσκων ἐν τῷ ἱερῷ, "while he was teaching in the temple." Donahue characterizes Mk 12:13-34 as "Jesus'' Jerusalem *didachē*.[18] This characterization nicely captures not only the events of 12:13-34 but also those of 12:1-40 in their entirety. The focus in this subsection is upon Jesus' status as messianic teacher.[19]

---

[15] Although ἀποκριθείς is often left untranslated, I have translated it because it seems to fulfill a similar function to that of the other participle in this verse (διδάσκων), that is, that of providing the setting for Jesus' question (see II.b.).

[16] See Joel Marcus' outline, *Mark 1–8: A New Translation with Introduction and Commentary* (Anchor Bible 27; New Haven, CT: Yale University Press), vol. 1, p. 64.

[17] Joel Marcus, *Mark 8–16: A New Translation with Introduction and Commentary* (Anchor Bible 27a; New Haven: Yale University Press, 2009), vol. 2, pp. 767–779. For a brief but helpful discussion of Mark's account in relation to those of the other evangelists, see Robert H. Stein, *Mark* (Baker Exegetical Commentary on the New Testament; Grand Rapids: Baker, 2008), pp. 499–502. Concerning Mark's "Holy Week," Stein concludes: "Whether Mark intended his readers to understand all of 11:1-16:8 as taking place within this tight chronological framework is unlikely" (p. 499). Stein then cites "The famous quotation of Papias," which says, "Mark . . . wrote accurately all that he remembered, not, indeed, in order, of the things said or done by the Lord (Eusebius, *Eccl. Hist.* 3:39:15)" (p. 499 n 1).

[18] John R. Donahue, SJ, "A Neglected Factor in the Theology of Mark," *JBL* 101 (1982), p. 570.

[19] Some form of διδάσκω or διδάσκαλος appears 5 times in 12:1-40 with reference to Jesus, representing a little over 20 percent of their occurrences in Mark's Gospel. Other words and phrases in these verses also emphasize Jesus' status as teacher, including "speaking in parables" in 12:1 and "answering" in 12:28, 29, 35. On the theme of Jesus as messianic teacher in Mark, see Adela Yarbro Collins, *Mark: A Commentary* (Hermeneia; Minneapolis, MN: Fortress, 2007), pp. 73–79.

Jesus' Jerusalem teaching occurs in the context of increasingly heightened conflict between himself and the authoritative teachers of Israel.[20] Though their opposition to his ministry has been apparent from the beginning (e.g., 2:6-7, 16, 24; 3:2, 6), it is now growing stronger. As Jesus predicted (8:31), the time of the Son of Man's rejection has come (cf. 12:10).[21] Furthermore, the conflict between Jesus and Israel's teachers is now unfolding on the latter's home turf, the temple.[22] Mk 12:1-40 presents Jesus' extended response to the challenge to his authority raised by "the chief priests, the scribes, and the elders" (11:27-28) on the heels of his astonishing words and actions in the temple on the previous day (11:12-19).[23] The function of 12:1-40 in this regard explains the presence of ἀποκριθεὶς in 12:35. Jesus' riddle in 12:35-37 represents his last public "answer" to the question concerning his authority before his trial.

As the structure of 12:1-40 demonstrates (see II.C.), the themes of Jesus' teaching in the temple include his authority to act as God's agent (12:1-12, 35–37) as well as his authority as an interpreter of Israel's scriptures (esp. 12:18-34). The last question asked of Jesus in this subsection measures his orthodoxy by the standard of what his contemporaries understood to be the first principle of scriptural teaching: the requirement to acknowledge and honor the one true and living God (12:28-34; cf. Philo *Decal.* 65; Josephus *Ant.* 3:91).[24] Jesus' answer reveals his (and the evangelist's) firm commitment to Jewish monotheism, as he provides the New Testament's only direct quotation of Deut. 6:4 (12:39-40; cf. 10:18).[25] Jesus' rhetorical question for "the scribes" in turn concerns whether they have sufficiently acknowledged the lordly status of God's messianic king, in accordance with the divine revelation given through David in Psalm 110 (12:35-37). Have they "respected" God's "beloved Son" (cf. 12:6)? The subsection of 12:1-40 concludes in verses 38–40 with a warning against the spiritual vices that will keep readers of sacred scripture from acknowledging this scripturally promised divine Son and thus from entering into the kingdom of God (12:38-40; cf. 12:7).

[20] Those engaging Jesus in 12:1-40 include the scribes, the Pharisees, the Herodians, and the Sadducees (see 12:13, 18, 28, 35, 38).

[21] A form of ἀποδοκιμάζω is used in both 8:31 and 12:10, thus linking Jesus' prediction regarding his rejection with the events described in the parable.

[22] Cf. Josephus' characterization of the experts in the Law as "scribes of the temple" (*Ant.* 12:142). See also Collins, *Mark,* p. 73.

[23] So Joanna Dewey, *Markan Public Debate: Literary Technique, Concentric Structure, and Theology in Mark 2:1-3:6* (SBL Dissertation Series 48; Chico, CA: Scholars Press, 1980), pp. 164–165.

[24] As Jerome Neyrey observes, the theme of "giving God his due" pervades 12:13-34 (*Render to God: New Testament Understandings of the Divine* [Minneapolis: Fortress, 2004], pp. 16–17). Donahue notes with respect to 12:13-34 that "*Theos* is used 13 times in 21 verses, the most intense concentration in the gospel" ("Neglected Factor," p. 570 n 21).

[25] M. Eugene Boring, "Markan Christology: God-Language for Jesus?" *NTS* 45 (1999), p. 456.

## II.c. Structure

Mark 12:1-40 and 12:35-37 exhibit symmetrical patterns. In 12:1-40, Jesus responds to questions regarding his authority (cf. 11:28) in two fundamental ways.[26] The first type of response (A, A') takes an antagonistic stance toward the Jewish leaders and addresses Jesus' authority as God's beloved/lordly Son, coupled with a warning against those who reject him. The second type of response (B, C, B') takes a more affirmative stance toward the Jewish leaders—or at least toward the teaching of the Pharisees, and displays Jesus' commitment to some of biblical Judaism's most basic beliefs. In 12:35-37, the structural emphasis falls upon the citation of Ps. 110:1, which serves as inspired evidence of the Messiah's lordly status and therefore as the basis for rebuking the scribes' failure to appreciate what David "in the Holy Spirit" declared.

### II.1. An outline of Mark 12:1-40[27]

A   vv. 1–12   The authority of God's beloved Son plus a threat of divine judgment

B   vv. 13–17   Giving God his due: money

C   vv. 18–27   God's power to raise the dead

B   vv. 28–34   Giving God his due: the love of God and neighbor

A   vv. 35–40   The authority of God's lordly Son plus a threat of divine judgment

### II.2. An outline of Mark 12:35-37[28]

A   And while he was teaching in the temple, Jesus answered and said,

B   "How can the scribes say that the Messiah is the son of David?

C   David himself, in the Holy Spirit, declared,

D   'The Lord said to my Lord, Sit at my right hand, until I put your enemies under your feet.'

C   David himself calls him Lord;

B   so how is he his son?"

A   "And the great crowd heard him gladly."

---

[26] Cf. Dewey, *Markan Public*, pp. 162–163.

[27] Ibid., p. 162.

[28] Here I follow Joel Marcus, *The Way of the Lord: Christological Exegesis of the Old Testament in the Gospel of Mark* (Louisville, GA: Westminster/John Knox, 1992), pp. 130–131.

# III. Commentary

Set in the midst of the ongoing conflict in the temple between Jesus and Israel's teachers, and having just responded successfully to three questions in the preceding verses (12:13-34), Jesus now responds with a question of his own. The question concerns the filial descent of the Messiah. At issue is the view of the scribes, who say the Messiah is David's son, versus the view uttered prophetically by David himself, who calls the Messiah his Lord. Though Jesus' understanding of the Messiah's pedigree remains implicit in this passage, the immediate context (12:1-12), as well as the context of Mark's Gospel as a whole, leaves room for no doubt concerning his viewpoint. The Messiah is not merely David's son. He is God's lordly Son, sent into the world to inaugurate God's long awaited kingdom and destined to share in God's kingly glory.

*And while he was teaching in the temple, Jesus answered and said.* As discussed previously (see II. A–B.), the two participles in 12:35 (ἀποκριθεὶς and διδάσκων) provide the setting for Jesus' question concerning the Messiah's descent. The chief priests, the scribes, and the elders have questioned Jesus' authority to speak and act as he did in the temple on the previous day (11:27-28), and Jesus has already addressed this question indirectly in two ways: first with a question about the source of John the Baptist's authority (11:29-33), and then with a parable regarding "a beloved son" (12:1-12). He has also vindicated himself as an authoritative teacher of Israel's scriptures by showing his commitment to giving the one Lord God his due. According to Jesus, Caesar deserves what belongs to him and God deserves what belongs to him (12:13-17), including the acknowledgment of his "power to raise the dead" (12:18-27) and his identity as the one true and living God (12:28-34).[29] Jesus now addresses the question about his authority one last time by posing a conundrum regarding the Messiah's filial descent: *"How can the scribes say that the Messiah is the son of David?"*

The belief that the Messiah would be of Davidic stock was commonplace by the time of the New Testament. This belief was rooted in a host of Old Testament scriptures (e.g., 2 Sam. 7:12ff; Isa. 11:1ff; Jer. 23:5-6) and reflected in other Jewish writings as well (e.g., *Pss. Sol.* 17:21; 4QFlor[174] I, 7–19).[30] According to some interpreters, Jesus' question is designed to sever the link between the Messiah and David in one of two ways. His question is taken either as an affirmation of his own messianic status while denying his Davidic lineage[31] or, from the opposite side, as an affirmation of his Davidic lineage

---

[29] Neyrey, *Render to God*, pp. 18–19.

[30] See Christopher Burger, *Jesus als Davidssohn: Eine traditionsgeschichtliche Untersuchung* (Göttingen: Vandenhoeck & Ruprecht, 1970), pp. 16–24, and the literature cited therein.

[31] Paul J. Achtemeier, "'And he followed him': Miracles and Discipleship in Mark 10:46-52," *Semeia* 11 (1978), pp. 115–145; followed recently by Elizabeth Struthers Malbon, *Mark's Jesus: Characterization as Narrative Christology* (Waco, TX: Baylor University Press, 2009), p. 159. Malbon considers this interpretation to be the "obvious conclusion."

while denying his messianic status.[32] Both interpretations fail, however, not only because they do not fit Mark's overarching characterization of Jesus as both Messiah and son of David (e.g., 1:1, 8:29; 10:47-48; 11:10; 14:61-62),[33] but also because they do not appreciate how questions function in Markan discourse more broadly and in this text more specifically.[34] In certain key examples related to the issue of his identity in the latter half of Mark's Gospel, Jesus' questions are not designed to reject categorically the position held by his interlocutors, but to demonstrate the position's insufficiency, taken on its own. Jesus' question in 8:29 is not meant to deny his prophetic vocation (cf. 6:4).[35] Nor is his question in 10:18 meant to deny his status as a "Good Teacher."[36] As the preceding examples suggest, Jesus' questions often function to accomplish rhetorically what his two-stage healing of the blind man in 8:22-26 accomplished symbolically, that of moving someone from partial to fuller vision.[37] In the present text, then, the point of Jesus' question seems to be that the Messiah is "more than David's son."[38]

Gundry presents a unique variation on the interpretation that Jesus is denying the Messiah's Davidic descent. He understands Jesus to be inquiring after the scriptural source of the (mistaken) scribal belief that the Messiah would be a son of David.[39] This interpretation rests however upon too narrow an understanding of πόθεν in 12:37, which can mean not only "whence" in terms of *location* but also "whence" in terms of *origin* and of *cause* (as in, "How can it be?").[40] Moreover, Gundry's interpretation saddles Jesus with exactly the sort of hermeneutical narrowness that he has just rebuked in the Sadducees in

[32] Bruce D. Chilton, "Jesus ben David: Reflections on the *Davidssohnfrage*," *JSNT* 14 (1982), pp. 88–112.
[33] For an extended argument in this regard, see Burger, *Jesus als Davidssohn*, pp. 42–71.
[34] For a helpful discussion of the role of questions in Mark's Gospel, see Robert M. Fowler, *Let the Reader Understand: Reader-Response Criticism and the Gospel of Mark* (Minneapolis: Fortress, 1991), pp. 131–134. According to Fowler's count, "there are 114 questions in Mark's Gospel, 77 of them unanswered" (p. 132 n 8).
[35] See Marcus, *Mark*, vol. 2, p. 611, who, following Räisänen, describes Jesus' question as "Socratic."
[36] See Joel Marcus, "Authority to Forgive Sins Upon the Earth: The *Shema* in the Gospel of Mark," in *The Gospels and the Scriptures of Israel* (eds, Craig A. Evans and W. Richard Stegner; Sheffield: Sheffield Academic Press, 1994), pp. 208–210.
[37] As Fowler puts it, "questions sow seeds of thought" (*Let the Reader Understand*, p. 132).
[38] Burger, *Jesus als Davidssohn*, p. 66 (cf. pp. 168–169). Joel Marcus takes an interesting approach to this text, suggesting that Mk 12:35-37 in its immediate context denies the Messiah's Davidic sonship but that in its broader Markan context only serves to qualify the adequacy of the Messiah's Davidic sonship as an explanation of his identity: "Jesus is *not (just)* the Son of David *but (also)* the Son of God" ("Identity and Ambiguity in Markan Christology," in *Seeking the Identity of Jesus: A Pilgrimage*, eds, Beverly Roberts Gaventa and Richard B. Hays [Grand Rapids, MI: Eerdmans, 2008], pp. 139–140).
[39] Robert H. Gundry, *Mark: A Commentary on His Apology for the Cross* (Grand Rapids, MI: Eerdmans, 1993), pp. 718–719, 722–723.
[40] *A Greek-English Lexicon: Compiled by Henry George Liddell and Robert Scott* (9th edn with a revised supplement; Oxford: Clarendon, 1996), s.v.

12:18-27. Surely Jesus does not require the Sadducees to make good and necessary inferences from scriptural premises in one moment only to rebuke the scribes for doing so in the next! Jesus' question is not intended to deny the Davidic descent of the Messiah or to challenge the scriptural foundations for this belief. His concern is to question the adequacy of this belief as an explanation of the Messiah's identity and authority.

In order to demonstrate the inadequacy of the scribal perspective, Jesus cites what *David himself* (αὐτὸς Δαυὶδ) *declared* about the matter in Ps. 110:1: *"The Lord said to my Lord, 'Sit at my right hand, until I put your enemies under your feet.'"* The authority of David's perspective lies in the fact that he speaks *in the Holy Spirit*. The use of similar language elsewhere suggests a visionary experience (Ezek. 11:24; 37:1; Rev. 1:10; 4:2; 17:3; 21:10) or prophetic utterance (Neh. 9:30; Mic. 3:8; Zech. 7:12) enabled by the Holy Spirit.[41] David's perspective on the matter thus represents God's perspective on the matter.

Mark's citation of Ps. 110:1 follows the LXX of Ps. 109:1 with two exceptions. Mark lacks the article before κύριος and has ὑποκάτω instead of ὑποπόδιον (so Mt. 22:44).[42] The latter discrepancy likely signals a conflation of Ps. 110:1 and Ps. 8:6 (8:7 LXX), a conflation present in other New Testament writings as well (1 Cor. 15:25-27; Eph. 1:20-22; Heb. 1:13.2–8).[43] This conflation in turn suggests that Mark may be drawing his citation from a messianic *testimonium*.[44] Whatever Mark's relation to the LXX and to possible *testimonia* collections may be, it is clear that he wishes to trace the use of one of early Christianity's most important messianic prooftexts back to Jesus himself. The question is, why? What role does Ps. 110:1 play in the present context?

Psalm 110 seems to have played little to no role in the messianic expectation of pre-Christian Judaism.[45] However, it takes on a dramatic new role in early

---

[41]  The examples cited have ἐν πνεύματι instead of ἐν τῷ πνεύματι, as we have it in 12:36. The meaning, nevertheless, seems to be equivalent.

[42]  For a discussion of the various text forms of Ps. 110:1 that are cited in the New Testament, see David M. Hay, *Glory at the Right Hand: Psalm 110 and Early Christianity* (Nashville, TN: Abingdon, 1973), pp. 34–38.

[43]  On the theological significance of this conflation, see Martin Hengel, "Sit at My Right Hand!" in *Studies in Early Christology* (Edinburgh: T & T Clark, 1995), pp. 163–172.

[44]  See Martin C. Albl, *"And Scripture Cannot be Broken": The Form and Function of the Early Christian* Testimonia *Collections* (Leiden: Brill, 1999), pp. 222–228, 236.

[45]  Hengel, "Sit at My Right Hand!" p. 179. Hengel suggests that Psalm 110 influenced the Similitudes of 1 Enoch (pp. 185–189). However, Bauckham argues against such an influence, noting the lack of direct allusion to the text ("The Throne of God and the Worship of Jesus," in *The Jewish Roots of Christological Monotheism* [eds Carey C. Newman, James R. Davila, and Gladys S. Lewis; Leiden: Brill, 1999], pp. 57–60). On the basis of the common themes that appear in 11QMelchizedek and Psalm 110, Marcus argues that the former "should be considered a chapter in the history of the interpretation of Ps. 110" (*Way*, p. 133; similarly, Hengel, "Sit at My Right Hand!" p. 182). However, the themes Marcus identifies are common to a host of Old Testament eschatological texts. Furthermore, as John J. Collins notes, our fragments of 11QMelchizedek do not contain any direct verbal allusions to Psalm 110 (John J. Collins, *The Scepter and the Star: The Messiahs of the Dead Sea*

Christianity, becoming the most commonly cited Old Testament messianic proof-text in the New Testament[46] and providing the exegetical foundation for a host of Christological topics treated in both the New Testament and beyond.[47] According to early Christian writers, Psalm 110 predicts the Messiah's heavenly vindication, glory, and enthronement (Mt. 26:64; Acts 2:33-36; Eph. 1:20-23; Heb. 1:3-4, 13–14; etc.), as well as his priestly ministry at the Father's right hand (Heb. 5:10; 6:20; 7:21-28 *et passim*). It is also taken as evidence of the Messiah's eternal generation and divinity.[48] In our passage, Ps. 110:1 functions as a prophecy of the Messiah's vindication and glory, a prophecy that, as such, includes an implicit threat against his enemies.[49] In this regard, its function is very similar to that of Ps. 118:22-23 in Mk 12:10-11. However, the main function of this psalm lies in the inference that Jesus draws in verse 37 regarding the Messiah's sonship: *David himself calls him Lord; so how is he his son?*

The first part of the inference concerns the inadequacy of the scribal understanding of the Messiah's descent. The line of reasoning is this: Because David calls the Messiah his "Lord," a merely Davidic understanding of the Messiah's ancestry is inadequate. The question for us concerns how this line of reasoning works. What is it about the servant/Lord relation between David and the Messiah that relativizes the father/son relation between David and the Messiah? The answer, it seems, cannot be that 'Lord' and 'my Lord' are simply functioning here as honorific titles for the promised eschatological king. To be sure, both terms are commonly ascribed to anointed human kings in the

---

*Scrolls and Other Ancient Literature* [New York: Doubleday, 1995], p. 142). *T. Job* 33:3 does speak of Job's throne at God's right hand, and thus undoubtedly alludes to Ps. 110:1. However, Job is not cast in the role of God's eschatological agent/Messiah in this text. His enthronement instead seems to function as a reward for his piety (so Bauckham, "Throne of God," p. 62 n 37), the latter being a common theme in pre-Christian Jewish literature (see Hay, *Glory*, p. 55). The most notable exception to the dearth of messianic reflection upon Psalm 110 (also noted by Hengel, "Sit at My Right Hand!" p. 179) lies in the canonical edition of the Psalter itself, where the exaltation of "my Lord" to God's right hand in Psalm 110 follows the psalmist's plea for deliverance from his adversaries in Psalm 109. See especially 109:26-31. Verse 31 states that the Lord "stands at the right hand of the needy, to save him from those who condemn his soul to death." This example is particularly interesting for the interpretation of Mk 12:36 because earlier in this subsection (12:10-11) the evangelist cites Ps. 118:22-23 as a prophecy of the Messiah's suffering and vindication.

46 Hay identifies 22 citations of or allusions to Psalm 110:1 in the New Testament: Mt. 22:41-46; 26:64; Mk. 12:35-37; 14:62; 16:19; Lk. 20:41-44; 22:69; Acts 2:33-36; 5:31; 7:55-56; Rom. 8:34; 1 Cor. 15:25; Eph. 1:20; 2:6; Col. 3:1; Heb. 1:3, 13; 8:1; 10:12-13; 12:2; 1 Pet. 3:22; Rev. 3:21 (*Glory*, pp. 45–46). See also Martin Hengel ("Sit at My Right Hand!" p. 133) and Richard Bauckham (*Jesus and the God of Israel*: God Crucified *and Other Studies on the New Testament's Christology of Divine Identity* [Grand Rapids: Eerdmans, 2008], p. 173), who identify 21 and 20 citations or allusions respectively.

47 For much of the following, see Hay, *Glory*, pp. 45–51.

48 Ibid., pp. 48–50.

49 So Marcus, *Way*, pp. 134–137; and Rikk E. Watts, "Mark," in *Commentary on the New Testament Use of the Old Testament* (eds, G. K. Beale and D. A. Carson; Grand Rapids, MI: Baker, 2007), p. 222.

LXX without any connotation of divinity whatsoever (see, e.g., 1 Sam. 26:18-19; 2 Sam. 1:10; 3:21; 9:11; 11:11; 13:32, 33; etc.). Moreover, generally speaking, it would have sounded strange in the ancient world to hear a father call his son "Lord."[50] However, in this instance, we are not talking about just any father or about just any son. We are talking about David, the recipient of covenant promises, and about the Messiah, the ultimate eschatological object of those promises. And if we consider this fact, it seems that no Second Temple Jew would have been surprised to hear David call his promised son—*the* promised son, "Lord."[51] After all, the point of the Davidic Covenant is that the one who will enjoy an everlasting throne, and thus an everlasting lordly status, is none other than the filial offspring of David (2 Sam. 7:14, 16)! Therefore, it is not clear how interpreting "Lord" as merely an honorific title for the promised eschatological king accounts for the supposed inadequacy of the scribes' understanding.

In this passage, the significance of the title "Lord" does not lie primarily in the title itself. The significance lies in the place where the recipient of this title sits—on God's throne, at God's right hand. In order to appreciate the point, we must consider the symbolic function of God's throne in Second Temple Judaism. During this period, God's heavenly throne serves as a symbol of his unique and unrivalled deity.[52] While the Judaism of this era knows of many heavenly figures who enjoy an exalted status in God's presence, their exalted status is clearly distinguished from that of God's. Two examples are worth mentioning. In some texts these figures sit on thrones that are distinguished from God's throne (e.g., *2 En.* 20:1-3; *T. Levi* 3:8; Col. 1:16). In other texts, they are depicted as standing in God's presence, that is, taking "the posture of servants" (e.g., *2 Bar.* 21:6; 4 Macc. 17:18; Heb. 1:13-14).[53] Both sorts of portrayals thus preserve in different ways the Jewish monotheistic belief in God's singular sovereignty. Consequently, for a figure to sit on God's own throne, as a handful of figures in pre-Christian Jewish literature do—including the Danielic Son of Man (Dan. 7:9-14; *1 En.* 45:3; 51:3; 69:27; 84:3), Wisdom (Wis. 9:4), and the messianic king of Psalm 110—is for that figure to share in God's singular sovereignty and to exercise a prerogative that is uniquely God's.[54] For in an ultimate sense God *alone* is king (cf. *Sib. Or.* 3:11; *1 En.* 9:4; Philo, *Spec.* 1, 30; *Virt.* 179; 1 Tim. 6:15).[55] Understood in this historical context, then, the

[50] Marcus, *Mark*, vol. 2, p. 847.
[51] In the *Psalms of Solomon*, the coming "son of David" (17:21) is called "the Lord Messiah" (18:1).
[52] See especially Bauckham, "Throne of God."
[53] Ibid., pp. 52–53. It is the latter stance, interestingly, that characterizes Metraton (who also, however, is enthroned) and Melchizedek, two of intertestamental Judaism's most exalted heavenly figures. See Hengel, "Sit at My Right Hand!" pp. 192–194.
[54] Hengel, "Sit at My Right Hand!" pp. 156–157; Marcus, *Way*, p. 134; Bauckham, "Throne of God," pp. 52–53.
[55] Paul Rainbow identifies the ascription of exclusive sovereignty to God as one of "ten forms of explicit monotheistic speech" in Jewish Second Temple literature ("Monotheism and

lordship of Psalm 110's Messiah is an exalted one indeed. And it is *this* under-standing of the Messiah's lordly status which poses a problem for an exclu-sively Davidic understanding of his descent. How is *he*—this lordly co-regent of God's singular divine kingship—merely David's son?

This leads us to a second aspect of the inference that Jesus draws from Ps. 110:1. In Jesus' question in verse 37, αὐτοῦ is fronted (πόθεν αὐτοῦ ἐστιν υἱός), indicating emphasis: "how is he *his* son?" The line of reasoning seems to be as follows: Given the Messiah's status as God's lordly co-regent, how can he be *David's* son? The point, in other words, is not to deny the Messiah's son-ship. The point is to deny that a merely Davidic ancestry could account for the Messiah's sovereign supremacy. Matthew draws out the logic of Mark's ques-tion more straightforwardly, "*Whose* son is he?" (22:42). According to Jesus' riddle in Mk 12:35-37, the Messiah's lordly session in Ps. 110:1 requires us to conclude that he is ultimately "the son of someone other than David."[56]

Though Jesus' riddle only implies an answer to the question concerning the Messiah's sonship, the truth regarding his filial descent is not a mystery for the attentive reader of Mark.[57] At the beginning, middle, and end of his Gospel, Mark identifies Jesus the Messiah as *the Son of God* (1:1, 11; 9:7; 15:39).[58] The structural location of these identifications within Mark's narrative lends support to Kingsbury's argument that the primary secret which Mark seeks to disclose to his readers is not so much the so-called *messianic* secret as it is the secret concerning Jesus' "divine sonship."[59] This is the secret that God and Jesus know (1:11; 9:7), and that the unclean spirits know as well (3:11; 5:7). It is moreover the secret that, for Mark, cannot be revealed fully within the context of Jesus' temple teaching, but only as he breathes his last on the cross (15:39).[60] It is in his lordly self-offering as a ransom for many (cf. 10:45), wherein he fulfills the role scripturally patterned in the *Aqedah*,[61] that the Messiah's divine sonship is fully and finally unveiled: "Truly this was the Son of God!" (15:39).

It is worth noting that, for Mark, the secret of Jesus' status as God's lordly Son is intimated in the Old Testament scriptures as well. Though the secret is *hidden* there, it is *there* (cf. Rom. 16:25-26). This, of course, is why Mark quotes Psalm 110, for verse 1 exhibits the lordly nature of God's anointed king. An

---

Christology in 1 Corinthians 8:4-6" [D.Phil. Thesis, Oxford University, 1987], pp. 45–46).
[56] Marcus, *Way*, p. 141.
[57] Ernest Best, *The Temptation and the Passion: The Markan Soteriology* (2nd edn; Cambridge: Cambridge University Press, 2005), p. 168.
[58] Joachim Gnilka, *Das Evangelium nach Markus* (Zürich/Neukirchen-Vluyn: Benziger/Neukirchener, 1979), vol. 2, p. 171.
[59] Jack Dean Kingsbury, *The Christology of Mark's Gospel* (Philadelphia, PA: Fortress, 1983), p. 14.
[60] Cf. Gnilka, *Markus*, vol. 2, p. 172.
[61] See Best, *The Temptation and the Passion*, pp. 167–172. For other associations of the *Aqedah* with divine sonship, see *T. Levi* 18:6-7; Jn 3:16; Rom. 8:32.

interesting question concerns whether or not the evangelist sees in Psalm 110, *taken as a whole*, the answer to Jesus' riddle. In verse 3 of the LXX, God speaks of the messiah's eternal generation: "From the womb, before the morning star, I have begotten you."[62] Is this perhaps Mark's ultimate answer to the *Davidssohnfrage*? It is difficult to decide. A number of patristic interpreters certainly took it as such and concluded that God had revealed his eternally begotten Son, even before the incarnation, to those like David who were his "friends and favorites."[63]

In response to Jesus' teaching, Mark tells us *the great crowd heard him gladly.* Once again, the contrast between the teaching of Jesus and that of the scribes is evident in the reaction of the crowd (cf. 1:22).

## IV. Exegetical and Theological Synthesis

One question remains for those who would follow the implications of this text to the point of theological understanding and confession: What does it *mean* within a Markan context to assert that Jesus is God's lordly Son? The answer to this question comes to light when we consider our passage in relation to both its immediate and broader contexts.

Jesus' parable in Mk 12:1-12 distinguishes his identity as God's "beloved son" from that of God's "servants" (esp. 12:2-6). Not only does the beloved son come last in the series of emissaries (12:6). He also stands in a relationship to the vineyard that is different from those who precede him. With his father, he owns the vineyard. He is "the heir" of its fruits (12:7). The distinction between the owner's beloved son and his servants is telling. And when this distinction is juxtaposed with Mark's monotheistic emphasis in 12:13-34, its significance becomes clear: Whereas it belongs to servants to gather the fruits that are due to *another*, it belongs to a beloved son to gather the fruits that are *his own*. The beloved Son alone is worthy, with his Father, to receive the fruits that are due him (cf. 12:32). Consequently, the failure to "respect" the beloved Son (12:6) is tantamount to the failure to "render to God the things that are God's" (12:17).

The characterization of Jesus' divine sonship within the immediate context of 12:35-37 corresponds to what we find within the broader context of Mark's Gospel as well. In Mark's Prologue, we learn that the "way" of the one sent

---

[62] Psalm 110:3 in the MT is difficult to translate. Though it does not as clearly suggest the idea of eternal generation, Collins and Collins conclude that it does refer "to the begetting of the king" (Adela Yarbro Collins and John J. Collins, *King and Messiah as Son of God: Divine, Human, and Angelic Messianic Figures in Biblical and Related Literature* [Grand Rapids, MI: Eerdmans, 2008], p. 19).

[63] John Chrysostom, *Homilies on the Gospel According to St. John*, Homily 8. Commenting on Jn 1:9, Chrysostom cites Mk 12:36 as evidence for David's vision of the preincarnate Son.

by God to inaugurate the kingdom is "the way of the Lord" himself (1:2-3). Accordingly, as Mark's story unfolds, God's beloved Son appears as one who exercises the Lord's unique and incommunicable authority: forgiving sin (2:7, 10), perfecting the Sabbath (2:28), quieting the storm (4:41), walking on the sea (6:45-52), and so forth. The messianic Son who "comes *in the name of* the Lord" (11:9) comes *as* the Lord.[64] Moreover, the consummation of his coming is realized when, having given his life as a ransom for many, God's beloved Son sits enthroned as Lord at his Father's right hand (cf. 12:10-11; 35–37; 14:62).

According to Mark's characterization, therefore, Jesus' identity as God's lordly Son signifies his status as one who, with God his Father, is the one true and living God. While this lordly characterization provides new meaning to the title "Son of God," which in the Old Testament can be accommodated to the title "son of David" (cf. 2 Sam. 7:12, 14), it provides this new meaning in a way that does not compromise biblical monotheism.[65] Mark does not wish to say that the Son is *another* god alongside God the Father (perhaps in the manner of an apotheosized emperor), but that he is one God *with* his Father. Just as Mk 12:35-37 presents two regents who share one divine throne, so Mark's Gospel as a whole presents two dramatis personae who share one divine life, power, and glory.[66] In doing so, Mark's Gospel exhibits the same trinitarian grammar that is enshrined in the Nicene *homoousion*.[67] The Markan Son of God is "one of the Trinity."[68] Herein lies the glory of his identity; and herein lies the gravity of the decision with which those who meet him are confronted: Will they respect and receive him, and thereby enter into his kingdom and blessing, or will they disregard and reject him, and hence be trampled under his feet (cf. Mar 12:36).

---

[64] Rikki Watts offered a very similar reading of Mark's Gospel to that summarized in this and the two preceding sentences in a paper delivered at the Annual Meeting of the Society of Biblical Literature in November 2009 ("In the Power and Authority of God: A Preliminary Exploration of Yahweh Christology in Mark"). For another similar reading, see Bauckham, *Jesus and the God of Israel*, chapter 8.

[65] Contra William Bousset, *Kyrios Christos* (trans. John E. Steely; Nashville: Abingdon, 1970), pp. 146–147.

[66] C. Kavin Rowe speaks of a *Verbindungsidentität* of Jesus and God in Luke's characterization of Jesus (*Early Narrative Christology: The Lord in the Gospel of Luke* [Berlin: Walter de Gruyter, 2006], p. 27). This notion applies to Mark's characterization as well.

[67] Cf. David S. Yeago, "The New Testament and the Nicene Dogma: A Contribution to the Recovery of Theological Exegesis," *Pro Ecclesia* 3 (1994), pp. 152–164.

[68] While Mark has relatively little to say about a third character who shares the singular life of God, it is instructive to note what he does say. According to Mk 12:36, it is "in the Holy Spirit" that David perceives and confesses the lordly nature of God's beloved Son (cf. 1 Cor. 12:3). The same Spirit who descends with God's fatherly approbation upon Jesus at his baptism (1:10), and who overshadows him on the Mount of Transfiguration (9:7), is the one who unveils the glory of God's lordly Son to and through David. Given that only God can unveil God (cf. 1 Cor. 2:10-13), Mark's portrait of the Spirit confirms his identity as "one of the Trinity" as well.

The present interpretation further illumines the function of Mk 12:35-37 within the Markan plot line as a whole. Jesus' question regarding the Messiah's pedigree comes at the conclusion of his last public confrontation with the Jewish authorities on the stage of Mark's Gospel.[69] The next time Jesus faces this group is at his arrest and trial. There his accusers bring a number of charges against him that do not stick (14:55-59) until at last the charge of "blasphemy" prevails (14:60-64). At a minimum, the charge of blasphemy implies that Jesus had assumed certain unique divine prerogatives.[70] With respect to the present discussion, it is interesting to note that this charge is linked with Jesus' acceptance of the title "Son of the Blessed [One]," as well as his prediction of the Son of Man's enthronement "at the right hand of Power" (14:61-62), two themes that also appear in 12:35-37. The question is: From whence did Jesus' accusers get the idea that his self-identification as the Son of God entailed a claim to unique divine prerogatives, thus opening him to the charge of blasphemy? In terms of the Markan narrative, it seems that Jesus' accusers derived this entailment from Jesus' own question in Mark 12:35-37. By proposing the idea of a lordly Son of God who shares God's singular sovereignty, Jesus introduced his opponents to a new understanding of messianic sonship and thus provided them with the very rope that they would use to hang him. Of course, it is a matter of no little dramatic irony that in providing his accusers with the grounds for his execution, Jesus also set the stage for the completion of his mission (cf. 10:45) and the climactic unveiling of his identity as the Son of God on the cross (15:39). Mark 12:35-37 thus proves to be quite pivotal in Mark's characterization of Jesus as God's lordly Son.

## V. Postscript

It is a great pleasure to participate in this tribute to Henri Blocher. Few have labored as a "scribe trained for the kingdom" (Mt. 13:52) with the fidelity, wisdom, and excellence of Professor Blocher. May God continue to grant such gifts to the church.

[69] Cf. Mark 12:43, where Jesus calls his disciples to himself for private instruction. Jesus is not occupied with the Jewish leaders between 12:41-14:42.
[70] Adela Yarbro Collins, "The Charge of Blasphemy in Mark 14:64," *Journal for the Study of the New Testament* 26 (2004), pp. 379–401.

Chapter 8

# John 1: Preexistent Logos and God the Son

## Henri Blocher

One enters Holy Scripture through a majestic porch: the Heptameron synthesis, the overview of God's creation, with its artful symmetry of the Seven Days (Gen. 1:1-2:3). The fourth Evangelist wished his reader to proceed and receive his testimony after being similarly introduced: he provided as an entrance into his gospel what is commonly called a *prologue*. The first 18 verses offer a panoramic picture (and maybe more than that) of the Jesus story that is being told from 1:19 onwards. The first words, *in the beginning*, signal the intention of "answering" the Genesis canonical opening: laying down the foundational truth, defining the right perspective, attuning spiritual ears to the meaning of the message.[1]

The awesome grandeur of the prologue "arch" should not intimidate us. Even if we are able only to gather a few specks from the structure, they will be a treasure of life-giving teaching. The remarks that follow will bear the mark of my[2] special calling: I am a "systematic" theologian. I try always to remember, however, that the theologian's *principium cognoscendi externum* is none other than the divine discourse written down in Scripture, interpreted after the analogy of faith—through philological exegesis and "biblical theology." These

---

[1] In intriguing fashion, the same word "beginning" keeps recurring in another writing belonging to the Johannine corpus, 1 John (also twice in 2 John), with the preposition "from": ἀπ'ἀρχῆς, 1:1; 2:7, 13, 14, 24; 3:8, 11. The reference seems to oscillate between the beginning of the readers' Christian life, the saving events proclaimed in the Gospel (the beginning of the Christian economy), the beginning of human history (3:8, cf. John 8:44), and even the Absolute Beginning (1:1, which may correspond to John 1:1). I suggest that such a fluidity is deliberate: the three of four "beginnings" involved have deep connections, probably reflecting the divine priority. They are highlighted as a condemnation of the false teachers' hunger for *novelty* (this human inclination has grown paroxysmal in our late modernity!). Though less overtly, we cannot rule out kindred associations in the Fourth Gospel.

[2] Regarding the slightly irritating problem of choosing between the first singular and the first plural pronouns, the authorial "I" and "we," I follow Paul Ricoeur and will use both: "I" when personal commitment is foremost, "we" when I wish to associate readers and feel I can; cf. his *La Mémoire, l'histoire, l'oubli* (l'Ordre philosophique; Paris: Gallimard, 2000), p.III.

remarks, little technical in the main, will focus on the Christological titles, Λόγος, usually translated the "Word," and "Son" μονογενής; but they will not forgo all interest in the context of their use. Cheer up: the richness and power of the material will compensate for inadequate approach and treatment.

## I. A Parabolic Structure

We may start with the question of shape and arrangement: it often sheds light on a writer's purpose. Unfortunately, scholarly proposals vary considerably. We should take for granted that the prologue was the object of careful planning, and also there was no intention to reproduce the pattern of Genesis 1 (if the Fourth Gospel tries to work with "seven days," it does so in the section 1:19-2:12, but this falls short of convincing proof). Since the first verse proclaims the *preexistence* of the one who is called Jesus Christ in v. 17, and v. 14 his coming in the flesh, his *incarnation,* one is tempted to adopt a diptych disposition: v. 1–13 devoted to the Logos not yet incarnate, 'άσαρκος, and v. 1418 to the Logos incarnate, 'ένσαρκος; this would correspond to the great Colossians "hymn" with its studied diptych parallelism (firstborn of all creation/firstborn from the dead, Col. 1:15-20). But insuperable objections arise: why is John the Baptist so present in the first part already, since his ministry is bound with the incarnation? Why, in vv.12-13, the famous statement on becoming the children of God through faith in Christ's name?

Pretty obvious: the symmetry between the first and the last verse, according to the *inclusio* device which one often meets in Scripture: the same unusual ascription of the title "God" to Jesus Christ, "the Word was God" and "God μονογενής" (it is also used for an *inclusio* of the whole gospel: the third occurrence is found at the end, just before the epilogue, in Thomas' confession, 20:28). Then, it is quite striking that the mention of John the Baptist in the first part is matched by several lines devoted, again, to his testimony in the second one (v.15): could we take it as a hint of an intended symmetry? Actually, the proposal I find most persuasive finds a kind of *parabola*, with elements on the right and on the left hand sides symmetrically answering to each other (this geometrical figure better represents the outline than the *chi* of chiasm).[3] The themes are organized after an ABCDEF/A'B'C'D'E'F' pattern, with FF' central: about the decision everyone is to make before Jesus Christ.

Can we flesh out the scheme? A (vv.1–2) and A' (v.18) tell of *God with God.* B (v.3) and B' (v.17) of Christ's *mediator's role*: first in *creation,* second in *redemption.* C (vv.4–5) and C' (v.16) of the *benefits* he thus bestows on humankind. D (vv.6–8)

---

[3]  I am basically following André Feuillet's presentation in his masterly article "Prologue du quatrième évangile," *Supplément* au *Dictionnaire de la Bible,* Henri Cazelles & André Feuillet, eds (Paris: Letouzey & Ané, 1969) VIII:623–688 (fasc. 44).

and D' (v.15) of *John the Baptist's witness*. E (v.9) and E' (v.14) of Christ's *coming into the world*. F (vv.10–11) of those who *receive him not* and F' (v.12–13) of those who *receive him indeed*: an implicit invitation to personal decision.

## II. Why John the Baptist?

The clarity and harmony of this construction rules out the idea (Bultmann's) that the prologue was first a hymn that celebrated John the Baptist and was subsequently recast to serve Christian ends,[4] or, contrariwise, that the verses on the Forerunner's witness were clumsily interpolated into a "poem" which had been previously composed.[5] Yet, the modern reader is a bit surprised by the DD' elements of the "parabola." Why such an emphasis? Can we account for the weight put on the Baptist's ministry? Should we find here food for our reflections?

We cannot rule out a trace of polemics. Decades after Easter, there may well have been disciples of the Desert Preacher who still refused to admit that he had "told the people to believe in the one coming after him, that is, in Jesus" (Acts 19:4, NIV); the whole chapter of Acts 19 reflects the existence of not-yet-Christian "disciples," with Apollos representing the most intelligent and open among them. If we follow Oscar Cullmann's reading of Mt. 11:11, we must realize that in the eyes of many contemporaries, Jesus was the "smaller" one, compared with John the Baptist.[6] The point emphasized in the prologue may have been a live issue when the gospel was written. It is an effect of historical distance that we tend to forget or minimize trends or figures that later disappeared from the stage . . .

If the author of the Fourth Gospel was John the Apostle, the son of Zebedee, as tradition emphatically affirms him to be, he had a personal interest in the topic, for he himself had started as a disciple of John the Baptist. Indeed, I believe he was the author. Against winds of scholarly opinion still heavily

---

[4] A highly technical study by Jean Irigoin, "La Composition rythmique du prologue de Jean (I,1–18)," *Revue Biblique* 78 (October 1971): 501–514, firmly reaches that conclusion; it shows that the prologue rigorously obeys the laws of Greek metrics.

[5] Though I confess a measure of embarrassment with the transition from v. 8 (the subject, ἐκεῖνος, is John) to v. 9 (the subject is Christ, without even a pronoun to signal the change).

[6] The argument is based on the fact that μικρότερος is comparative, not superlative: the smaller or lesser *of the two*, John the Baptist and Jesus. The meaning of the proposition, then is not: "the smallest one in the kingdom of heaven has greater privileges than even John the Baptist," but rather: "the one who is thought smaller than John, myself Jesus, is greater in the kingdom of heaven, in the truth of God and fulfillment of prophecy." Cullmann affirms his choice in his *Christologie du Nouveau Testament* (Bibliothèque Théologique; Neuchâtel & Paris: Delachaux & Niestlé, 1958), p. 33; he agrees with Fr. Dibelius in a 1910 article, and with several in the ancient church according to Jerome's testimony (Cullmann refers to Origen, Hilary, and Chrysostom).

blowing, I consider the substantial[7] apostolic authorship of the gospel as established beyond doubt: by such demonstrations as we owe, in Westcott's footsteps, to Leon Morris, Donald Carson, and not long ago, with all nuances
and through a thorough sifting of possible arguments, to Craig S. Keener.[8]
Remembering John the Baptist's witness to Jesus makes manifest the existential and historical roots of Johannine theology. And since some contacts, at
least, between John the Baptist and the Qumran community are likely (in
the same Judean desert area), affinities between the Dead Sea Scrolls and the
Fourth Gospel are easily explained—for example, on the opposition of the
Spirit of truth and the spirit of error.

The reference to John the Baptist goes beyond biographical interest: it is
loaded with theological significance. It is found in all four canonical gospels;
it belongs, we could say, to the gospel "genre" and constitutes "the beginning
of the gospel about Jesus Christ" (Mk 1:1, NIV). John the Baptist was sent to
prepare the way of the Lord, as the New Elijah (Mal. 3:1 and 4:5; Mt. 11:13f; Lk.
1:17). As such, he *recapitulates* the witness of all "the servants the prophets," who
foretold the coming deliverance and Deliverer. John the Baptist represents the
Promise, he stands for the Old Testament. As he points his finger to Jesus, he
defines the relationship between the Old and the New. Still a man of the older
economy (the greatest among those born of women, Mt. 11:11), standing on
the threshold of the new one, in the nearness of the Kingdom breaking in, he

---

[7]  This qualification means that I don't commit myself on the role of a possible amanuensis
or even editor.
[8]  *The Gospel of John: A Commentary* (Peabody, MA: Hendrickson, 2003), I:81–139. One of
the key methodological issues in the debate is the weight one should place on tradition
(tradition so loud and clear on Johannine authorship from the second half of the second
century). Without making tradition infallible, I suggest that discounting old testimony/
memory and trusting, instead, subjective appreciations (often purely hypothetical recon-
structions) betrays a strange absence of self-criticism; it is marred by more than a tinge of
modern arrogance at the level of epistemology. Internal evidence, however, is also strongly
in favor of John, the son of Zebedee, as the "beloved disciple" and as the author—*provided*
one approaches the text with the trust and respect it deserves. I just mention one element
of that evidence which enchants my mind: the use of proper names (for the twelve), as
highlighted by dom John [christened "Henry" in the Anglican Church] Chapman, OSB,
"Names in the Fourth Gospel," *Journal of Theological Studies* 30/1 (October 1928):16–23 and
summarized by A. Feuillet in his *Introduction à la* Bible, II:656. The Fourth Gospel mentions
the apostles by name *much more often* than the other Gospels: 40 times in Matthew (if we
include the phrase "the sons of Zebedee"), 74 times in the Fourth Gospel; Peter is named
26 times in Matthew (25 times in Mark), and 40 times in the Fourth Gospel. And *yet* the
sons of Zebedee are named 7 times in Matthew, 18 times in Mark, 10 times in Luke, are only
named *once* in the Fourth Gospel (the phrase "the sons of Zebedee," ‘οι τοῦ Ζεβεδαίου, in
21:2); the name "John," 9 times in Mark, *never* occurs in the Fourth Gospel! This omission is
so glaring that it is worth a signature. It is a negative signature, in the photographic sense of
"negative": so elegant, from the literary and also the spiritual point of view! (Of course the
Fourth Gospel mentions "John" several times, but John *the Baptist*: precisely, there was not
need for the title to be added, since no confusion was possible.) Why is the non-apostolic
origin of the Fourth Gospel still a majority view? I suspect that applying the tools of sociology and social psychology to the academic "tribe" would be enlightening.

shows in the Good News of Jesus the *fulfillment* of everything that went before. Indeed this is a major intention of the prologue (and of the whole Fourth Gospel). The incarnation was not a bolt from the blue. It also signifies, against all Gnostic evasion, the historical density of revelation and redemption.

I will freely venture further suggestions. If, unfettered by Enlightenment (secularizing) presuppositions, we dare search for some *design* in the providential leading of history (as drawn for us in Scripture), if we try to revive typological considerations, a remarkable pattern emerges. Elijah appears in the Old Testament as "a" new Moses, with a Sinai experience recounted in 1 Kings 19 that matches Moses': he is the outstanding representative of the line of prophets who had been promised in Deuteronomy 18. Yet, he was not "the" New Moses, of equal size and even greater, he was not *the* Prophet. This had been understood by the Old Testament faithful, and they were still hoping for the Prophet like unto Moses. The New Testament, then, proclaims the Prophet's name: Jesus (Acts 3:22, etc.).[9] Elijah was there to relay the promise. A fine symmetry thus obtains: John the Baptist was not "the Prophet" (John 1:21b) but he was a new Elijah, who was to recapitulate the promise Elijah had relayed, and thus to open the way for the Fulfiller. As it were for a warning, the traits of these figures exhibit marked differences. In many respects, Elijah is a prophet most *unlike* Moses. He is not in the least a lawgiver, he has no share in the government of the people, he does not look as one trained in all the wisdom of Egyptians. You could not mistake him for *the* New Moses. Similarly, the contrast between John the Baptist and Jesus is conspicuous, and Jesus himself underlined it (Mt. 11:18f). Divine pedagogy.

We can even discern additional refinements. Some scholars have sensed (Augustin George on Luke) some reticence before the full and strict identification of John the Baptist and Elijah. It may help to explain John's denial that he was Elijah (John 1:21a).[10] In a sense, ultimately, *all* the promises are "Yes and Amen" in Jesus Christ: *he* is the Antitype of all the types, as he recapitulates all things. In a sense, *he* is also the New and Greater Elijah—and it may be a reason why John the Baptist, contrary to Elijah, did *not* work miracles. Jesus did. It is true that Jesus' miracles call to mind those of Elisha (e.g.

[9] I argued elsewhere that the Servant prophecies in Isaiah develop the promise of the New and Greater Moses (*Songs of the Servant: Isaiah's Good News* [Vancouver: Regent College Publications, 2005]; the prominence of the title παῖς, the LXX word for the Servant, in the first chapters of Acts (Isaiah 53 in the background), therefore implies the New Moses Christology. It is also in the background in John 4: Samaritans based their expectation of the *tàhév*, the Restorer (v.25), on Deuteronomy 18, and Jesus answers: "I who speak to you am he" (v.26, NIV).

[10] John, of course, may simply ward off the misunderstanding that he was Elijah the Tishbite in person, redivivus, or more probably disown ideas that were associated, among Jews, with the promise of Malachi. But among those, precisely, there may have been some ascribing him undue prominence and independence, a mission whose purpose would not have been simply "preparing the way of the Lord."

the multiplication of loaves, cf. 2 Ki 4:42-44) even more than those of Elijah, but this is no contradiction: Elisha was Elijah's heir and successor, "a" new Elijah after him (2 Kgs 2:9-15), and therefore a type of *the* New Elijah![11] We are not unfaithful to the "mood" of the prologue if we confess that in him, Jesus Christ, all the fullness resides.

# III. Antecedence

It is important for the prologue that a preparation should have preceded the coming of Jesus Christ, but the most original feature is the proclamation of his *absolute antecedence*. It is skillfully expressed with the tenses of Greek grammar (v. 15): the paradox of Christ's coming *after* John the Baptist, and getting ahead of him (γέγονεν), is that he *was* before, before John, before all the prophets, before all creatures—in the beginning, the Absolute Beginning ('ἦν, the imperfect tense of unlimited duration, as in v. 1). In Genesis 1:1, the LXX (correctly) translates the verb in the aorist tense; the prologue wishes to go back higher, earlier. It affirms eternal preexistence.

Better to hammer it in, the prologue distinguishes between the Preexistent One and *all things created*: he was the Agent of their creation, and, in a typically Johannine repetition, nothing came into being apart from his agency (v. 3). The style and very diction of the repetitious statement are reminiscent of the Qumran *Community Rule*: "Everything came into being through his science and he establishes everything that exists through his thought, and apart from him nothing was made."[12] If we follow the punctuation choice which I unreservedly advocate, if we put the full stop at the end of v. 3 and join the last two words 'ὁ γέγονεν to the preceding sentence,[13] there is a clear demarca-

---

[11] The case also illustrates another "law" of biblical typology. Types often go by pairs, and the second one in the pair looks *less* glorious than the first one (because we are still in the Old Testament) though he is *more* directly typical of Jesus Christ (because the Antitype comes after the type: the second one in the pair signifies that order). So Moses with Joshua: the law was given by Moses, but Jesus is our Joshua (same name!) who causes to enter into the land of promise, the true Rest of God. So David with Solomon: though he is also the New David, Jesus is obviously the *son of David*, the Prince of peace, who is able to build the temple. So the first temple (Solomon's) and the second one (Zerubbabel's): Jesus *re*-builds (John 2:19), he restores the true temple for the Remnant coming back from exile . . .

[12] 1 QS 11:11, my translation of ובדעתו נהיה כול וכול הווה במחשבתו יכינו ומבלעדיו לוא יעשה. It is striking that מחשבה *could* be translated λόγος in Greek.

[13] Despite Kurt Aland's influential choice of the other possibility, I consider Bruce M. Metzger's arguments persuasive, in his handy and helpful *A Textual Commentary on the Greek New Testament* (London & New York: United Bible Societies, 1971), pp. 195f. I surveyed the debate in a short article, "Mise au point johannique (Jn 1.3–4)," *Théologie Évangélique* 1 (2002): 77–80, and I added an argument which I have not seen elsewhere and which I offer for consideration. It is based on a numerical pattern, apparently intentional on the part of the Evangelist, in the first paragraph of the prologue (v. 1–5, by almost universal consent).

tion between all the beings who once began to exist—a valid paraphrase of the clause—and the One who ever *was*, and *is*. Only prejudice would blind the reader to the presence of a true *ontological* interest here (even in the Old Testament, it would be simplistic to deny it altogether). It will also surface in the recurrence of the I AM formula in the Fourth Gospel (especially in 8:58; maybe that interest is involved in the riddle of 8:25). The prologue brings us back *before* the Old Testament preparation; it affirms the roots and foundations in Eternal Being of the Gospel Events. It thereby gives the lie to *functional* reductionism. It thereby suggests that history needs a metaphysical grounding and framework to be meaningful: otherwise it is impossible to prevent a crumbling into meaninglessness, as a dust of instants, dust of death (one cannot ensure that a sufficient connection be left, even for an idiot's tale).

The One who was, and is, and is to come (and is coming) dwells in unapproachable light, but causes his life-giving light to shine for humans. He discloses the mystery of his being. The prologue shows a *work of reflection* on that mystery. In the AA' parts of his parabola, John *the Theologian*, as he was called in the ancient Church, shows that he has pondered the mystery later to be called the mystery of the Trinity, of the divine Tri-Unity. The paradox is deliberate: monotheism being nonnegotiable, the Word is both God and with God (v. 1). No one has ever seen God, and the one we have seen is God—with the personal title added μονογενής (v. 18). The thrust of the prologue is opposed to the lame attempt to solve the paradox in the way of Arius, by making the Word and Son *inferior* to the absolute God: the absence of the article with *theos* in v. 1 does not imply a mere "divinity" lower than full deity—it is required by grammar, to indicate the predicate[14]; the article is *not* used for the God

The Evangelist used "lines" of *twelve* words each, except the last one (v.5) which has 13— maybe to mark the completion of the paragraph. Using a hyphen (-) to bind together several words if they translate only one in Greek, we read: *In the-beginning was the Word, and the Word was with the God* (12 words) / *And God was the Word, this-one was in the-beginning with the God* (12 words), and at the end: *and the light in the darkness shines, and the darkness suppressed it not* (13 words). If we take ὁ γέγονεν with the preceding sentence, we also find 12 words in lines 3 and 4: *Everything through him came-to-be, and without him not one-thing came-to-be which came-to-be* (12 words) / *In him was life, and the life was the light of the humans* (12 words). This pattern is lost with the other (Aland's) punctuation; as the Italians say: *e peccato!* In line 3 (v. 3), my translation fails to indicate the difference of verbal tenses: not one thing "came to be" (ἐγένετο, bespeaking a past event) which "has existence as a result" (γέγονεν, describing an enduring state of affairs as a consequence of past events); there is no idle repetition, we might paraphrase: all contingent being owes its existence to the creative agency of the Word. (By my reckoning, that total number of words in the prologue is 3x7x12; it may be significant, with the intention of imitating Genesis—the number of words in Gen. 1:1-2:3 is a multiple of 7; incidentally, a mistake has crept into the English version of my book on the opening chapters of Genesis, *In the Beginning*, p. 53 n.49: it should not read 7x63 but 7x67).

[14] A proposition in the reverse order, with God as subject and Logos as predicate, would not be consonant with later trinitarian orthodoxy, for "God" (often with the article) is either the name for deity without consideration of the Persons, or used as a personal name for

"no one has ever seen" in v. 18, and it *is* used for Jesus in Thomas' confession "My Lord and my God" (20:28). So θεός in v. 1, implies the full deity of the Logos, Jesus Christ. If the text hints at a way of *thinking* the mysterious harmony of identity (one God) and distinction, beyond the two main titles and the orientations they determine, it points to the importance of *relation*. This will become the key concept of trinitarian theology—starting with the Cappadocian fathers and their use of σχέσις, central for Augustine (*relatio*) and for Thomas Aquinas, who defined the Persons as "subsisting relations." The Word is "with" (πρός, also near, toward) God the First Person, "in ('εις) the bosom" of the Father, an image that tells both of union and distinction. The prologue does not offer an elaborate trinitarian theology, but it sets the stage for the later labors of the doctors God was to give the Church through the Christian era.

The two titles are Λόγος and μονογενής. Roughly considered, the first title predominates in the first part, ABCFEF, with the metaphor of light, the role in *revelation*; the second title predominates in F'E'D'C'B'A', with *grace* communicated, and filial glory. But "life" is present in C, the title Logos in E' and the theme of revelation comes back in A' ('εξηγήσατο, "he has made known"). The two titles must not be separated, and probably interpret each other. Our comments will not forget it, though dealing with each in turn.

# IV. Logos

Calling Jesus Christ Λόγος, is uniquely Johannine. As apocalyptic *Christus Victor* the Lord is named "the Logos of God" (Rev. 19:13), and as the object of apostolic witness, "the Logos of life" (1 John 1:1): only in the prologue of the gospel is he called Logos, absolutely. What is the meaning and import of such a use? What is the background, the knowledge of which may help us to come nearer the meaning?

Scholarly opinions have differed widely, to this day. The discovery of early manuscript fragments of the Fourth Gospel (first part of the second century), Qumran affinities, have ruined the views that saw the gospel as born of Gnostic influences and "Greek" speculation, in the second century. Privilege goes to the Jewish setting, with the role of the *Word* of God in the Old Testament and Jewish tradition (Aramaic *memra*'; preexistent Torah in later Judaism), in special missions (Isa. 55:11), sometimes personified (Wisdom of Solomon 18:15f). Since, in order to create, God "spoke, and it came to be" (Ps. 33:9), the agency of the Word in creation fits the reference. But a second one looks also promising. God created, through his word, *in and with his Wisdom*. In the Old

the Father, whereas Logos is a personal name, which cannot be used for the Father and would not be adequate for deity as such.

Testament, Wisdom is personified more insistently then the word. It enjoys a filial relationship to the Lord God and the role of the "master workman" (אָמוֹן) in the creation of the universe (Prov. 8:22-31). Second Temple Judaism power-fully developed the theme. There is sufficient evidence that a "Wisdom Christology" played an important part in New Testament Christianity, in Paul's epistles, and even on the lips of our Lord himself (compare, e.g., Mt. 23:34 and Lk. 11:49). Wisdom pursuits, third, were characteristic of *Hellenistic* Judaism, and implied exchanges, and mutual influences, with Greek philosophy. Philo of Alexandria constructed a magnificent synthesis of biblical teaching and Greek concepts, with elements borrowed and recast from Platonism and Stoicism: he made the Logos central—sometimes nearly identifying him with God (the Lord), sometimes stressing the distinction, a mediating role in cre-ation, and a name of "son." One can even go beyond Philo's work as a third determinative background for John's prologue, and consider that the writer had to confront directly *Greek modes of thought* (it was the surrounding culture) and responded first and foremost to ideas that were current about the Logos.

I can only register here my tentative conclusion—or, maybe, conviction. It is safer to retain the meaning "Word" (*verbum, sermo* were translations among Latin fathers), in accordance with the ordinary use of the word throughout Scripture, for "divine discourse" or utterances, and with the occurrences in the Epistle and in Revelation. Through the Logos, God makes himself known. Yet, I cannot get rid of the suspicion that the pendulum, in recent years, may have gone too far, too far from interest in Hellenistic/Greek connections. Stressing Jewishness is so fashionable these days! But Judaism was to a large extent "Hellenistic," even in Palestine, and there were crosscurrents; Philo's achievement is so powerful that we may imagine that it exercised a wide influ-ence (at least indirectly); at the end of the apostolic period, enough educated Gentiles had become Christians to make it possible and relevant for evangelists to meet "head-on" common beliefs and representations. I suggest the meaning of Logos in the prologue is richly composite.

The Word shares so remarkably the privileges of personified Wisdom in Proverbs—much more closely than those, in any passage, of the דבר יהוה– that I cannot doubt the sapiential reference. Wisdom was with God in the begin-ning.[15] She was begotten before the foundation of the world.[16] She was the agent of creation, she had a special link with humankind, a *mediating* role: she was "delight" (I understand, with the LXX: for God), and she found *her* "delight" in the children of Adam (Prov. 8:30f)—though the metaphor of light

---

[15] ראשית in Pr 8:22 implies more than mere beginning (I favor rendering it "principle"), but a reminiscence of Gen. 1:1 is nevertheless likely (some ancient interpreters understood the word with the connotations of "principle" also in Genesis), and a reminiscence of both in Jn 1:1 (the LXX uses 'αρχή, also found in Rev. 3:14).

[16] The verb קנה, in Prov. 8:22 should probably be translated "to procreate" (it is the verb of Gen. 4:1 and its pun); at any rate חוֹלָלְתִּי, in vv. 24 and 25 means "I was given birth."

is not used, we are not far from Jn 1:4! Was she also "life"? Indeed, she claims: "Whoever finds me, finds life" (Prov. 8:35). A reference to biblical Wisdom is thus quasi certain. But it is allowable to make one step beyond, to postbiblical Wisdom. The Evangelist probably remembered how the seeds of Proverbs 8 had germinated in the sapiential tradition of Judaism. Many scholars have noted how the prologue agrees with the book of Wisdom, with God addressed: "Thou hast made all things in/by your Logos, and in/by your Wisdom thou hast established the human being" (Wis. 9:1b–2a). At other points the Fourth Gospel shows that the author was acquainted with the sapiential apocrypha (see, e.g., 6:35 with Ecclesiasticus, Sir 24:21). True, one does not taste a Philonic flavor in John (as many have found in Hebrews, though there have been strong objections against too close a connection). However, it remains possible that the Alexandrian philosopher was responsible for the substitution of Λόγος to Σοφία, which allowed for the synthesis of the two Old Testament strands (the Mosaic–Prophetic and the Sapiential). There was a further advantage for the gospel: a masculine title was more fitting for the *man* Jesus.[17]

And "Logos" was meaningful for Greek readers. We should realize that the notion was as widespread and self-evident in their world as that of "person-hood" in ours.[18] Teachers and missionaries of Stoicism had successfully propa-gated their view of the Logos, the cosmic Principle, Reason divine and Soul of the universe, responsible for the order and cohesion of the All, Reason in which humankind participates in a special fashion. Middle Platonism had assimilated elements of this vision. How could a Greek reader enter the Fourth Gospel through the prologue "porch" and *not* understand that the preexistent Christ exercised the functions of the Greek Logos? John's original presenta-tion not only unites the Word and Wisdom lines, but it finds the appropriate cultural translation, long before Lesslie Newbigin. It offers the paradigm of faithful and "creative" contextualization. If we did not prefer to speak of divine inspiration, we would exclaim: What a stroke of genius!

The synthesis binds together creation and revelation, before the wit-ness moves to redemption and incarnation (of which neither Ben Sira, nor Chrysippus, nor Philo, had any inkling: I do not minimize the gap). It pro-vides a basis for the *universal* destination of the message—an important topic in the Fourth Gospel (4:42; 10:16; 11:52; 12:32 . . . ).[19] Inasmuch as Wisdom

---

[17] Gender, as a grammatical category, has little to do with sex as a real determination (and as a social reality); sound linguistics should dispel the confusion of recent decades over this matter; but in the case of Wisdom, a full-fledged literary personification had been associated with the feminine gender of the name.

[18] I was struck by the comparison when I first read it in Hendrik Kraemer, *La Foi chrétienne et les religions non chrétiennes* (Bibliothèque théologique; trans. Simone Mathil; Paris & Neuchâtel: Delachaux & Niestlé, 1956), p. 57.

[19] V. 9 in the prologue expresses the universal intention, but it has been understood in two different ways (accepting, anyway, that "coming into the world" qualifies the Light, rather than "every human being"). Most theologians, in tradition, see here the revelatory activity

belongs more obviously to the inner life of God than "speaking," it suggests the foundation of revelation within the divine being itself. Though attributing the thought to John is speculative, it seems that being "in the bosom of the Father" is the condition for the perfect making him known. Revelation requires both *distinction* (it is unthinkable in Parmenidean identity, there can only be deceptive "opinion") and *union*. Because, in the beginning, God has his Word *with* him, God is not imprisoned in the silent abyss of his absoluteness; because the Word *is* God, he makes him known truly, the Word is not confined to speaking negatively of some Unknown Other.

Since the author was clearly conscious of a mystery and paradox when affirming (monotheistic) deity and distinction, there may still be another intention in the original choice of the title Logos, Word—and, at least, there is food for theological thought. It may help us to understand how the one God can have a "son" (the usual title, prominent in the Fourth Gospel). The human image of God implies an intimate self-differentiation, consciousness of self with the production of an inner word. Analogically, can we accept that God expresses himself within himself, through an inner Word? And since he is God, his self-expression is perfect and absolute: his alter ego, who possesses everything God possesses. In this sense, he is the Son, the perfect expression of the Father, who possesses everything the Father possesses—the only difference being that he is the Son, and the Father is the Father.

This leads us to the second title, μονογενής.

## V. Unique (Son)

The time-honored rendering of the second title, "only-begotten," *unigenitus* in the Vulgate, has come under heavy fire in recent scholarship. Μονογενής is *not* derived from γεννάω, "to beget," but from γίνομαι, "to become, to come into being." Therefore, it only means "unique of its kind," with no thought of generation. The LXX uses it to translate יחיד, which may even mean "solitary" (Ps. 25[LXX 24]:16; in 68[67]:7, the LXX uses another word), but often implies endearment, uniqueness in value (Gen. 22:2, etc.). Therefore, most schlars will say, "only-begotten" is misleading. These critical considerations are solid and relevant; yet, I fear they may oversimplify the issue.[20]

of the pre-incarnate Word, through creation, providence, and (for several exegetes) also through special revelations. The other reading sees the mission-incarnation itself, the coming into the world as a man—and the verse, then, stresses the universal import of the *Christian* message. Elsewhere in the Fourth Gospel, the phrase always refers to the special incarnation coming: 11:27; 12:46 (I am the Light); 18:37 (in 1 Jn 4:1, it is the coming of false prophets); this appears to be decisive in favor of the second reading.

[20] I appreciate the courage of the nonconformist plea by John V. Dahms, "The Johannine Use of *Monogenès* Reconsidered," *New Testament Studies* 29(1983): 222–232. I am also

Etymology may be left aside, since it is no sure guide to meaning. From a lexicographic point of view, the fact is that it *can* be used outside of the filial relationship, but this happens in a small minority of occurrences compared with the frequent association with sonship. This avails in classical Greek.[21] It remains true in the LXX, although less conspicuous. It is the case for *all* New Testament occurrences: always used for a son or a daughter (one never reads of a μονογενής, brother or sister). One can therefore expect the thought of sonship to be near at hand, except if there are indications to the contrary. Indications in the prologue confirm the filial connotations: the term is used *in correlation* with "Father" in v. 14 and in v. 18,[22] and this implies that "Son" (expressly in 3:16,18) is to be understood. Technically, μονογενής is not strictly equivalent to "only-begotten"; it may have been suggested by its use for the Spirit of Wisdom, in Wis. 7:22 (again the sapiential stamp); but we should not separate it in the Fourth Gospel from the filial relation.

Through faith in his name, those who receive him as Word and Light, are extended the privilege of sonship (vv. 12–13). There may be here an invitation to discern a kind of reciprocity: the Logos-Son became flesh in order that we, who are flesh, may become children, may be born of God. Actually, some late witnesses (almost all Latin writers) read a *singular* verb at the end of v. 13 (and a singular pronoun at the beginning): "the one who was not born of bloods, nor of the will of the flesh, nor of the will of a husband, but of God," and the clause then qualifies Jesus Christ. The criteria of textual criticism lead to a rejection of this variant, but it illustrates, in the dimension of *Wirkungsgeschichte*, to what sort of a meditation the terms of the prologue can give rise. The thought of Jesus Christ's sonship is present indeed.

The prologue highlights two themes together with the sonship of the μονογενής. And ultimately, the two are one: *glory* and *grace*, and both involve a contrast with the greatest servant God had raised to that day, the Man of God Moses. John seems to follow the same logic as the writer to the Hebrews: "Jesus has been found worthy of greater honor than Moses, just as the builder of a house has greater honor than the house itself . . . Moses was faithful as a servant in all God's house. . . . But Christ is faithful as a Son over God's house" (Heb. 3:3-6, NIV). We may add that the Christological concentration of typology enables the Son to be also the House itself, for we are the God's "house" in him.

---

impressed by the judgment of a scholar I admire, Ignace de La Potterie, *La Vérité dans saint Jean* (Analecta Biblica; Rome: Biblical Institute Press, 1977), I:181–191.

[21] For example, A. Bailly's *Dictionnaire grec-français*, revised by L. Séchan & P. Chantraine (Paris: Hachette, 1981), p. 1295. It offers the following meanings: (1) only-begotten, only child (with many references to Greek authors, not to John); (2) from the same race, blood-relative (one reference); (3) term of grammar, of one gender only.

[22] In v. 18, the term distinguishes the revealing God from the invisible God, the Father; one does not imagine that the term could be used for the Father (as it could if it meant nothing but uniqueness).

The last point emerges in v.14 of the prologue. Moses erected the Tabernacle, that God may dwell in the midst of his chosen people, but the Logos-Son *became* one of his people, and he "tabernacled" among us, his own flesh (ours he shared) being the final "tent-of-meeting." The verb σκηνόω derives from the noun σκηνή, used for the Tabernacle; many have supposed that assonance justified a reference to the שכינה, a favorite word in Judaism for the Most Holy Presence: the word is not found in the Bible itself, but, of course, the verb שכן frequently occurs, and the noun derived משכן is typical for the sanctuary, the divine Residence. The presence of Jesus Christ among humankind is the Antitype of the Exodus Glory-Cloud.

Such language shows that the incarnation was *conceptualized*—and we remember how stupendous a thought it must remain! The Logos who was God did not forgo his deity, since his glory was still being "contemplated" through the veil of his flesh: therefore, he *added* the flesh, as Chalcedon correctly confessed centuries later. But this is the only case of *one* being and *two* natures; for a "nature" is the whole *quidditas*, "whatness," of that nature's bearer. It is impossible for a creature to bear two natures at once! Only God could do it—because God's relationship to his creature is unique: *interior intimo meo*,[23] and the one in whom "we live, we move, we *are*" all what we are (Acts 17:28). Only because the Logos was God could he become flesh. And at the same time, continuity obtains: This metaphysical impossibility, except for God, the sovereign God, *fulfills* the Old Testament type; it brings to perfection the divine Covenant move: God in the midst of his own, God-with-us. Though many tenets of his theology (as far as I know of them) are cause for great worrying, I can underwrite Mark S. Kinzer's quotation: "The Christian doctrine of the incarnation is an intensification, not a repudiation, of traditional Jewish teaching about the dwelling of the divine presence in the midst of Israel."[24]

What do we see when we behold the glory? The glory of the unique Son is the glory of the Father, for they are one: the fullness of *grace and truth*. We immediately recognize the well-known Old Testament pair, חסד ואמת. In the earlier use, the two words probably overlapped in meaning, colored each other, as a quasi hendiadys; in rabbinic Judaism, we are told, a stricter distinction was introduced and אמת, sometimes took on a more juridical sense (truth as right or just judgment).[25] It is difficult to tell how the Evangelist exactly took the words: "truth" probably evoked sure revelation and the fulfillment of figures, while "grace" may have referred first of all to the gift of sonship. At any rate,

---

[23] Augustine's beautiful saying, *Confessions* III,vi,11 (more interior than the most inner part of me).

[24] Kinzer himself quotes from Bruce Marshall, and I owe the quote to Richard Harvey, *Mapping Messianic Jewish Theology: A Constructive Approach* (Milton Keynes: Paternoster, 2009), p. 129, as he expounds Kinzer's theology.

[25] According to Gerhard Kittel, "Ἀλήθεια, B.1," in the *Theologisches Wörterbuch zum Neuen Testament* he edited (Stuttgart: W. Kohlhammer, 1933), I:237f.

the promise of Psalm 85 was probably on his mind: the Glory dwelling in the land (the verb is שכן), and meeting each other (חסד ואמת, v.10f [9f in English bibles]). And above all, he was thinking of the most famous account of God's revelation: when the Lord reveals his *glory* to Moses (Exod. 33–34). The glory of YHWH is the contents of his name: the Lord rich in חסד ואמת (Exod. 34:6). Moses could receive a glimpse of that glory. As a faithful servant, he could teach and testify about that glory. Yet, what he, himself, could "give" was only "the law": *grace and truth came through Jesus Christ* (John 1:17).

How was Moses granted a glimpse of the glory? God had warned him: "no one may see me and live" (Exod. 33:20); but God had found a solution: "I will put you in a cleft in the rock and cover you with my hand until I have passed by. Then I will remove my hand and you will see my back; but my face must not be seen" (v. 22f). The prologue also recalls the awful warning: "No one has ever seen God" (Jn 1:18a). What corresponds to the mysterious passing by and the hand protecting is now the coming of the Word in the flesh, of the Son become one of us: "God μονογενής, who is in the bosom of the Father, THAT ONE has made him known." He, who sees the Father face to face, has brought us into his knowledge. God's "back," as Augustine rightly perceived, is none other than the human nature, the human body of Jesus Christ, who was born of the Virgin Mary, crucified, buried and gloriously raised from the dead![26] We know God when Jesus Christ has passed and we follow him; we know him in truth, for he is God, and whoever has seen him has seen the Father; we know him by grace, and we marvel not only that we escaped destruction by the blaze of the Glory, but that in him, through faith in his name, we receive eternal life as sons and daughters of God.

Is this to receive "grace for grace" (v. 16)? John did not explain what he meant precisely. Maybe precision is not needed. It is enough to be lost in wonder and gratitude, as we benefit from the superabundant overflow of grace and truth! The theological wealth of the prologue of the Fourth Gospel, of which we have caught but a glimpse, serves as a mirror of what is ours in Christ, our Lord and Savior, the eternal Word and God the Son.[27]

[26] *De Trinitate* II,xvii,28.
[27] This article originally appeared in *Ichthus* 47–48 (Nov–Dec 1974), pp. 2–7.

Chapter 9

# Ephesians 4:1-16: The Ascension, the Church, and the Spoils of War

## Michael Horton

Not without reason C. H. Dodd regards Ephesians as "the crown of Paulinism."[1] Anchored in the eternal election, redemption, and effectual calling of the Triune God (chapter 1), God's program—"the mystery of the ages"—is to make out of the two peoples (Jew and Gentile) one new body with Christ as its head. The letter weaves together soteriology and ecclesiology, biblical and systematic theology, doctrine and practice in a unified yet variegated tapestry.

Characteristic of Paul's letters, the transition from doctrine to exhortation is announced by the "therefore" of 4:1-3: "*I therefore, a prisoner for the Lord, urge you to walk in a manner worthy of the calling to which you have been called, with all humility and gentleness, with patience, bearing with one another in love, eager to maintain the unity of the Spirit in the bond of peace*" (vv. 1–3). And yet the dramatic narrative and doctrine of the gospel is never left behind even in this extended exhortation. The entire paraclesis (running from 4:1 almost to the end of the letter) is one long imperative to grow up in unity in Christ, and yet it is charged throughout by the powerful indicatives of Christ's earthly and heavenly ministry.

As Douglas Farrow has argued, the ascension is "the point of intersection in Christology, eschatology, and ecclesiology"?[2] Nevertheless, the ascension seems to receive far less attention than the other themes that are central to the ecclesiology of Ephesians: namely, election, redemption, and calling. Our passage raises the ascension of Christ to its proper place as a genuinely new event in the history of salvation. However, first Paul exposes the sinews of ecclesial unity.

---

[1] Quoted by F. F. Bruce, *The Epistles to the Colossians, to Philemon, and to the Ephesians* (New International Commentary on the New Testament; Grand Rapids, MI: Eerdmans, 1984), p. 229. Given the remarkably close parallels between statements in Ephesians and Paul's farewell speech to the Ephesian elders in Acts 20:17-38, it seems most plausible that the letter (or sermon) could not have been written without at least Paul's personal supervision, probably from a Roman prison around 64 CE.

[2] Douglas Farrow, *Ascension and Ecclesia* (Edinburgh: T & T Clark, 1999), p. 16, citing R. Maddox, *The Purpose of Luke-Acts* (T&T Clark, 1982), p. 10. I draw significantly on Farrow for my own interpretation of the ascension in *People and Place: A Covenant Ecclesiology* (Louisville and London: WJK, 2008), chapter 1.

# I. From the Father, in the Son, through the Spirit: the Trinitarian Source

**4** *There is one body and one Spirit—just as you were called to the one hope that belongs to your call—***5** *one Lord, one faith, one baptism,* **6** *one God and Father of all, who is over all and through all and in all.* **7** *But grace was given to each one of us according to the measure of Christ's gift. (Eph. 4:4-7)*

The imperative to maintain (eagerly) the unity of the Spirit in the bond of peace is based on the objective indicatives of the gospel: "*There is* one body and one Spirit . . . one hope . . . one Lord, one faith, one baptism, one God and Father . . . " Far from obscuring the importance of personal faith, experience, and obedience, Paul understands the external gospel and its ministry as the basis for his exhortations. Further, without suggesting a fully developed dogma, it is impossible to miss the trinitarian structure of Paul's argument throughout this epistle. Especially in chapter 1, God's grace is given to sinners from the Father, in the Son, through the Spirit: a point that is reiterated in 3:14-18. Although the Son and the Spirit are also identified as God, the Father is given ontological and economic priority among the persons. In the context of early trinitarian formulations, Gregory of Nazianzus wrote, "No sooner do I conceive of the One than I am illumined by the Splendor of the Three; no sooner do I distinguish Them than I am carried back to the One."[3] For Paul, this is just as true of the unity and plurality of the church. Plurality is not accidental but essential to the unique kind of unity that this God creates in his church, as the apostle teaches elsewhere: "For the body does not consist of one member but of many" (1 Cor. 12:14). The Triune God is always the giver, while his ecclesial image-bearer is a always a recipient in relation to God. All believers share equally in the saving gift of grace. "*But* to each one of us grace has been given as Christ apportioned it" (v. 7). The gospel constitutes the unity, while the diversity of spiritual gifts given to each member for the common good underscores the plurality of persons. It is the former that is stressed in the clauses that follow.

*First, the church is constituted as "one body."* It is constituted neither hierarchically nor democratically. It is united neither by the will of an earthly head nor by the will of the people, but from above, by the electing, redeeming, and sanctifying work of the Triune God. And yet this heavenly work touches down in history, through the covenant of grace.

*Second, the church comes into existence through "one Spirit."* The "one God and Father" is "over [*epi*] all" in his sovereign grace, but is also "through [*dia*] all"

---

[3] Gregory of Nazianzus, "Oration 40: The Oration on Holy Baptism, chapter 41," in *A Select Library of Nicene and Post-Nicene Fathers*, 2nd Series, Volume 7 (ed. Phillip Schaff; Peabody, MA: Hendrickson, 2004), p. 375.

in the Son and "within [en] all" by the Spirit (v. 6). The prophets announced that the outpouring of the Spirit on all flesh will be the evidence that we are now living in "these last days" (Joel 2:28-32; cf. Isa. 32:15; 44:3; Ezek. 39:29; Mic. 4:1) and this even is now associated with Pentecost (Acts 2:17-21). Paul's eschatology presupposes this inextricable connection between the Spirit and "these last days" (1 Cor. 10:11; 2 Tim. 3:1; cf. Heb. 1:2; Jas. 5:3; 2 Pet. 3:3). In his upper room discourse (Jn 14–16), Jesus prepared the disciples for his departure, promising to send his Spirit who will make them sharers in Christ and all of his gifts (see also 1 Cor. 12:3-7).

*Third, the church is driven by "one hope."* It is the indwelling Spirit who places us in the tension between the already and not-yet of redemption. Although he unites us to Christ and all of his blessings, so that we are already co-sharers in the harvest of which he is the firstfruits (see 1 Cor. 15), the "already" tantalizes us with the "more still" awaiting us in the future. "For who hopes for what he sees? But if we hope for what we do not see, we wait for it with patience. Likewise, the Spirit helps us in our weakness" (Rom. 8:23-26).

*Fourth, the apostle teaches that the center of the church's unity is "one Lord."* The unity of the church is not tied to an earthly head, whether pope or bishop—or a charismatic leader, movement, beloved pastor, shared experiences and friendships, or ethnic and social affinities. It is always easy for the church to look away from its ascended Lord and to base its unity on someone or something else that seems more tangible, visible, and realized here and now. In these cases, the existence and identity of the church would derive from below, from us, rather than from above, from the Triune God. It would be either a false unity that downplays plurality or a false plurality that can never achieve genuine unity. However, the unity of the church derives from "one Lord": the risen and ascended Christ, who is its only head.

*Fifth, the substance of the church's unity is "one faith."* With good exegetical reason, theologians distinguish between the faith that believes (*fides qua creditur*) and the faith that is believed (*fides quae creditur*). Especially with the definite article, "the faith" refers to the latter (Acts 6:7; Eph. 4:5; 1 Tim. 1:19; 3:9; 5:8; 6:12; Jude 3). "One faith" surely falls into this second class. The church is bound by a common body of truth, through which the whole body is being built up (as Paul will argue in verses 12–15). Elsewhere, Paul reminds Timothy of the importance of "sound teaching" (2 Tim. 4:3), even "the pattern of sound words": a common confession (2 Tim. 1:13). By grounding the church in a common confession—a body of truth delivered once and for all as a deposit for the saints in all times and places, both hierarchical and democratic extremes are avoided. On one hand, Paul consistently teaches that each of us has been given faith to trust in Christ—in contrast to the unicity of a church that believes and acts *for* its members. On the other hand, "one faith" in this context directs us not to each person's act of faith but to the creed that Christians confess in all times and places. Therefore, ecclesiology is not allowed to smother soteriology, yet one's personal relationship with Jesus Christ does not dissolve ecclesiology. To belong to Christ is to belong to his church, confessing the one faith together with all of the saints in all times and places.

*Sixth, the church is claimed by God through "one baptism."* Even baptism is God's work, pledging Christ and all of his benefits—ratifying the covenant of grace. The deepest social bond is not blood or political ideology, socioeconomic demographics, cultural tastes, or generational affinities, but baptism. In the waters of baptism we discover our true brothers and sisters, with Christ as the bond. Baptism is the primordial sacrament of this objective unity of the visible church, just as Paul elsewhere argues that the Supper strengthens and confirms it (1 Cor. 10:17). Like these other bonds of unity, "one baptism" ensures that the church's identity comes to it from outside of itself. *"There is* one Lord, one faith, one baptism," quite apart from an individual's act of faith. Baptism is valid even if one does not receive the reality through the sign.

If the tendency in Roman Catholic ecclesiologies is simply to *collapse* the believer's faith into the faith of the church and the Spirit's work of uniting us to Christ into an *ex opere operato* efficacy of the sacraments, the opposite tendency in Anabaptist and evangelical approaches is to *separate* them. For example, Lewis Sperry Chafer and John Walvoord argue that "one baptism" here means "Spirit baptism," distinct from water baptism.[4] Harold Hoehner offers two reasons for rejecting a connection with water baptism in this verse: "(1) the rite of baptism, with all its different modes, seems to be more divisive than unifying (certainly in the later centuries); and (2) there is no mention of the other ordinance, the rite of the Lord's Supper, as a unifying element as Paul did in 1 Cor. 10:17. Nevertheless, it was the one rite that outwardly demonstrated the believers' faith in their Lord."[5] The dualism between objective means and subjective reality is presupposed rather than defended in Hoehner's exegesis of the passage: "Hence, the 'one baptism' most likely refers to the internal reality of having been baptized into (identified with) the 'one Lord' by means of the 'one faith' mentioned in this verse."[6] So, in Hoehner's view, both the "one faith" and the "one baptism" are purely inward, invisible, and individual acts of the believer, rather than the external, public, and corporate word and act of God.[7] The implications for ecclesiology more generally are significant, as I point out in the last section of this chapter.

---

[4] John Walvoord *The Holy Spirit: A Comprehensive Study of the Person and Work of the Holy Spirit* (3rd edn; Findlay, OH: Dunham, 1958), p. 140.

[5] Harold Hoehner, *Ephesians: An Exegetical Commentary* (Grand Rapids: Baker Academic, 2002), p. 517.

[6] Ibid., p. 518.

[7] I find these arguments puzzling. First, the fact that Christians have divided throughout history over the proper interpretation of the "one faith" does nothing to vitiate the fact that there is a common confession, so why should tragic divisions over baptism determine its meaning or importance in this verse? Second, there is no reason to conclude that the absence of the Lord's Supper in Ephesians 4 eliminates the significance that the apostle

Anticipating his emphasis on the ascension, all of Paul's clauses move from the Triune God (cause) to us (effect) rather than vice versa. Like the weapons that Paul mentions in chapter 6, all of these clauses refer to something objective, external to the believer. This is what Paul means when he exhorts believers repeatedly to "put on Christ." "For as many of you as were baptized into Christ have put on Christ" (Gal. 3:27; cf. Rom. 13:14). This is why the churches of the Reformation identify the visible church by the marks of the proper preaching of the Word and the administration of the sacraments. "*The* faith" is the content of each believer's faith, rather than vice versa.

*Seventh, the source of the church's existence is also its end: "one God and Father."* Rudolf Schnackenburg comments, "Only with the look up to the one God and Father of all does the enumeration of unity-motifs reach its peak."[8] As James writes, "Every good gift and every perfect gift is from above, coming down from the Father of lights with whom there is no variation or shadow due to change" (Jas 1:17). All good gifts come from the Father, in the Son, and by the Spirit. It is the Father who chose us in Christ, sent his Son in love to redeem his people, and sent the Spirit to unite us to Christ. Obviously, we do not find in Paul refined formulations of trinitarian dogma. Nevertheless, we do find material from which the latter emerged. Without discounting the ontological unity of the essence, the source of the Godhead is a person—namely, the Father. There is a unity of essence, which is not plural or capable of division and is shared equally by each person. Yet each person of the Godhead possesses a unique and incommunicable identity that contributes to the mutual good and purposes of the one God. By analogy, it may be said that the church simultaneously is one, sharing equally in the grace of salvation—the "one Lord, one faith, one baptism," and many members in communion.[9] The one gift of salvation and the many gifts for the common good highlight this analogy.

## II. The Ascension: Distributing the Spoils of Victory

**8** *Therefore it says, "When he ascended on high he led a host of captives and gave gifts to men." **9** (In saying, "He ascended," what does it mean but that he had also*

---

gives it elsewhere. Paul does not mention elders and deacons in Ephesians 4, yet clearly identifies and defines these crucial offices in other epistles. Third, Hoehner assumes here that the Supper is also a subjective act of the believer's testimony rather than an objective means of God's grace (ibid.).

[8] Rudolf Schnackenburg, *Ephesians: A Commentary* (trans. Helen Heron; Edinburgh: T&T Clark, 1991), p. 166.

[9] Markus Barth notes, "In harmony with 4:4-6 and 1 Cor. 12:4-7 Paul refers to the trinity of God as the archetype of unity in diversity." See Markus Barth, *Ephesians: Translation and Commentary on Chapters 4–6* (Anchor Bible; Garden City, NY: Doubleday & Co., 1974), p. 477.

*descended into the lower parts of the earth?* **10** *He who descended is the one who also ascended far above all the heavens, that he might fill all things). Eph 4:8-10*

The heart of Paul's argument turns not on a philosophical principle or political ideal, but on the redemptive-historical event of Christ's ascension. Before focusing directly on these verses, it may be helpful to place them in the wider context of Israel's exodus-conquest motif.

## II.a. God's ascent from Sinai to Zion: biblical theological exploration

Jewish scholar Jon D. Levenson develops the theme of Yahweh's march (Israel in tow) out of Egypt to Sinai and then on to Zion.[10] Psalm 68 (probably dated somewhere between the thirteenth and tenth centuries BCE) is a war psalm, recounting a march through the wilderness led by "the God of Sinai," where the camp is fed and its thirst quenched by Yahweh himself (vv. 7–10). Rich with a combination of martial and liturgical elements, the verses that follow "record a march of YHWH from Sinai, a military campaign in which the God of Israel and his retinue . . . set out across the desert."[11] (It is this Psalm that Paul will cite in our passage below.)

As important as Sinai is in the march, it lies midway between Egypt and Canaan (Zion). It is a covenant of law, prescribing the work to be done, rather than the Sabbath rest; the place of trial rather than the place of victory and consummated blessing. Levenson observes that the focus shifts from Sinai to Zion, for example, in Psalm 97, but also in Ps. 68:8-9 (cf. Ps. 50:2-3). In fact, the shift can be seen already in Deut. 33:2. "The transfer of the motif from Sinai to Zion was complete and irreversible, so that YHWH came to be designated no longer as 'the One of Sinai,' but as 'he who dwells on Mount Zion' (Isa. 8:18) . . . The transfer of the divine home from Sinai to Zion meant that God was no longer seen as dwelling in an extraterritorial no man's land, but within the borders of the Israelite community."[12] And in the Zion traditions, "there will emerge something almost unthinkable in the case of Sinai, a pledge of divine support for a human dynasty."[13] In other words, God's unilateral promise to Abraham is similar in form and content to his pledge to David's heirs (2 Sam. 7:1-17).

---

[10] Jon D. Levenson, *Sinai and Zion: An Entry Into the Jewish Bible* (San Francisco: HarperSanFrancisco, 1985), p. 19.
[11] Ibid., p. 19.
[12] Ibid., p. 91.
[13] Ibid., p. 92.

Thus, the march from Sinai to Zion also speaks of a progress in covenantal history from conditionality and temporality to unconditional and everlasting blessing, notes Levenson.[14] While the Sinai covenant is always threatened by the unfaithfulness of Israel to its conditions, the heavenly Zion exists "by his grace alone."[15] This is why Jeremiah 7 faults those who "have taken the cosmos out of the cosmic mountain," turning it "into a matter of mere real estate." They do not long in joy and awe for the mountain. "Why should they? They are standing on it. The edifice on Mount Zion does not correspond to the gate of heaven; it *is* the gate of heaven. In other words, they have lost the sense of the delicacy of relationship between the higher and lower Jerusalem, and have assumed that the latter always reflects the former perfectly."[16]

I have argued elsewhere that this failure to see the earthly Zion as merely a type or foreshadowing of the heavenly Zion that would descend from heaven is the result of confusing the Abrahamic and Sinaitic covenants.[17] Levenson comes close to saying something identical, yet he concludes that for Judaism Sinai always has the last word.[18] Hence, "Even in modern Israel, the Judaism practiced is not that of the Hebrew Bible, but the continuation of its rabbinic successor, which fashioned a tradition that could deal with a world without a Temple, Jewish sovereignty, or, increasingly, a homeland."[19] After richly exploring the contrast between the Sinai and Abrahamic/Davidic covenants (as conditional treaty and unconditional grant, respectively), Levenson concludes, "In fact, the Davidic theology is the origin of Jewish messianism and the Christology of the church."[20]

Recapitulating the trial of Adam in Eden and Israel in the desert, Jesus Christ leads the exiles out of the ultimate bondage into the liberation of the Sabbath rest (Heb. 4:1-13), with the powers of the age to come penetrating this evil age through word and sacrament (Heb. 6:4-19). The march from Sinai to Zion is at last completed by Jesus Christ: those who look to Christ, Jews and Gentiles, have arrived not at Sinai but at Zion, the heavenly Jerusalem in festive assembly (Heb. 12:18-24). For Paul, too, Sinai and the earthly Jerusalem correspond to Hagar and bondage, while all who trust in Christ are citizens of Zion, the heavenly Jerusalem, and children of Sarah (Gal. 4:21-31). With Christ's fulfillment of the work of new creation-and-conquest, all prior history—including the Sinai theocracy—now belongs to the old order that is "passing away," "fading," "becoming obsolete." Christ's resurrection has inaugurated the age to come,

---

[14] Ibid., p. 165.
[15] Ibid., p. 166.
[16] Ibid., p. 169.
[17] Michael Horton, *Covenant and Salvation* (Louisville: Westminster John Knox, 2007), pp. 11–36.
[18] Levenson, *Sinai and Zion*, p. 180.
[19] Ibid., p. 180.
[20] Ibid., p. 194.

so that the Abrahamic promise—and Israel's commission to the world—can finally be fulfilled. As Robert Jenson finely puts it, "By Jesus' Resurrection occurring 'first,' a sort of *hole* opens *in* the event of the End, a space for something like what used to be history, for the church and its mission."[21]

In Eph. 4:8, Paul appeals to Psalm 68, especially verse 19, although I will quote verses 15–20 for a fuller context:

> O mountain of God, mountain of Bashan; O many-peaked mountain, mountain of Bashan! Why do you look with hatred, O many-peaked mountain, at the mount that God desired for his abode, yes, where the LORD will dwell forever? The chariots of God are twice ten thousand, thousands upon thousands; the Lord is among them; Sinai is now in the sanctuary. You ascended on high, leading a host of captives in your train and receiving gifts among men, even among the rebellious, that the LORD God may dwell there. Blessed be the LORD, who daily bears us up; God is our salvation. Our God is a God of salvation, and to GOD, the Lord, belong deliverances from death.

> Verse 1 ("God shall arise, his enemies be scattered; and those who hate him shall flee before him") echoes the battle cry in Numbers 10:35. In that event, the ark of the covenant was leading the people of Israel through the wilderness on their way to Zion.

It may be that Psalm 68 was composed to commemorate the arrival of the ark in the sanctuary at Zion. In any case, it celebrates the procession: "O God, when you went out before your people, when you marched through the wilderness, the earth quaked, the heavens poured down rain, before God, the One of Sinai, before God, the God of Israel" (vv. 7–8). The fighting men sleep while the Lord lays the enemies to waste and scatters kings, and the women announce, "The kings of the armies—they flee, they flee!" and "divide the spoil" of precious treasures from the Lord's victory (vv. 11–14). Housing the sacred tablets, the ark is a portable Sinai, which has now moved into its sanctuary. Verses 24–27 report "the procession of God, my King, into the sanctuary," with singers and congregation. "Summon your power, O God, the power, O God, by which you have worked for us" (v. 28). The days are envisioned when God will break the spears of his enemies and bring many captives to worship on his holy hill in peace (vv. 32–33). "O kingdoms of the earth, sing to God; sing praises to the Lord . . . Awesome is God from his sanctuary; the God of Israel—he is the one who gives power and strength to his people. Blessed be God!" (v. 35).

The God of Sinai is now the God of Zion. Although Sinai is not forgotten, it yields to a broader, fuller, and richer future, when a remnant of all the warring nations will find safety and peace in the presence of the God of Israel. God

---

[21] Ibid., p. 85.

ascends his own mountain in conquest and enters his sanctuary in triumph, while the mighty men of Israel slept.

Some have argued that this Psalm was part of the Jewish liturgy of Pentecost, since it was this annual feast that celebrated the giving of the law at Sinai.[22] According to Rudolf Schnackenburg,

> "You have received gifts among humanity" was understood as "received gifts for humanity," so that he (Moses) might give the gifts to them. . . . Originally taken [in the OT and Judaism] to apply to God who, coming from Sinai majestically rises to Zion, and in Judaism taken to mean Moses who climbs the Mountain of God (Sinai) and there receives the Tables of the Law, the text is now interpreted in the style of a midrash and is understood in a Christian way as referring to Christ.[23]

> Already the transfer from Moses to Jesus may be seen in Peter's Pentecost sermon: " 'Exalted at the right hand of God, he received the promise of the Holy Spirit from the Father and poured it forth, as you [both] see and hear' " (Acts 2:33; cf. 5:32-33).

Paul's otherwise puzzling editing of the Psalm from "you received gifts" to "he gave gifts" makes perfect sense, therefore, in the light of the ascension as the fuller reality to which the Psalm pointed.[24] In the light of Christ's ascension after having defeated his enemies, he is now distributing the spoils of victory to his people. Consequently, there is no way to interpret this event other than to refer to Jesus Christ as the gift-giver rather than the recipient. Christ has ascended in triumphant procession, not to an earthly Zion but to its heavenly archetype. He enters not with the ark of the covenant and its sacred tablets—Sinai in miniature (Ps. 68:17) or with the sacrifices it prescribed—but with his own blood (Heb. 9:11-12). It is a covenant founded on better promises, since

---

[22] For sources on this point, see Peter O'Brien, *The Letter to the Ephesians* (Pillar New Testament Commentary; Grand Rapids, MI: Eerdmans, 1999), p. 291.

[23] Schnackenburg, *Ephesians*, p. 177.

[24] Commentators observe that there are traces in the Targum and rabbinical tradition that substantiate the translation of Ps. 68:19 as "he gave" rather than "he took," and some Syriac and Aramaic manuscripts of the LXX support it as well (Schnackenburg, *Ephesians*, p. 177; cf. M. Barth, *Ephesians*, pp. 472, 475; Peter O'Brien, *The Letter to the Ephesians*, p. 290; R. A. Taylor, "The Use of Psalm 68:18 in Ephesians 4:8 in Light of Ancient Versions," *Bibliotecha Sacra* 148 [1991], pp. 332–335). Given Paul's extensive rabbinical training, however, it seems unlikely that he would have relied upon a version of Psalm 68 that was less widely available and attested among contemporary Jews. Hoehner thinks it might simply be a summary, not an exact quotation (*Ephesians*, p. 528). However, it is more than inexact; it changes the subjects of giving and receiving. The simplest answer is that Paul is interpreting this psalm christologically, just as the psalmist interpreted the history recounted in Numbers 10 in the light of the reign of David and the temple. Paul is not engaging in mere typology, using Psalm 68 as a proof-text for the antitype. Rather, like other NT writers, he is interpreting redemptive history in the light of its greater fulfillment.

they are based on God's faithfulness rather than the people's, extend to all nations and not only Israel, and pertain to an everlasting rest rather than a temporary land of blessing.

Just as ancient rulers would divide the spoils of conquest (see Genesis 14; Judg. 5:30; 1 Sam. 30:26-31), and then erect a temple-palace in honor of their victory, Zion's sanctuary is the house that the conquering King of Israel builds to celebrate his victory over all the earth. The captives in the victorious train of the conquerors (Yahweh/Christ) are Satan, death, and hell.[25] Paul adds that there is no ascent without a prior descent, which I take to refer not to a literal descent into hell, but into the depths of the earth.[26] There is no conquest without the exodus, no victory without the battle, no ascension without the incarnation, cross, and resurrection.

## III. The Gifts That He Gave

*11 And he gave the apostles, the prophets, the evangelists, the pastors and teachers, 12 to equip the saints for the work of ministry, for building up the body of Christ, 13 until we all attain to the unity of the faith and of the knowledge of the son of God, to mature manhood, to the measure of the stature of the fullness of Christ, . . .*

*Eph.4:11-13*

The presence of "each one" in vv. 7 and 16 form an *inclusio.* "We move from the stress on unity (vv. 4–6) to diversity in vv. 7–10, and back again to unity in vv. 11–16," O'Brien notes.[27]

---

[25] Who are the captives? Probably Satan, sin, and death (the view of Chrysostom, Theophylact, Calvin, Bengel, Alford, Eadie, Dieblius, et al.) rather than the people rescued by Christ (the view of Justin Martyr, Theodore of Mopsuestia, Aquinas, Murray, et al.). Nevertheless, especially in light of Ps. 68:30-35, the triumph over the violent enemies of God results in their being included in the procession to the holy sanctuary. The most obvious interpretation of the "captives" in Psalm 68 are, as G. V. Smith argues, rebellious Israelites (G. V. Smith, "Paul's Use of Psalm 68:18 in Ephesians 4:8," *Journal of the Evangelical Theological Society* 18 [1975], pp. 181–189). However, Paul frequently has in mind the satanic "powers" that hold us in bondage. Ephesians 6 supports this interpretation. Obviously, Satan and his minions are not converted into true worshipers, but many "captives" of his domain are transferred to Zion.

[26] See John Calvin, *The Epistles of Paul the Apostle to the Galatians, Ephesians, Philippians and Colossians*, (Calvin's Commentaries; trans. T. H. L. Parker; Grand Rapids: Eerdmans, 1972), p. 176. O'Brien notes, "The unusual expression 'the lower parts of the earth' is better interpreted as 'the earth below' than as the abode of the dead" (*The Letter to the Ephesians*, p. 294). Ralph P. Martin follows G. B. Caird's intriguing suggestion that "ascent" / "descent" refers to Christ's ascension and the descent of the Spirit (Martin, *Ephesians, Colossians, and Philemon* [Interpretation: A Bible Commentary for Teaching and Preaching; Atlanta: John Knox Press, 1991], p. 50). However, this does not seem plausible. Christ is the subject of both actions. Furthermore, as Hoehner points out, this interpretation of verse 9 "makes verse 10 useless" (Hoehner, *Ephesians*, p. 532).

[27] O'Brien, *The Letter to the Ephesians*, p. 286.

## III.a. The gifts are ministers

In Romans 12 and 1 Corinthians 12, Paul's list of gifts is broader, but in Ephesians 4 Paul's focus is narrower. The gifts are not abilities in this case, but people: namely, apostles, prophets, evangelists, and pastor–teachers. The broader gifts highlight the diversity and plurality of the "many" who serve the common good, while these gifts serve to create the unity of the one body in "one Lord, one faith, one baptism." Paul has underscored that Christ is the giver of these gifts (vv. 7–8), and he does so again, this time adding *autos* for emphasis: "And *he himself* gave the apostles," and so on. This too parallels Psalm 68, where the Lord gains his victory *even as his warriors slept* and salvation is repeatedly attributed therefore to Yahweh alone. It is Christ who is raised and ascended, assuring us that we too will share fully in his heavenly triumph: not by imitating his ascension, but by receiving its benefits.

All of the "gifts" named are ministers of the Word. In the early church, the apostles were uniquely authorized by Jesus Christ directly and prophets elucidated God's Word in concrete contexts. Apostles were to be heeded, while new covenant prophets were to be tested by the Word—including the teaching of the apostles (1 Thess. 5:20). Similarly, all of the apostles were evangelists, but not all evangelists were apostles.[28] As Paul wrote in 1 Corinthians, some plant, some water, but the Spirit gives the increase (1 Cor. 3:5-9). Paul was not a settled pastor of any church—and pointed out that even administering baptism was the exception rather than the rule in his ministry (1 Cor. 1:14-17). Associates like Titus were left behind to establish the proper order of a particular church, with pastor–teachers and elders (Tit. 1:5). Each of these offices in Eph. 4:11 is distinguished by a definite article, but there is only one definite article for "the pastors and teachers," suggesting that this is one office: namely, pastor–teachers.[29]

## III.b. The goal of the gifts is growth together in Christ

The rest of this section (vv. 12–14) provokes more exegetical debate. In fact, Schnackenburg notes, "It is one of the most compact and also most difficult

---

[28] O'Brien points out that "evangelist" is never mentioned elsewhere as a distinct office. Timothy is to fulfill "the work of an evangelist" as pastor (2 Tim. 4:5). And Philip, a deacon, is "the evangelist" in Acts 21:8. Although found in verbal form elsewhere (Acts 20:28; 1 Pet. 5:2), this is the only place in the NT where "shepherd" is a noun (*Letter to the Ephesians*, p. 299). "They manage the church (1 Thess. 5:12; Rom. 12:8) and are to be regarded in love 'because of their work'" (Ibid., p. 300). "Shepherds" is broader than "teachers": all teachers are shepherds, but not all shepherds are teachers.

[29] John Eadie, *A Commentary on the Greek Text of the Epistle of Paul to the Ephesians* (Grand Rapids, MI: Baker, 1979), p. 304.

and problematic sections in the whole letter."[30] Essentially, it comes down to the question as to whether these ministers are given for the completion of the saints (as the older English translations, like the KJV, render it) or whether they are given for the equipping of the saints to be ministers in their own right (as new translations, like the ESV above, render it). According to the older translation, it is the aforementioned officers who are given for (a) completing/perfecting the saints, (b) the work of ministry, and (c) the edification of Christ's body. The three clauses repeat the same purpose in different words.

In terms of syntax, the question comes down to the best translation of the verb *katartismos* and the preposition *eis*. In classical Greek literature, the verb *katartizein* is used to refer to refitting a ship, setting a bone, building a house, and the like. It is used in similar ways in the New Testament (Mt. 4:21; Mk 1:19; Heb. 10:5; 11:3).[31] Therefore, older translations seem preferable: Christ gave ministers for the purpose of completing the saints as God's building project, for the work of the ministry, and for the edification of the whole body.[32] This also fits better with the results that Paul elaborates in vv. 13–15, where the saints are by this ministry built up in "the unity of the faith and of the knowledge of the Son of God, to mature adulthood . . . ," "no longer children, tossed to and fro by the waves and carried about by every wind of doctrine," and "speaking the truth in love" so that they "grow up in every way into him who is the head, into Christ." Other gifts are necessary for the *well-being* of the church; the ministry of Word and sacrament is necessary for the *being* of the church.

Rudolf Schnackenburg supports this reading: the aforementioned ministers are gifts that Christ gave "for the preparation of the saints," "for a work of service," and "for the building-up of the Body of Christ."[33] Everyone receives a spiritual gift, but Paul distinguishes ministers as God's gift to the whole body for its ever-maturing unity in Christ. Schnackenburg points out that elsewhere in Paul *katartismos* had "more the sense of 'make perfect,' be it in faith (1 Thess. 3.10), in a common conviction (1 Cor. 1.10), or in 'everything good' (Heb. 13.21)."[34] "There is consequently no necessity to think of instruction and training of the rest of the faithful for active service in the congregation."[35] The clear sense of the argument is that Christ is the one giving; pastors and teachers are the ones serving, and the whole body is the one growing, "until we all attain unity in the faith."

---

[30] Schnackenburg, *Ephesians*, p. 171.
[31] Ibid., p. 308.
[32] Eadie, *Ephesians*, p. 307.
[33] Schnackenburg, *Ephesians*, p. 172.
[34] Ibid., p. 182. Also with *eis*, in Rom. 9:22, "made for destruction."
[35] Ibid., p. 183.

However, this exegesis is by no means standard among contemporary commentators, beginning with J. A. Robinson's 1904 commentary.[36] In this now widespread interpretation, Paul's point is that the gifts that Christ gave are meant to equip all of the saints for the work of the ministry. The purpose is "to equip the holy ones for the work of ministry, in other words, to prepare the members of the church, particularly the laity, to accomplish all that ministry entails."[37] The application is clear: "every-member-ministry."[38]

I conclude with Markus Barth that "The wording of the Greek text of vs. 12 does not permit a decision" one way or the other.[39] However, I do think that some determination can be made concerning the meaning of *katartismos* and the flow of Paul's argument.[40] In addition it may be said that within the context of Paul's "building" metaphor, "complete" makes more sense than "equip." Paul is not arguing that every member builds the church through his or her ministry, but that through the ministry of the Word each member is built up into one body through the truth.

Allowing that the argument can fall either way syntactically, advocates of "equipping the saints for the work of ministry" nevertheless tend to base their conclusion on a commitment to every-member-ministry. For example, O'Brien judges, "If it is only the leaders of v. 11 who perfect the saints, do the work of ministry, and edify the body of Christ, then this is a departure from Paul's usual insistence that every member is equipped for ministry."[41] However, this seems to beg the question. Of course, service (*diakonia*) is sometimes used in a broader sense in the New Testament, in terms of loving and serving each other (1 Cor. 12:5; Gal. 5:13; Eph. 6:6; 1 Pet. 2:16; 4:10). Yet the apostle draws a clear distinction between this general office of all believers and the particular offices of service in the church: namely, pastors, elders, and deacons (1 Cor. 4:1; 2 Cor. 6:4; Col. 1:24-25; 1 Tim. 3:10). These members function in an official

---

[36] J. A. Robinson, *St. Paul's Epistle to the Ephesians* (London: Macmillan, 1904), p. 99, "was the first in recent times to challenge the older view . . . that Christ had three distinct purposes in mind in giving gifts to his church." Instead, Robinson argues that there were two purposes, one immediate—"to equip the saints for work in his service"—and the other ultimate—"for building up the body of Christ."

[37] Peter S. Williamson, *Ephesians: Catholic Commentary on Sacred Scripture* (Grand Rapids: Baker Academic, 2009), p. 117.

[38] Ibid., p. 119.

[39] Barth, *Ephesians*, p. 478.

[40] It is significant that advocates of the more recent consensus recognize that the verb typically means to put in order, complete, establish, restore, or instruct rather than equip. For example, see Hoehner, *Ephesians*, pp. 549–50: In the LXX, it means "'to establish' (Ps 74:16 [LXX 73:16]), 'to equip, restore' (Ps 68:9 [MT 68:10; LXX 67:10]), and 'to complete, finish' (Ezra 4:12, 13, 16; 5:3, 9, 11; 6:14). It appears thirteen times in the NT and can mean 'to restore or mend' fishing nets (Matt 4:21 = Mark 1:19), 'to restore' a fallen brother (Gal 6:1; cf. 1 Pet 5:10), 'to prepare' (Rom 9:22; Heb 10:5), 'to put into proper order, complete, furnish' (1 Thess 3:10; 1 Cor 1:10; Heb 13:21), 'to perfect' (Matt 21:16), or 'to instruct' (Luke 6:40)."

[41] O'Brien, *Letter to the Ephesians*, pp. 302–303.

capacity, ministering in Christ's name to the needs of his people. They are set apart and ordained for this purpose (1 Tim. 3:1-5:25; 2 Tim. 1:1-3, 14–4:8; 4:14; 5:7; Tit. 1:5-2:15). In fact, "Let the elders who rule well be considered worthy of double honor, especially those who labor in preaching and teaching" (1 Tim. 5:17). Paul pleaded with the Ephesian elders, "Pay careful attention to yourselves and to all the flock, in which the Holy Spirit has made you overseers, to care for the church of God, which he obtained with his own blood" (Acts 20:28).

Additionally, there are parallels in Paul where the same body-building metaphor is used. In 1 Corinthians 3, Paul clearly indicates that there is a distinction between his official ministry and the rest of the body that he serves in Christ's name. "What then is Apollos? What is Paul? Servants through whom you believed, as the Lord assigned to each. I planted, Apollos watered, but God gave the increase . . . For we are God's fellow workers. You are God's field, God's building" (vv. 5–6, 9). Here Paul mixes the metaphors of field and building, but the point is the same as in Ephesians 4: the servants of the Word— whether apostles or ordinary ministers—are builders, and the church is the building. The apostles have laid the foundation, and the ordinary ministers build on it (1 Cor. 3:10-17; cf. Col. 1:24-28).

We have no reason to conclude that Paul comes to his subject matter in Ephesians 4 with any different paradigm. For him, then, there is no false choice to be made between clericalism and "every-member-ministry." As Andrew Lincoln reminds us,

> An active role for all believers is safeguarded by vv. 7, 16, but the primary context here in v. 12 is the function and role of Christ's specific gifts, the ministers, not that of all the saints. Rendering *katartismon* 'completion' has a straightforward meaning which does not require supplementing by a further phrase, and *diakonia*, 'service,' is more likely to refer to the *ministry* of the *ministers* just named . . . [It is] hard to avoid the suspicion that opting for the other view is too often motivated by a zeal to avoid clericalism and to support a 'democratic' model of the Church. . . .[42]

Lincoln's suspicion concerning the democratic-egalitarian bias of contemporary exegesis of this verse seems undeniable.[43] For example, according to

---

[42] Andrew Lincoln, *Ephesians* (Word Biblical Commentary 42; Dallas: Word, 1990), p. 253; cf. T. David Gordon, " 'Equipping' Ministry in Ephesians 4," *Journal of the Evangelical Theological Society* 37, no. 1 (March 1994), pp. 69–78. It is also interesting to read Calvin's commentary on this passage (*Commentaries on the Epistles of Paul to the Galatians and Ephesians,* [Calvin's Commentaries; trans. William Pringle; Grand Rapids, MI: Baker, 1996], pp. 277–286), especially since the more recent translation does not even occur to him. For this very reason, he seems to capture the flow of the passage's argument.

[43] Like Lincoln (above), Ralph Martin observes, "This is a popular view today, enforcing the democratic nature of the church in which all the members are called ministers, some 'ordained' but all with shared ministry" (*Ephesians, Colossians, and Philemon,* p. 52).

G. B. Caird, Christ's ministry is entrusted "to the whole membership of the people of God, not to a group of clergy within the church."[44] Markus Barth reads these verses as a manifesto for the abolition of the clergy–laity distinction, celebrating the grace and love of God that "transcend the confines of the church."[45] "The epistle looks beyond the church and does not suffocate in ecclesiology; it proclaims that God's kingdom is greater than the church."[46] One almost forgets the syntactical questions of Eph. 4:12 amid the sweeping polemic. The older translation "has an aristocratic, that is, a clerical and ecclesiastical flavor."

Certainly the needs of the laymen saints are cared for; they receive salvation, eternal life, ethical instructions through the saving word, the seal of the sacraments, the doctrinal decisions, the disciplinary measures administered by the officers. Yet two implications of this interpretation are inescapable: (1) the laymen are ultimately only beneficiaries, and (2) the benefits of the clergy's work remain inside the church—though people and power outside the church may witness the clergy's successes and failures.[47]

However, Barth presses a false choice. I readily concede that the older translation implies that the laity "are ultimately only beneficiaries" of this ministry of Word and sacrament, but is that not precisely the marvelously evangelical point that Paul is making? These ministers are gifts to the whole body, servants of Christ to his people, not aristocrats or oligarchs. The ascended Christ is dispensing the spoils of his victory to his sheep through his shepherds. Yet Barth's second point does not follow—namely, that "the benefits of the clergy's work remain inside the church," and the rest remain mere spectators. By analogy, one could say that an auto mechanic's *work* takes place in the shop, but this hardly means that its *effects* remain there. Rather, its effects are evident wherever the repaired vehicle is driven. Believers do not need to "find a ministry" in the church, but to be fitted by the ministry for their gift-exchange in the body and in the world. Barth believes that unless the clergy–laity distinction is abolished, the pieces of armor in Ephesians 6 are the exclusive property of the ordained.[48] However, once again, this presses a false choice, as if the official ministry of the Word were somehow an impediment to rather than the very means of providing "the training and the necessary arms to all the saints." He even conjectures, "The ordination mentioned in I Tim 4:14; 6:12; II Tim 1:6 may well refer to the confession and laying-on-of-hands connected with baptism," rather than to a separate rite of ordination.[49] Where the Reformers

---

[44] G. B. Caird, "Ephesians" in *Paul's Letters from Prison* (Oxford: Oxford University Press, 1977), p. 76

[45] Barth, *Ephesians*, p. 471.

[46] Ibid., p. 472; cf. pp. 496–497.

[47] Ibid., p. 479.

[48] Ibid., pp. 479–481.

[49] Ibid., p. 481.

affirmed simultaneously the priesthood of all believers (baptism ordaining them as such) and the distinct calling of some members as overseers and deacons, Barth collapses the latter into the former. Yet once again Barth seems not only to qualify but to contradict his argument: "The resulting democratic character of the church does not obliterate the roles which specific servants must and may play within the church."[50] These inconsistencies are confusing, to say the least.

Similarly, Harold Hoehner's exegesis is constrained by an assumption that "to make such a distinction between clergy and laity goes against the thrust of this passage that promotes unity in the body of Christ."[51] However, if the church's unity is generated by "one Lord, one faith, one baptism," it is unclear why the ministry of pastor–teachers should be an impediment to rather than instrument of its realization. In evaluating all semantic alternatives, the chief factor in each case is whether it encourages a distinction between clergy and laity.[52] Hoehner does not even believe that the "gifts" in v. 11 are officers, but general-office gifts. "This eliminates the distinction between clergy and laity, a distinction with little, if any, support in the NT . . . Thus, every believer must do the work of the ministry."[53] "Paul is listing gifts and not offices."[54] Not even "apostles" here refers to an office, but to a gift for missionary activity.[55] Even if one concludes that this verse means "equipping the saints for the work of ministry," there can be no question that Paul treats ministers of the Word as the ones who prepare them for it.[56]

## IV. Theological and Practical Implications

It seems to me that contemporary ecclesiological discussions are often ranged between two extremes that generate exaggerated reactions. I have explored these trajectories in detail elsewhere, so must restrict myself in this brief space to conclusions rather than arguments.[57]

---

[50] Ibid., p. 482.
[51] Hoehner, *Ephesians*, p. 548.
[52] Ibid., pp. 548–549.
[53] Ibid., p. 549.
[54] Ibid., p. 539.
[55] Ibid., p. 547.
[56] Some, like Gordon Fee, go so far as to insist that "pastors/teachers" is a function, not an office (*God's Empowering Presence: The Holy Spirit in the Letters of Paul* [Peabody, MA: Hendrickson, 1994], pp. 706–707). James Dunn also sees "charisma" as a spontaneous gift for an event, in a particular instance, rather than an office (J. D. G. Dunn, *Jesus and the Spirit* [London: SCM, 1975], p. 254). However, there is no exegetical reason to set function and office in antithesis (see O'Brien, *Letter to the Ephesians*, p. 301).
[57] Horton, *People and Place*, chapters 6–8.

On one hand, there is the tendency simply to collapse the many into the one, the sign into the reality, the visible into the invisible, and the head and members. This trajectory, identified especially with Roman Catholic ecclesiologies, treats a hierarchically constituted church (with an earthly head) as a substitute for Jesus Christ in the flesh. Just as in transubstantiation the earthly signs of bread and wine are annihilated and replaced by the reality (Christ's body and blood), the visible church simply *is* Jesus in his now-visible activity in the world. Augustine's expression, *totus Christus*, which he used to refer to the intimate union of Christ and his body, downplayed crucial differences. Interpreted in even more deeply Neoplatonic terms throughout the Middle Ages, this idea justified a hierarchical ecclesiology according to which grace flowed down the ladder of being from its highest to lowest rungs. Indebted to Fichte, Hegel, and Schelling, nineteenth-century "Reform Catholicism" (as well as liberal Protestantism in the wake of Schleiermacher) also spoke of the church as an extension of Christ's incarnation and redeeming work in the world.

Douglas Farrow shows the extent to which this paradigm is generated by a failure to recognize the significance of Christ's bodily ascension. Origen represents the extreme limits to which a thinly Christianized Platonism can go. If Jesus Christ's own glorification was, as Origen said, "more of an ascension of the mind than of the body,"[58] then it follows that ours is as well. As the spiritual educator of the human race, Jesus leads us away from the shadows of time and matter into the reality of being. Even in less radical accounts (such as that of Athanasius and Augustine), the absence of Christ in the flesh is no longer a loss but becomes the occasion for his "return" in and as the church. Increasingly, the particular person, Jesus of Nazareth, was forgotten, yielding to a cosmic Christ whose visible-earthly existence was now transferred to the church. "Indeed, it meant that the church now controlled the parousia," notes Farrow. "At the ringing of a bell the *Christus absens* became the *Christus praesens . . .* Seated comfortably with the Christ-child on its lap, the church soon became his regent rather than his servant. In short, its Marian ego, already out of control at the beginning of the eucharistic debates, afterwards knew no bounds."[59]

With the rise of German Idealism (especially Fichte and Hegel), the synthesis of christology and ecclesiology seemed complete in many Roman Catholic and Protestant systems. In our own day, this synthesis is pursued to its fullest extent by writers like Graham Ward, who scolds those who grieve over and long for "a lost body"—"the body of the gendered Jew," instead of realizing that in his ascension Christ's body is not loss but expansion. His natural body

---

[58] Ibid., p. 97, citing Origen's *de princ.* 23.2.
[59] Ibid., p. 157.

becomes transcorporeal; he returns (has already returned) in and in fact as the church.[60]

However, Paul's "body of Christ" analogy is to be taken neither literally, in the sense of replacing Christ, nor as a mere figure of speech. Taken univocally, the theory of the church "as 'the extension of the Incarnation,'" as Lesslie Newbigin observes, "springs from a confusion of *sarx* with *soma*." "Christ's risen body"—that is, his ecclesial distinguished from his natural body—"is not fleshly but spiritual." "He did not come to incorporate us in His body according to the flesh but according to the Spirit." Hence, his promise that when he ascends he will send the Spirit.[61] Newbigin's point reminds us of the importance of both the ascension of Christ in the flesh and the descent of the Spirit. Our union with Christ does not occur at the level of fused natures, but as a common participation of different members in the same realities of the age to come by the same Spirit. Miroslav Volf properly argues, against Cardinal Ratzinger (now Pope Benedict), "A *theological interpretation* going beyond Paul himself is needed to transform the Pauline 'one *in* Christ' into Ratzinger's 'a single subject *with* Christ,' or certainly into 'a single . . . Jesus Christ.'"[62]

It is the difference as much as the affinity between Head and members that constitutes Paul's ecclesiology. Just as husband and wife become "one flesh" without becoming one person or "fusion of existences," so also with Christ and his church (Eph. 5:31-32). In fact, Avery Cardinal Dulles recognizes, "The root of the metaphor," he says, "is the kind of treaty relationship into which a suzerain state entered with a vassal state in the ancient Near East." In addition to providing the background for the body of Christ analogy, "That kind of military and political treaty afforded the raw material out of which the concept of 'People of God' was fashioned."[63] Overlooking this covenantal context of the body analogy, warns Dulles, may lead "to an unhealthy divinization of the Church," as if the union "is therefore a biological and hypostatic one" and all actions of the church are ipso facto actions of Christ and the Spirit.[64] Drawn from the realm of politics rather than philosophy, the analogy of a covenantal body makes otherness and plurality as essential as unity. It is that unity that is so deeply dependent on the work of the ministry that Paul describes as God's gift.

As John Webster points out, the emphasis on the church as an extension of Christ's person and work, which owes "as much to Hegelian theory of history as

---

[60] Graham Ward, *Cities of God* (Radical Orthodoxy; London and New York.: Routledge, 2000), pp. 93–116.

[61] Lesslie Newbigin, *The Household of God: Lectures on the Nature of the Church* (Eugene, OR: Wipf & Stock, 2009), p. 80.

[62] Miroslav Volf, *After Our Likeness: The Church as the Image of the Trinity* (Grand Rapids, MI: Eerdmans, 1998), p. 34.

[63] Dulles, *Models of the Church*, pp. 22–23.

[64] Ibid., p. 51.

to theology, . . . has become something of a commonplace in some now dominant styles of modern theology and theological ethics." God's work of reconciling the world in Christ merges with the church's moral action.[65] Interpreted
within a more cultural-linguistic paradigm, Stanley Hauerwas, Timothy
Gorringe, and others join this trajectory. They still speak of the Trinity and
grace, but the emphasis falls on the acts of the church, "often through the
idiom of virtues, habits and practices."[66] According to Timothy Gorringe,
"the community of reconciliation" is "the means through which atonement
is effected, which is the reason, presumably, Christ bequeathed to us not a
set of doctrines or truths, but a community. . . . "[67] The force of Christ's completed work, Webster judges, "is simply lost" in this inflated talk of the church's
redemptive activity.[68] Christ's person and work easily becomes a "model" or
"vision" for ecclesial action (*imitatio Christi*), rather than a completed event to
which the church offers its witness.

At the other extreme—often in reaction against this first paradigm, is the
tendency to separate the invisible, eternal, and spiritual reality from everything visible, temporal, and creaturely. The democratic reaction against special offices is consistent with an anti-institutional and anti-sacramental bias. As
a result, however, the logic of Paul's argument, namely, that Christ is delivering
the spoils of *his* victory to his people is easily exchanged for a model of the
church that focuses on the activity of believers. "One Lord" easily becomes
assimilated to a one-sided emphasis on "my personal Lord and Savior." "One
faith" succumbs to my act of believing. "One baptism" no longer refers to the
objective sacrament, but to the inner experience of new birth. Identified by the
Reformers as "enthusiasm," this radical Protestant trajectory is especially evident in the history of various groups ranging from the most extreme (e.g., the
Gnostics) to more orthodox (e.g., the Montanists and Spiritual Franciscans).
This heritage reaches us today through Anabaptism, pietism, and evangelical
as well as Pentecostal groups.

Though less subjective, this more "Anabaptist" approach is also evident in
Karl Barth's sharp criticism of the Roman Catholic and neo-Hegelian ecclesiologies. The church is not an extension of Christ's incarnation and redeeming
work, Barth properly emphasizes.[69] While offering salutary warnings against
assimilating christology to ecclesiology, Barth frequently set these in opposition. Against Hegelian synthesis, he preferred Kierkegaardian paradox,

---

[65] John Webster, *Word and Church* (Edinburgh: T & T Clark, 2001), p. 226.
[66] Ibid.
[67] Timothy Gorringe, *God's Just Vengeance* (London: Verso, 1991), p. 268.
[68] Ibid.
[69] Karl Barth, *Church Dogmatics*, IV/3: *The Doctrine of Reconciliation* (eds, G. W. Bromiley and
T. F. Torrance; Edinburgh: T & T Clark, 1961), pp. 7, 327; idem, *Church Dogmatics*, IV/2:
*The Doctrine of Reconciliation* (eds, G. W. Bromiley and T. F. Torrance; Edinburgh: T & T
Clark, 1958), p. 132.

verging on absolute contradiction. The true church belongs to the "submarine island of the 'Now' of divine revelation" that lies beneath observable reality.[70] In *Romans*, he speaks explicitly of "the *contrast* between the Gospel and the Church" (emphasis added).[71] Christ is the only sacrament. In fact, not only is there a difference between the sign and its eschatological fullness; the "invisible church" is taken to extreme limits when Barth writes, "In the heavenly Jerusalem of Revelation nothing is more finally significant than *the church's complete absence*: 'And I saw no temple therein'" (emphasis added).[72] Therefore, "the activity of the community is related to the Gospel only in so far as it is no more than a crater formed by the explosion of a shell and seeks to be no more than a void in which the Gospel reveals itself."[73]

A weak view of the means of grace is inextricable from a weak view of the church's outward ministry. Karl Barth denies that baptism is a "means of grace." "Baptism *responds to* a mystery, the sacrament of the history of Jesus Christ, of His resurrection, of the outpouring of the Holy Spirit. *It is not itself, however, a mystery or sacrament*" (emphasis added).[74] This means, of course, that baptism is no longer God's gracious action toward us, but is merely our personal response of faith and obedience. In this respect (as in his rejection of infant baptism), Barth's position is even more radical (or perhaps more consistent) than Zwingli's. Reflecting on this fact, Barth wrote, "The Reformed Church and Reformed theology (even in Zürich) could not continue to hold" to Zwingli's teaching, and took a "backward step" toward Calvin's "sacramentalism." "We for our part cannot deny that both negatively and positively Zwingli was basically right."[75] Despite considerable technical skill and knowledge of a wide variety of classical and contemporary interpretations of each passage (acknowledging in the preface the debt to his son, Markus Barth, in this regard), Barth's exegesis presupposes from the outset that these passages cannot be interpreted in a sacramental manner. Barth's "contrast between the Gospel and the Church" is inextricably connected to (perhaps generated by) a contrast between the sacraments and God's saving action.[76] Similarly, Markus

---

[70] Karl Barth, *The Epistle to the Romans* (trans. Edwyn C. Hoskyns from the sixth edition; London: Oxford University Press, 1933), p. 304.

[71] Ibid., p. 340.

[72] Ibid.

[73] Barth, *Romans*, p. 36.

[74] Karl Barth, *Church Dogmatics*, IV/4: *The Doctrine of Reconciliation* (eds, G. W. Bromiley and T. F. Torrance; Edinburgh: T & T Clark, 1969), pp. 73, 102.

[75] Ibid., p. 130.

[76] Even as sympathetic an interpreter as John Webster concludes concerning Barth's treatment of baptism in the final fragment of the *Church Dogmatics*: "The exegesis is sometimes surprisingly shoddy, dominated by special pleading, as well as by what seems at times an almost Platonic distinction between water baptism (an exclusively human act) and baptism with the Spirit (an exclusively divine act). . . . Clearly the Reformed tradition on sacraments had lost its appeal for him, though what replaced it lacked the nuance and

Barth's polemic against ordained ministry includes a gratuitous critique of the significance of the sacraments.[77]

However, these two paradigms are not our only options. What is missing is the perspective of Luther, Calvin, and the Reformation confessions that speak of the Spirit binding himself in his ordinary operation to the creaturely ministry of weak and sinful ambassadors. The Triune God works when and where he will, remaining sovereign in his gracious activity. Nevertheless, he condescends to work through means. Just as there is a "sacramental union" between sign and reality in the means of grace, there is a sacramental union between Christ and his church. This union is never determined by epistemological or ontological distance, but by the eschatological coordinates of "already" and "not-yet"—coordinates that are set by the concrete events of our Lord's descent, ascent, and return in the flesh.

The ascension highlights the paradox of our Lord's real absence in the flesh and his real presence in saving action in the power of the Spirit. This parenthesis in redemptive history cannot be mapped onto a Platonic ontology, whether in the direction of Hegelian synthesis or Kierkegaardian antithesis. Rather, the ascension keeps us in the tension between the already and the not-yet, as subjects of and witnesses to Christ's saving action rather than co-agents of it. Neither the sacramental body of Christ (baptism and the Supper) nor the ecclesial body of Christ can be allowed to substitute for the personal body of Jesus of Nazareth. Christ cannot be made present in the flesh by the church or by pious believers. As Paul argues in Romans 10, it is "the righteousness that is by works" that seeks to ascend into heaven to bring Christ down or descend into the depths to bring him up from the dead, while "the righteousness that is by faith" receives Christ as he delivers himself through his Word (vv. 5–17). Jesus Christ cannot be made bodily present on earth until his second coming, and all attempts to jump the eschatological gun end up reinterpreting Christ as someone other than the particular "gendered Jew" (to borrow Ward's phrase) who as the first-fruits determines the nature of our own future bodily existence.

Farrow suggests that Calvin, like Irenaeus, brought attention back to the economy and thus to the *problem* of Christ's absence. " 'But why,' asked Calvin, 'do we repeat the word "ascension" so often?' To answer in our own words, it was because he found it necessary to reckon more bravely than the other reformers with the absence of Christ as a genuine problem for the church."

Especially in the eucharistic debates, Calvin returns our focus to the economy of redemption. Like Irenaeus, he challenges every docetizing tendency in christology by focusing on the actual history of Jesus of Nazareth from descent

---

weightiness of earlier discussion." See John Webster, *Barth* (New York: Continuum, 2000), p. 157.

[77] Ibid., p. 483.

(incarnation and his earthly ministry of redemption), to his ascension and heavenly ministry, to the parousia at the end of the age.

To maintain a real absence is also to maintain a real continuity between the savior and the saved. All of this demonstrates that Calvin had a better grasp on the way in which the Where? question is bound up with the Who? question. That indeed was his critical insight into the whole debate. Calvin saw that neither a Eutychian response (Jesus is omnipresent) nor a Nestorian one (absent in one nature but present in the other) will do, since either way Christ's humanity is neutralized and his role as our mediator put in jeopardy. It is the God-man who is absent and the God-man whose presence we nevertheless require . . . A "species of absence" and a "species of presence" thus qualify our communion with Christ, who remains in heaven until the day of judgment. It is *we* who require eucharistic relocation.[78]

Instead of moving from Eucharist to Ascension, Calvin moved in the other direction and this led him to stress "the particularity of Jesus without sacrificing sacramental realism." In other words, Calvin took with equal seriousness both Christ's real absence from us in the flesh until he comes again and his real presence in Word and sacrament. If Christ is truly absent from us in the flesh, and our entire salvation depends on being united to him (the whole person, not just his divinity), then we are completely dependent on the Spirit's work. This "forced him to seek a *pneumatological solution* to the problem of the presence and the absence" (emphasis added).[79]

Jesus Christ did not ascend spiritually, leaving behind his body and world history; rather, he ascended in the flesh, opening up space within history for the in-breaking of the powers of the age to come. Our personal and ecclesial existence is determined not by supra-historical realities, but by the history that Jesus has opened up for us in these last days. The gift of salvation comes to us *extra nos*, outside of us. We dare not divert our attention from Christ and his gift-giving reign by focusing on the church and its activity, whether conceived in hierarchical or democratic terms.

There is a widespread assumption in evangelical churches today that the church is primarily a platform for every-member-ministry.[80] Yet this reverses the flow of gifts, forgetting that we cannot be active gift-givers among the

---

[78] Ibid., pp. 176–177.
[79] Ibid., pp. 177–178.
[80] A study conducted by the Willow Creek Community Church found that its most active members expressed dissatisfaction with the depth of worship and instruction—and consequently, with their own spiritual growth. "Why is there this disconnect?" the authors ask. "The quick answer: Because God 'wired' us first and foremost to be in growing relationship with him—not with the church" (Greg Hawkins and Callie Parkinson, *Reveal: Where Are You?* [South Barrington, IL: Willow Creek Association, 2007], pp. 40–41). The leadership concluded that the more Christians grow, the less they depend on the church and need to become "self-feeders." For mature Christians, the "church's primary role is to provide serving opportunities" (p. 42). "We want to transition the role of the church

saints and in the world unless we are first passive gift-receivers of Christ's ministry to us. Furthermore, if everyone is to find a ministry in the church (or in parachurch ministries), a new monasticism emerges and our gifts are not actually used where they are needed most: out in the world throughout the week—in our families, neighborhoods, and wider society. Taken to its logical conclusion, the shift from Christ's gift-giving through the means of grace to "every-member-ministry" invites the question as to why we should belong to a local church.[81]

Whether conceived in hierarchical and clerical or democratic and lay-oriented terms, both views downplay the identity of the church as a community of receivers. The bodily ascension of Christ is a historical narrative, not an allegory. It opens up space for the church to come into being and grow up into its head, expanding to the nations, rather than to replace its Lord as if it were his ongoing incarnation or an extension of his redeeming work. Ephesians 4 reminds us that it is Christ's conquest that has secured the blessings of the age to come, and that he is now dispensing the treasures of his victory to his church here and now through the ministry of Word and sacrament. Drawing on the Antiochene emphasis on "ambassadorship," Orthodox theologian John Zizioulas points out that ministers receive grace *to serve others.* "This does not imply that the minister himself is not in need of that grace. The point is that he needs it precisely because he does not 'possess' it but gets it himself as a member of the community."[82] For this reason, Zizioulas suggests, we should be cautious about such terms as "vicar," as if it were "a representation of someone who is absent."[83] Christ is the priest, but in the Holy Spirit he creates a community of priests. In this way, "the community itself becomes priestly in the sense of I Peter 2:5, 9," not by grace flowing from the priest or the church, but from the Head to his whole body as it is gathered for Word and sacrament.[84]

This present evil age, dominated by the flesh, is under judgment that is nevertheless postponed until the unfolding mystery of his plan for the church is

---

from spiritual parent to spiritual coach." The authors suggest the analogy of a trainer at the gym who provides a "personalized workout plan" (p. 65).

[81] This is precisely the conclusion that George Barna encourages throughout his book, *Revolution: Finding Vibrant Faith Beyond the Walls of the Sanctuary* (Carol Stream, IL: Tyndale House Publishers, 2005). Beginning from the premise that the church is basically a resource center for believers to pursue their own personal relationship with Christ, he argues that the local church will soon be replaced by Internet resources and informal gatherings of believers (e.g., Christian concerts and conferences). "So if you are a Revolutionary, it is because you have sensed and responded to God's calling to be such an imitator of Christ. It is not a church's responsibility to make you into this mold. . . . The choice to become a Revolutionary—and it is a choice—is a covenant you make with God alone" (*Revolution*, p. 70).

[82] John Zizioulas, *Being as Communion: Studies in Personhood and the Church* (Crestwood, NY: St. Vladimir's Seminary Press, 1997), pp. 227–228.

[83] Ibid., p. 230.

[84] Ibid., p. 231.

fully realized. In the meantime, it is the historical career of Jesus Christ that determines world events. The Father raised his Son "and seated him at his right hand in the heavenly places, far above all rule and authority and power and dominion, and above every name that is named, not only in this age but also in the one to come. And he put all things under his feet and gave him as head over all things to the church, which is his body, the fullness of him who fills all in all" (Eph. 1:20-22). A church that does not acknowledge Christ's absence is no longer focused on Christ, but is tempted to idolatrous substitutions in the attempt to seize Canaan prematurely. The parallel with Moses is striking: "When the people saw that Moses delayed to come down from the mountain, the people gathered around Aaron, and said to him, 'Come, make gods for us, who shall go before us; as for this Moses, the man who brought us up out of the land of Egypt, we do not know what has become of him'" (Exod. 32:1). In view of this survey, Farrow seems quite justified in concluding, "Looking away from Jesus has become a natural reflex."[85]

The emphasis of Reformation traditions on the church's constitution as *creatura verbi* (creation of the Word) is not motivated by a clerical domination of the laity, but by the gospel. God serves sinners. The sovereign God is not "served by human hands, as though he needed anything." Rather, Paul declared, God is the giver of all gifts (Acts 17:24-25). "'[W]ho has given a gift to him that he might be repaid?' For from him and through him and to him are all things. To him be glory forever. Amen" (Rom. 11:35-36). James adds, "Every good gift and every perfect gift is from above, coming down from the Father of lights with whom there is no variation or shadow due to change. Of his own will he brought us forth by the word of truth, that we should be a kind of firstfruits of his creatures" (Jas 1:17-18). Precisely because the church exists in relation to God only as a receiver, it becomes caught up in a gift-exchange between human beings that grows until it is finally perfected in the consummation. The desert blooms and seeds are scattered. The Spirit creates faith through the Word and this same faith bears the fruit of the Spirit in works of love and service, not only among the saints, but as we live out our callings among our neighbors in the world. In fact, this is the burden of the rest of Ephesians, from verse 17 to the end of the letter.

We are "receiving a kingdom that cannot be shaken," not building one (Heb. 12:28), and the fully functioning and maturing body of Christ is the *fruit* of "the work of the ministry," which is nothing less than Christ's own exercise of his gracious reign in this present age. The eschatological–pneumatological mediation of Christ's reigning presence as constitutive for the church today can be as easily subverted by self-confident laity as by self-confident clergy. In our highly individualistic and activistic culture, it is difficult to be recipients;

---

[85] Farrow, *Ascension and Ecclesia*, p. 255.

we prefer to be the architects and builders. In sharp contrast to any hierarchical, clerical, legalistic, or authoritarian orientation, Ephesians 4 follows evangelical logic throughout. It is not the priority of the ministers over the laity, but the priority of Christ's ministry to his people that is highlighted in this passage. When the church either confuses itself with its head or divorces itself from its head in a cacophony of competing individuals, it fails to stand where Paul calls us to stand in this passage: under the reign of the gift-giving King.

Chapter 10

# Colossians 3: Deification, *Theosis*, Participation, or Union with Christ?

## Andrew McGowan

The passage which I want to consider in this chapter is Col. 3:1-4: "Since, then, you have been raised with Christ, set your hearts on things above, where Christ is seated at the right hand of God. Set your minds on things above, not on earthly things. For you died, and your life is now hidden with Christ in God. When Christ, who is your life, appears, then you also will appear with him in glory." In particular, I want to focus on the meaning of verse 3: "For you died, and your life is now hidden with Christ in God."

Ever since the occasion when I had to admit during a sermon that I was not at all certain as to the meaning of these words, it has been my intention to give some more serious attention to them. To have the opportunity to do so in a volume dedicated to one of our finest European Reformed theologians is a particular pleasure. Through his writing, his personal encouragement, his participation in conferences and in his leadership of the Fellowship of European Evangelical Theologians, as well as in a host of other ways, Henri Blocher has been an example, a help, and an inspiration to many of us on this side of the Atlantic.

Colossians 3:3 does present us with particular difficulties. Although it does appear to suggest that human beings are somehow caught up into the deity, we must recognize that there are at least two serious theological difficulties in the way of such a conclusion. The first concerns the doctrine of God and the second concerns the doctrine of humanity.

In any doctrine of God we must begin by insisting upon what has been called the "Creator–creature distinction." In other words, the recognition that God is the Creator and is not to be identified with creation. This stands in opposition to pantheism, the view that God is everything and everything is God, an old view which is enjoying a resurgence in some environmental "Green" philosophies and in some new age spirituality. It also stands in opposition to all forms of theology that would seek to bring God down and to deny his transcendence. The orthodox view has always been that God stands over against creation, which is made "out of nothing" (*ex nihilo*). We must also carefully state the relationship between God and creation. The Bible makes it clear that God is "transcendent" (above the created order) but also "immanent" (within the created order). He is above and beyond the creation in the sense that he is distinct from it and does not "need" it but he is also intimately involved in the upholding of creation and is presently involved in and with his creation. We might put this another way by saying that we must maintain at all costs the ontological distinction between God's being and human being.

In any doctrine of humanity we must first affirm that human beings were created perfect, in the image of God but we must then go on immediately to say that our first parents deliberately chose to disobey God and so were separated from the presence of God. Our doctrine of humanity, then, must give a serious account of sin. Indeed, it is not possible to understand what a human being is without an adequate doctrine of sin. In its essence it involves rebellion against God and the desire to be independent and autonomous. It results in the pollution of every aspect of human nature and renders man guilty before God. It is also the essential backdrop to any understanding of the gospel because it provides the reason for the work of Christ.

Both the ontological Creator–creature distinction and the separation between God and humanity as a consequence of sin are problematic when we are trying to explore the meaning of Col. 3:3. How can human beings be "caught up" into God if there is an ontological separation? How can sinful human beings come into the presence of a holy God? The former question is the more difficult, the latter question being answered in Christian theology by means of the doctrines of justification and sanctification, the one dealing with the "status" of the human being before God, the other dealing with the inner, sinful condition. Even so, does this reconciliation and renewal enable the newly constituted human being to be somehow caught up into God?

Colossians 3:3 also presents a problem of interpretation, in that it has been interpreted in a number of different ways by different theological traditions. For some Orthodox theologians it refers to deification, for some Catholic theologians it refers to the Beatific Vision, for some Protestants it means ingrafting into the life of God (or *theosis*) short of deification, to other Protestant theologians it is a "participation" in the life of God, and to most Reformed theologians it is simply another way of speaking about the doctrine of union with Christ. In order to open up this question, we shall do four things. First, we shall look at the text in its context; second, we shall ask in what sense believers have died with Christ and been raised with Christ; third, given Henri Blocher's status as a leading Reformed theologian, we shall focus in on the current debate among Reformed theologians on this issue; then fourth, we shall seek to draw some conclusions.

# I. The Text in Context

The city of Colosse was situated in an area of the Roman Empire which today is part of Turkey. It was one of a group of three cities that were very close together and that formed a little triangle: Hierapolis, Laodicea, and Colosse.

One hundred miles due west of this group was to be found the city of Ephesus. Colosse was quite an old city. There is a reference to it as a "great city of Phrygia" as far back as 480 BC. There is another reference from 401 BC that calls it "a city inhabited and prosperous and great." As Hierapolis and Laodicea grew, however, Colosse shrunk. Two generations before Paul, a writer describes it as "a small town." The city of Colosse became part of the Roman Empire around 133 BC and, in the twelfth century, it disappears completely.

It would seem clear from Col.2:1 that Paul did not found the church in Colosse, since many of the Christians there were unknown to him. The city was situated on a trade route and it would have been one possible route for him to take on his third missionary journey, up through the Lycus Valley but there is nothing in the description of that journey in the Acts of the Apostles to suggest that he did so. Perhaps, however, he did have an indirect influence. The Church at Colosse may have been founded during the period, while Paul was ministering in Ephesus. In Acts 19:10, we learn that, during Paul's ministry in Ephesus, he spent two years teaching about the Kingdom of God in the lecture hall of Tyrannus (probably AD 54–56). During this time, "all the Jews and Greeks who lived in the province of Asia heard the word of the Lord." No doubt this included some from Colosse.

It would seem, however, that Epaphras was the evangelist who was directly responsible for establishing the Church in Colosse (1:7). Did he hear the Gospel in Ephesus? He was a Colossian himself (4:12) and a "fellow prisoner" of Paul's (Philemon 23). His work extended throughout the Lycus Valley (4:13). We do not know very much about him although we are told that he was a man of prayer (4:12).

Paul wrote Colossians from prison, although there is no definitive agreement among the commentators as to which imprisonment this was. The balance of evidence, however, seems to favor Paul's imprisonment in Rome, at the end of his third missionary journey, an imprisonment of around 5 years. This would mean that Colossians was written from Rome, at the same time as Philemon, during Paul's imprisonment described in Acts 28:30-31, probably around AD 60–61. During this time, Epaphras made a trip to Rome and brought a report about the Church in Colosse (1:3-8). As a direct result of that report, Paul and Timothy wrote this letter (1:1) and Paul also wrote the letter to Philemon (4:7-9 & Philemon). It would seem from the content, vocabulary, and structure of Colossians that Timothy was, in this case, more than merely an amanuensis but rather shared with Paul in the writing of the letter.

It is clear that the letter to the Colossians was partly designed to counter a heresy that had arisen, now called the "Colossian heresy." This heresy consisted of a strange mixture of mysticism and legalism. Alexander MacLaren wrote, "It is a monstrous combination, a cross between a Talmudical rabbi and a Buddhist priest." The mystical or speculative side is attacked in 2:8-10, and the legalism attacked in 2:20-23. It would seem that within this heresy there were even such things as the worship of angels (2:18). To counter the heresy, Paul points out that in Jesus Christ all the fullness of the godhead lives in bodily form and that he has overall power and sovereignty above every other claimed authority. He also stresses that the way of Christ is the way of holiness, as opposed to any kind of dependence upon laws and regulations. In opposition to Greek notions of wisdom, he speaks of the mystery of God in Christ.

With that general background to the letter, let us now focus in on 3:1-4. The opening words of the text, 'Εἰ οὖν although literally translated as "if then" probably have the sense (with many of the modern translations) of "since then." That is to say, the believers, having been raised (or co-raised: 'συνηγέρθητε') with Christ, are to "seek the things that are above, where Christ is seated at the right hand of God." This is underlined in the second verse, where they are told to "mind" (φρονεῖτε) the things above. In other words, they are to direct (or set, or focus) their minds "on things that are above, not on things that are on earth."

There is a clear development here on what has previously been said in Col. 2:20. In 2:20 we read, 'Εἰ ἀπεθάνετε σὺν Χριστῷ' (If or "since" you have died with Christ) and in 3:1 we read Surrey 'Εἰ οὖ ν συνηγέρθητε τῷ Χριστω' (If, or "since" you have been raised with Christ). As Murray Harris writes, "one prostasis introduces the consequences of death with Christ (2:20-23), the other the consequences of resurrection with Christ (3:1-4)."[1] The key question arising out of the parallel here concerns the meaning of this identification with Christ. In what sense have believers died with Christ and been raised with Christ? We shall return to this question shortly but, leaving it aside for the moment, there are certain points we can make in the light of these two verses. First, something significant has taken place in the lives of these believers, which can be spoken of in terms of death and resurrection. Second, this death and resurrection is not to be understood except in the context of the historical dying and rising of Jesus of Nazareth. That is to say, the believers have not undergone some spiritual experience of death and resurrection that might be interpreted or explained by another set of religious beliefs or philosophical and theological commitments. Their dying and rising is related to the dying and rising of Jesus. Third, this experience of dying and rising ought to result in a redirection of their thinking, such that the things above become the controlling paradigm, rather than the things of the earth. As Michael Bird puts it, "The material in 3:1-17 is a distinct unit that is premised on the reality of union with Messiah and the various imperatives that such a union creates for the individual believer and for the new covenant community."[2] Since "the things

[1]  Murray J. Harris *Colossians and Philemon* (Exegetical Guide to the Greek New Testament; Grand Rapids, MI: Eerdmans, 1991), p. 136.
[2]  Michael F. Bird *Colossians and Philemon* (A New Covenant Commentary; Eugene, OR: Wipf & Stock, 2009), p. 95.

above" are described in terms of the place where "Christ is seated at the right hand of God," we can legitimately paraphrase this as "allow heavenly things to determine your thinking." That is to say, the believers are to develop a world-view whereby the heavenly things (the things of God) determine our attitude to and engagement with earthly things. As some of our best apologists have put it, we are to think out of a centre in God.

If we now turn to verse three of the passage, we find a further theological complexity in relation to the believers' dying and rising with Christ. The text reads, ἀπεθάνετε γὰρ καὶ ἡ ζωὴ ὑμῶν κέκρυπται σὺν τῷ Χριστῷ ἐν τῷ θεῷ᾽ ("for you died and your life is now hidden with Christ in God"). The sense seems to be that the old life has died and the believer now has a new life that is "hidden with Christ in God." Our key question concerning the dying and rising of believers with Christ is dramatically heightened by this verse. Before turning directly to that key question, however, we must first answer another question: what does hidden (κέκρυπται) mean in 3:3?

A range of possible answers has been given to this question. Derek Tidball argues that 3:3 refers to the fact that unbelievers cannot see the truth: "If living with Christ is such a good thing, why are believers in such a minority? Why aren't Christians understood and recognized in a positive light? Why don't people flock to become disciples? Why doesn't everyone agree with the gospel? The reason is that for the moment our lives are *now hidden with Christ in God*. The divine mystery, which has been disclosed to believers, has not been revealed to everyone and the truth lies concealed to many. If the truth of God's plan is hidden to them, then it follows that the true identity of the people at the centre of God's plan will also remain hidden to them."[3]

J. D. G. Dunn, arguing that 3:1-4 is practical and ethical rather than philo-sophical and theoretical, speaks of a "hidden resource." That is to say, in order to develop the new perspective required in 3:1-2, believers find help from the fact that their life is "hidden with Christ in God." He writes, "Paul and Timothy were evidently wholly confident that this perspective, this hidden resource, would provide all the wisdom needed to cope with the challenges and prob-lems of daily living."[4]

Perhaps Murray Harris is nearest to the truth when he writes that the life of believers is hidden or concealed "until the final revelation." As he notes, this would mean that "security as well as concealment is implied."[5] Certainly, if we go on to 3:4, we can see why the view of Harris seems consistent with the flow of the passage: ὅταν ὁ Χριστὸςφανερωθῇ, ἡ ζωὴ ὑμῶν, τότε καὶ ὑμεῖς σὺν

[3] Derek Tidball *The Reality is Christ: The Message of Colossians for Today* (Fearn: Christian Focus Publications, 1999), p. 137.

[4] James D. G. Dunn *The Epistles to the Colossians and to Philemon: A Commentary on the Greek Text* (New International Greek Testament Commentary; Grand Rapids, MI: Eerdmans, 1996), p. 207.

[5] Harris, *Colossians and Philemon*, p. 139.

αὐτῷ φανερωθήσεσθε ἐν δόξῃ' ("When Christ, who is your life, appears, then you also will appear with him in glory"). The life of the believer is "hidden" but one day it will be revealed. The suggestion seems to be that the "real life" of the believer must be understood as that life which is "in Christ" and which will only be revealed to the world when Christ is revealed to the world. At the moment, the only life that can be seen is the human, earthly life, with all its sin and frailty but there is another life, changed by its relationship to Christ (through death and resurrection) which will appear one day.

## II. Death and Resurrection with Christ

That brings us to the key question, namely, how are we to understand the dying and rising of believers with Christ such that their lives are "hidden with Christ in God?" We might sharpen the question slightly by noting that 3:3 says, your life is "hidden with Christ" and 3:4 says, Christ "is your life." In other words, there is such a close connection between the life of the believer and the life of Christ that we can be said to share in the very life of Christ in heaven. By and large, the commentators tend to view this as speaking metaphorically, sacramentally, or spiritually.

### II.a. Metaphorical view

Several significant answers to this key question have been suggested. Some have argued that we must understand the believer's dying and rising with Christ in a metaphorical way. As we have seen, Dunn insists that the passage has to do with ethics. He regards 3:1-4 not as some great ontological statement but as a "general principle" that ought to guide the ethical conduct of believers. He writes, 'The event of death-and-resurrection was two-sided for Christ himself (2:15); a message of the cross without the resurrection would not be gospel, and a call to embrace the implications of the cross without a call also to embrace the implications of the resurrection would be poor teaching."[6] Given this ethical interpretation of 3:1-4, it is not surprising that Dunn holds the language to be "metaphorical and not literal . . . what was in mind was a change of perspective, not (yet) a (complete) ontological change . . . It is the sort of change which follows from complete identification with another person or cause . . . "[7] Dunn insists, therefore, that the main thrust of 3:3 is "not toward some visionary or mystical preoccupation with what human eyes may or may

---

[6] Dunn, *Colossians and Philemon*, p. 203.
[7] Ibid., p. 203.

not see on a journey to heaven. The concern is wholly practical and everyday-lifeish and focuses on their 'life' . . . "[8]

## II.b. Sacramental view

Another view, although not entirely incompatible with that of Dunn, is that the dying and rising of the believer with Christ must be interpreted sacramentally. In other words, 3:1-4 must be interpreted as making much the same point as Rom. 6:1-10. That passage speaks of death and resurrection in Christ and, like Col. 3:1-4, also has ethical implications which Paul spells out in 6:11-14. Bird takes this view. He writes that 3:3 "signifies the destruction of their old identities through the cross. The aorist verb *apethanete* (you died) points back to baptism-confession as the moment of identifying with Christ's death and resurrection."[9]

Harris offers a paraphrase of 3:1-4 in which he clearly regards the passage as referring to what happened when these believers were baptized, even though the word "baptism" does not appear in the pericope:

> In your baptism, then, you came to share in Christ's resurrection. In light of this, always seek whatever belongs to that heavenly realm above, where the risen Christ now reigns, seated at God's right hand in the place of unrivaled honor and authority. Focus your attention and your thoughts exclusively and constantly on the heavenly realm above, not on the earthly realm below. This is appropriate and necessary, for in baptism you died with Christ to sin and the world and now your new, spiritual life, enjoyed in union with Christ, is concealed in the safekeeping of God in heaven. Although your life is now hidden, when this Christ, who is your very Life, appears at his second Advent and his glory is manifested, then you too will fully share in his appearance and in the open display of his glory.[10]

## II.3. Spiritual view

Many commentators and theologians interpret the dying and rising with Christ in terms of a spiritual union with Christ. This is particularly true in the ortho-dox Reformed tradition as represented by the *Westminster Confession of Faith*.

Herman Ridderbos is only one of a number of theologians to whom we could turn as representing this "Westminster Theology" but his engagement with Col. 3:1-4 at a significant number of points in his analysis of Paul's theology

---

[8] Ibid., p. 207.
[9] Bird, *Colossians and Philemon*, pp. 98–99.
[10] Harris, *Colossians and Philemon*, pp. 141–142.

renders him highly useful for this task. Ridderbos begins his section on "Death and Resurrection with Christ" in Romans 6. He notes that the pronounce-ment of Rom. 6:2 "is not an ethical or mystical reality." Rather, he argues, "As is apparent from the whole context, it is not a question of dying to sin in a metaphorical sense (conversion or something like it), but of the participation of the church in the death and burial of Christ in the onetime, redemptive-historical sense of the word."[11] A little later he shows from Col. 3:1-4 that, for the believer, "what is on earth must no longer hold their attention, but what is in heaven." He then repeats his statement that when Paul appeals to the fact that they have died with Christ, the appeal "is therefore not an appeal to their conversion or to their ethical or mystical experience, but to their belonging to Christ when he died."[12]

It is at this stage in his argument that Ridderbos deals directly with Col. 3:1-4, about which he can say this, "One can call this passage, together with Romans 6, the *locus classicus* for the 'objective,' redemptive-historical signifi-cance of having died and been raised with Christ. The new life of believers is that which comes forth with Christ out of the grave, has gone to heaven with him, is there hidden and will once more appear from there with the parou-sia . . . " What has happened to Christ will also happen to the church "by virtue of its corporate unity with him."[13] Ridderbos notes that this reality of dying and rising with Christ (with all its implications) is appropriated through bap-tism.[14] For Ridderbos, then, the new life of the believer is in heaven and will only be revealed when Christ is revealed. In one sense, this new life is a pres-ent possession, in that the life of the believer is now transformed and can be described as life in the Spirit, "nourished from heaven" but in another, more complete sense, it is a future, eschatological reality. Later Ridderbos will note that until that eschaton, faith is "the provisional mode of existence of the new life."[15] At this point in his argument, Ridderbos does use the language of "par-ticipation." He says that the "new life of believers" consists in "participation in Christ's life."

To explain what Ridderbos means by "participation in Christ's life" we must turn back to the section of his Pauline theology where he explains what it means to be "in Christ." In this section, he deals directly with the question as to whether or not the believer is somehow divinized or deified through having died and been raised with Christ. He notes that some have followed a Hellenistic cast of thought and spoken of "absorption with the deity" but insists that this is to follow a wrong track. Thus he can say that "the expression

---

[11] Herman Ridderbos, *Paul: An Outline of his Theology* (trans. J.R. de Witt; London: SPCK, 1977), p. 206.
[12] Ibid., p. 211.
[13] Ibid., p. 212.
[14] Ibid., p. 213.
[15] Ibid., pp. 249–250.

'dying and rising with Christ' does not have its origin in the sphere of the individual mysticism of experience, nor in the automatism of the initiatory rites of the Hellenistic mysteries, but is of an entirely different nature."[16] Rather, argues Ridderbos, the explanation of this dying and rising is to be found in the parallel between Adam and Christ in 1 Corinthians 15 and in Romans 5. Following fairly closely the basic parameters of this theme as found in the *Westminster Confession of Faith*, Ridderbos shows that the corporate identity of humanity in Adam led to the corporate fall into sin. That is to say, all who were in Adam died. Similarly, there is a corporate headship which Christ exercises, such that those who are in Christ will be made alive. He writes, "It is this corporate connection of the all-in-One that Paul applies to Christ and his people, and from which the pronouncements concerning (dying, etc.) 'with Christ' must be interpreted, at least as to their origin, as is plainly evident as well from the close connection between Romans 5:12-21 (Adam and Christ) and Romans 6:1ff. (being buried with Christ, etc.)."

Ridderbos does not neglect the core ethical imperative of Col. 3:1-4. The believers are truly being urged to live in a different way and to have a new perspective because of what they are now in Christ. He says, "Having once died with Christ does not render superfluous putting to death the members that are on earth, but is precisely the great urgent reason for it." "you have been raised" leads directly to the imperative "seek the things that are above."

For Ridderbos, then, the way to understand dying and rising with Christ (and hence the core meaning of Col. 3:1-4) is in the context of a doctrine of union with Christ, understood in terms of a federal solidarity with Christ. This federal headship involves the new life of the believer having been raised with Christ and having gone with Christ into heaven. One day that new life will be revealed when Christ returns.

We have seen that there are various ways in which we can understand what it means to have died and been raised with Christ. There is a sense in which aspects of each of these views (metaphorical, sacramental, and spiritual) could be drawn together to provide a coherent interpretation of Col. 3:3. In recent Reformed theology, however, there have been moves to go much further and explore ideas that were previously foreign (or certainly tangential) to orthodox Reformed theology.

## III. The Reformed Debate

The issues before us in Col. 3:1-4, and especially in 3:3, have been the focus of significant theological discussion recently in Reformed theology. Much

---

[16] Ibid., p. 60

of this has been generated by a new interest in Eastern Orthodox theology. Scholars in the Reformed tradition who might have been expected to interpret Col. 3:1-4 in terms of union with Christ (as symbolized in baptism) have recently begun to offer interpretations of this and other passages (especially 2 Pet. 1:4) which go some way toward accommodating key ideas from Orthodoxy. Whereas previously the divide between the western church and the eastern church could have been stated as the difference between a "spiritual union with Christ" approach and a "deification" approach, there have now developed at least four distinct positions within Reformed theology: first, deification; second, *theosis*, third, participation; and fourth, union with Christ. In each case, the claim is made that this is the position held by Calvin. Let's look at each of these in turn.

## III.a. Deification

The doctrine that, in salvation, human beings are absorbed into the being of God has long been the teaching of the Eastern Orthodox churches. Recently, however, Protestants have begun to appropriate this teaching. The Finnish Lutherans claimed to have found deification in Luther.[17] Then, in a challenging and provocative article, Carl Mosser argued that Calvin taught deification.[18]

Mosser draws attention to Calvin's comments on 2 Pet. 1:4 regarding "becoming partakers of the divine nature" arguing that Calvin's language is classical patristic deification language.[19] He goes on to look through Calvin's writings, pointing out language that can be seen as "deification language." He makes a particular point of interpreting Calvin's view of the Lord's Supper in this way.[20] In the same way, he examines Calvin's doctrine of glorification and again finds deification language.[21] Why has this not been spoken of before? Mosser argues that Calvin's use of the deification language of the Fathers has been overlooked through a lack of familiarity with the sources.[22] He concludes,

Though not as bold as the Church fathers sometimes are, Calvin's understanding of deification is simply the patristic notion of *theosis*. In this sense we should not speak of "Calvin's doctrine of deification;" he was simply teaching

---

[17] Carl E. Braaten and Robert W. Jenson (eds) *Union with Christ: The New Finnish Interpretation of Luther* (Grand Rapids, MI: Eerdmans, 1998).
[18] Carl Mosser "The Greatest Possible Blessing: Calvin and Deification" *Scottish Journal of Theology* 55, no. 1 (2002), pp. 36–57.
[19] Ibid., p. 40.
[20] Ibid., p. 44.
[21] Ibid., p. 45.
[22] Ibid., p. 55.

and, more often, presupposing the church's doctrine. Nor should we speak of "Calvin's doctrine of deification" as if he had substantively developed or systematized the doctrine beyond what the patristic writers wrote; on this subject, Calvin was quite unoriginal. In another sense, however, we can. The role deification plays in Calvin's theology, its relation to other doctrines, and the minor developments one finds warrant comparative study of "Calvin's doctrine of deification" with that of individual Church fathers, medieval mystics, Eastern theologians, Aquinas, Luther and other sixteenth-century figures.[23]

This argument by Mosser is not persuasive. The quotations from Calvin which he presents can easily be interpreted otherwise (and have been by other scholars). More significantly, the detailed evidence of alleged direct correspondence between Calvin and the sources in the Fathers is not provided. Indeed, despite this being a major plank in his argument, Mosser says that he "purposely refrained from quoting patristic parallels to focus attention directly upon Calvin's own statements (as well as to save space)."

## III.b. Theosis

Until fairly recently, *theosis* was simply another way of referring to deification. Indeed, one of the most significant Orthodox treatises on the subject of deification was called *Theosis: The True Purpose of Human Life*.[24] More recently, however, a number of scholars have argued that it is possible to hold to the idea of *theosis* while at the same time rejecting the doctrine of deification. Indeed, some of those who hold this position have argued that it is entirely compatible with Reformed theology and was the position held by John Calvin. This is the position advocated by Myk Habets.[25]

Habets distinguishes his own view from that of the eastern Orthodox theologians by appropriating a distinction from Gösta Hallonsten between a "doctrine" of *theosis* and *theosis* as a "theme." He is not suggesting that Calvin had a full-blown doctrine of *theosis* (or divinization or deification) but rather that he did use the thematic language of *theosis*. This enables him to argue that there is no incompatibility between *theosis* and the traditional Reformed doctrine of

---

[23] Ibid., pp. 56–57.
[24] Archimandrite George, *Abbot* (Mount Athos: Holy Monastery of St. Gregorios, 2006).
[25] Myk Habets "'Reformed Theosis?' A Response to Gannon Murphy," *Theology Today* 65 (2009), pp. 489–498; Myk Habets, *Theosis in the Theology of Thomas Torrance* (Surrey: Ashgate, 2009). I am also grateful to Myk Habets for the as yet unpublished paper, "*Theosis*, Yes, Deification, No: Calvin's Reformed Doctrine of *Theosis*," presented at the Calvin500 conference in Geneva in 2009.

union with Christ.[26] Notice, he specifically states that he is not equating these concepts, merely insisting that there is no incompatibility between them.

Habets also quotes Calvin on 2 Pet. 1:4, then spends a good deal of time on Calvin's doctrine of union with Christ. He makes the point, drawn from T. F. Torrance and his school, that in traditional "Westminster theology" Union with Christ is merely a mechanism for the transfer of "benefits" rather than a full engagement in the life and being of Christ.[27] He argues that Calvin's understanding of the mystical union with Christ was far deeper and richer than many have understood, such that it is perfectly reasonable to use the word *theosis* in respect of his position. Habets is careful to avoid any suggestion that there is a "hypostatic union" between the believer and Christ[28] but believes nonetheless that our engrafting into Christ involves more than imputation understood in an extrinsicist manner.[29]

As with Mosser, the argument for *theosis* is not fully convincing. One is left with the conviction that a more developed and sustained doctrine of union with Christ, which has a more developed ontology and yet retains a clear commitment to forensic categories and to imputation, would more adequately represent Calvin's position. It is also clear from Billings' argument, however, that although he advocates the term *theosis*, his position is very similar to that advocated by those who want to use the language of "participation" and so it is to that position we now turn.

## III.c. Participation

There are scholars within the Reformed tradition who do not want to speak about deification, divinization or *theosis* but who are happy to use the language of "participation." This was the position held by T. F. Torrance and can be traced through his core theological writings as well as in his ecumenical engagements on behalf of the Church. More recently, however, we are indebted to Robert Walker for producing the two volumes of Torrance's lectures on Incarnation and Atonement.[30] In these volumes, we see the notion of participation in Christ carried through as a theme from beginning to end.

For Torrance, the incarnation is the key to understanding salvation. At the incarnation, God and fallen humanity are united in the person of Christ and reconciliation takes place. Everything about human salvation is worked out

---

[26] Ibid., p. 4.
[27] Ibid., pp. 6–7.
[28] Ibid., p. 12.
[29] Ibid., p. 11.
[30] T. F. Torrance *Incarnation: The Person and Life of Christ* (ed. Robert T. Walker; Milton Keynes: Paternoster, 2008); T. F. Torrance *Atonement: The Person and Work of Christ* (ed. Robert T. Walker; Milton Keynes: Paternoster, 2009).

from this incarnational basis. When human beings are united to Christ, they share in that reconciled humanity. In one sense, the task is for believers to become in themselves what they already are in Christ. Torrance thus eschews notions of atonement viewed as the Father punishing the Son in the place of sinners, with the benefits thereby achieved being imputed to believers. These purely forensic categories are regarded not only as deeply inadequate but as deeply damaging to the gospel itself.

T. F. Torrance argued for most of his life that this position is more true to Calvin than the "Westminster Theology," which he regarded as having taken a wrong turning in its doctrines of individual human double predestination and its teaching on limited atonement. More recently, Julie Canlis has argued that Calvin held to a "participation" theology.[31] Canlis notes that Reformed theologians have been rather nervous about using "participation" language in relation to our union with Christ, preferring instead to speak of "fellowship." The language of "participation" "having been type-cast as 'mystical' or 'platonic' and therefore un-Reformed."[32] Much of this reluctance to use such language, argues Canlis, stems from Calvin's controversy with Osiander. She insists, however, that when this controversy is reviewed it can be seen that there are many similarities between Calvin and Osiander and that it is not necessary to overreact against participation language.

Keen to relate the language of "participation" to traditional Reformed categories, Canlis expounds participation with Christ in terms of the doctrines of union with Christ and adoption. Her argument is that the controversy with Osiander refined Calvin's theology of participation, which can be summed up as union with Christ *as* adoption. This is her conclusion:

> Many scholars are doubtful whether there is any room at all for a "real communion" between the divine and human in Reformed theology. My proposition is that there is more than "room" in Calvin's thought for real communion; rather, "participation in God" is how we make sense of his views on the Christian life. This is not Osiander's "inflowing of substance" into us, making us justified and sanctified. It is a non-substantial participation in the person of Christ, made possible by Calvin's innovative doctrine of the Holy Spirit who is a safeguard *against* substantial participation. Neither is participation the result of a latent platonic ontology that Calvin held, but must be seen more in light of Calvin's push towards communion. For this reason, Calvin does not put us *en Christo* merely as a way of appropriating the salvific benefits of Christ. To see it so is to miss the overarching significance of union as adoption, by which we are taken up to participate in (and

---

[31] Canlis, "Calvin, Osiander, and Participation in God," *International Journal of Systematic Theology* 6, no. 2 (2004), pp. 169–184.

[32] Ibid., 169.

be transformed by) God's trinitarian life and love. We must never forget that Calvin was first and foremost a concerned pastor. Union with Christ as adoption—living as children with a benevolent Father—this is the essence of the justified life that Calvin desired for his flock.[33]

If we return briefly to where we began, we might well argue that the Reformed doctrine of adoption does indeed provide a solid basis for approaching Col. 3:3. Adoption is the climax of a process whereby God changes an unbeliever into a believer, a sinner into a saint. The process begins with the new birth. When that takes place, the gift of faith is given. That faith when exercised leads to justification (pardon and acceptance) and then adoption. Taken on its own, justification is a legal concept and might sound cold or remote, but adoption, as the completion of the process, puts that right. It is the great wonder of the Christian gospel that we should not only be forgiven but actually taken into the very family of God.

Canlis' work has been taken up by others, most notably in an extended treatment of the subject by J. Todd Billings, whose recent book has caused considerable rethinking in Calvin studies.[34] Although Billings' work found its origin in a response to notions of "gift," particularly in Radical Orthodoxy, it is a wideranging study on Calvin's use of the language of participation. He begins by laying out the concerns of Milbank and others, not least in their strong objection to any forensic notion of imputation. For Milbank and others, this

> is seen as indicative of a nominalist metaphysic which stands in radical discontinuity with the patristic synthesis in Thomas's theology of participation. Imputation capitulates to the late medieval replacement of "divine decree" for "ontological infusion" in justification. As such it breaks down the fundamental analogy between God and creation, stressing a univocal understanding of being rather than an ontology of participation.[35]

Billings sets out to prove that Milbank and the others have misunderstood Calvin and that he does indeed have a strong doctrine of participation in Christ which was not at all damaged by his other theological commitments. In particular, he shows that Calvin's use of the *duplex gratia* of justification and sanctification, both of which flow out of the believer's union with Christ, answers many caricatures of Calvin's position.[36]

---

[33] Ibid., 184.

[34] J. Todd Billings *Calvin, Participation, and the Gift: The Activity of Believers in Union with Christ* (Changing Paradigms in Historical and Systematic Theology; Oxford: Oxford University Press, 2007).

[35] Ibid., p. 9.

[36] Ibid., pp. 15–16.

Billings' position is different than that of Canlis at one key point. Canlis argued that Calvin's view could be described as a "non substantial" participation in Christ, whereas Billings believes that Calvin held to a "substantial participation." For Canlis, "non-substantial participation" means that the human being and Christ share in one another's existence and lives by the Holy Spirit, whereas Billings wants to argue that Calvin held to the view that believers participate in the "substance" of Christ.[37] In support of his argument, Billings seeks to demonstrate that there was a steady increase in the language and theology of participation through successive editions of the *Institutes*. He writes,

> By the 1559 edition of the *Institutes*, Calvin's doctrine of participation has been expanded to an impressive scope. He has no fewer than thirty-two references in the Latin to believers participating in Christ (*participes*) with many more references in less direct language. The language of participation is used with regard to justification, baptism, the Lord's Supper, the Resurrection, the Incarnation, the Atonement, the *imago dei*, and "participation in God". In addition, Calvin has expanded the accompanying themes of union with Christ, union with God, engrafting into Christ, and adoption. The theme of participation has been broadened and intensified as Calvin's Pauline soteriological langauge is used to read and reread a great variety of credal *loci*.[38]

Billings believes that Calvin's doctrine of participation manages to hold together "organic images of transformation into Christlikeness by the indwelling of the Spirit with forensic images of God's free pardon . . . "[39] He also asserts that Calvin's view of participation takes seriously human sin and therefore "the eschaton is not collapsed into the present, and sinners are not said to be perfected in this life."[40]

Bruce McCormack has entered the lists in this debate.[41] He too calls for a theology of participation, along the lines advocated by Torrance and Canlis. The significance of McCormack's intervention, however, consists in the strong argument he presents for the important theological boundary line which he insists must be drawn between *theosis* and participation. In an article for the Jüngel *festschrift*, he expounds the respective positions of Barth and Jüngel on

---

[37]  Ibid., pp. 62–63.
[38]  Ibid., p. 101.
[39]  Ibid., p. 196.
[40]  Ibid., p. 196.
[41]  Bruce L. McCormack, "For Us and Our Salvation: Incarnation and Atonement in the Reformed Tradition" *The Greek Orthodox Theological Review* 43 (1998), pp. 281–316; Bruce L. McCormack, "Participation in God, Yes, Deification, No: Two Modern Protestant Responses to an Ancient Question," in *Denkwürdiges Geheimnis: Beiträge zur Gotteslehre. Festschrift für Eberhard Jüngel zum 70. Geburtstag* (eds, I. U. Dalferth, J. Fischer, and H-P. Großhans; Tübingen: Mohr-Siebeck, 2004), pp. 347–374.

the question of the ontological distinction between God's being and human being, showing how the Reformed Barth and the Lutheran Jüngel used the *anhypostasia* and *enhypostasia* distinctions (although in a slightly different way) to maintain a strong doctrine of the unity of the person of Christ in which there was no confusion of the divine and the human.[42] McCormack believes that any confusing of this ontological distinction between God's being and human being fundamentally damages Christian theology.

McCormack is also deeply concerned that any notion of deification, diviniza- tion, or *theosis* will inevitably lead to a weakening of the Reformed doctrine of the two natures of Christ. In his long article on Incarnation and Atonement (published in the *Greek Orthodox Theological Review*!), he writes,

> What we have established to this point is basically two things. The first is that for a Christology to be "Reformed," it must affirm the principle that the two natures remain distinct and their properties unimpaired after the union. On that point there is such overwhelming unanimity in the Reformed tradi- tion that a Christology which would set it aside or weaken it must, by doing so, cease to be Reformed. Secondly, we have established that the Subject who worked out our redemption is the God-man in his divine-human unity. In saying this, I am also suggesting that the language of "subject" should not be used to translate *hypostasis* into a more modern idiom. The "Subject" in this case is not the *hypostasis* as such, but the *hypostasis* together with the two natures which subsist in it. God as *human*—He is the Subject of our redemption.[43]

In his conclusion to this same article he writes,

> In conclusion: the Reformed understanding of incarnation and atonement distinguishes itself through its continuous emphasis on the distinction of divine being and human being as well as through the very prominent role it assigns to the Holy Spirit, as the Power which joins together divine being and human being without setting aside the distinction. It is the Spirit who brings divine nature and human nature together in the hypostatic union and in a very real sense, mediates between them; it is the Spirit who empow- ers and makes possible the obedience of the Son in and through his human nature; it is the Spirit who joins us to the Son, thereby effecting our sancti- fication and our justification; and it is the Spirit who "glorifies" believers by glorifying the Son in eternity.[44]

---

[42] McCormack, "Participation in God," pp. 36–37.
[43] McCormack, "For Us and Our Salvation," p. 294.
[44] Ibid., p. 311.

At the same time, however, McCormack is not satisfied with the categories of traditional "Westminster Calvinism." Like Torrance, he believes that a doctrine of union with Christ conceived as a vehicle for the transmission of the benefits of Christ, viewed exclusively in forensic categories, fails to do justice to the biblical language of participation in Christ and the theological need to root a doctrine of atonement in an ontology that takes seriously the significance of the incarnation, as opposed to reducing the atonement to something that essentially happened on the cross.

# IV. Conclusions

What are we to make of all this? I began this essay indicating that I had a pastoral issue: how to explain Col. 3:3 to my congregation in a way that, on the one hand, did not suggest deification and yet, on the other hand, did not reduce it to a somewhat shallow statement of the means whereby we receive certain benefits from God. It seems to me that if we take the contextual biblical interpretation of Col. 3:3, as provided by the biblical commentators, together with an analysis of the debates on the theological interpretation of the passage, not least in respect to the arguments concerning deification, participation, and union with Christ, then there are challenges presented to the Reformed theological community.

There are certain key theological affirmations which must be maintained. First, the Creator–creature distinction; second, the ontological difference between God's being and human being; and third, the doctrine of the two distinct natures of Christ under the one Person of the *Logos*. The affirmation of these doctrines will distinguish Reformed theology from various forms of deification theology. Beyond that, however, there are disagreements within the broad stream of Reformed theology. On the one hand, theologians like Ridderbos want to insist that the doctrines of incarnation and atonement as found in the Reformed confessions are fit for purpose. On the other hand, theologians like Torrance and McCormack believe that traditional Reformed categories fail to do justice to their biblical and theological understanding of inclusion and participation in the life of Christ. It seems to me that a more serious and direct dialogue is required between these two schools of thought.

In my view, Torrance et al. have failed to give sufficient place in their theologies to the forensic metaphors which are clearly present on the face of the New Testament. In addition, they tend to have a very weak doctrine of imputation. The notion of an "incarnational union" of all humanity with Christ, sometimes distinct from a "spiritual union" between Christ and believers, is often confused and confusing and does not seem to accord easily with the biblical language. Questions remain about the significance of the Cross if the incarnation is the primary driver in atonement theology.

On the other hand, the traditional "Westminster" version of Reformed theology has tended to reduce the doctrine of union with Christ to a means for the obtaining of certain benefits from Christ. The forensic metaphors have often failed to do full justice to the very real biblical language of participation in the life of Christ and made it difficult to deal with Col. 3:3 and other texts. In a determination not to be "Barthian" there has perhaps been an overreaction against some important biblical motifs.

Recently a group of theologians began to meet in Scotland to discuss these matters, forming a theological reading group and beginning with Torrance's two volumes on Incarnation and Atonement. The members of this small group are drawn both from the "Torrance" and the "Westminster" camps, with others who represent neither group, including a Catholic theologian. In my view, it is this kind of engagement, where we can challenge one another, which will help to move us forward on these vital theological questions.

Chapter 11

# What Is Theological Commentary?
# An Old Testament Perspective

Walter L. Moberly

## Introduction

The premise of this collection of essays is that it is possible, indeed desirable, to bring together the doctrines of the church and the reading of Scripture. The concern is not primarily to show historically how the doctrines arose, but rather to demonstrate the fruitfulness of Christian doctrine for good and wise readings and appropriations of the biblical text in the world of today. The bulk of the book has been devoted to providing examples of such readings. My task, by way of rounding off the project and complementing Don Carson's chapter, is to offer some programmatic reflections on some of the particular issues that arise as one attempts to read and comment on the Old Testament theologically.

Three initial caveats, however, must be sounded. First, I am writing this chapter "blind," that is without having seen the preceding essays on Old Testament passages, or Don Carson's essay. How well it will complement them is, therefore, unclear—and may be a challenge for editors and readers alike!

Secondly, it seems to me probably inevitable, but in fact constructive, that issues of theological commentary will tend to be approached differently, according to whether the commentator's primary intellectual and scholarly location is theology or Bible. However much we are seeking to hold these realms together, there are nonetheless legitimately differing perspectives, priorities, and debates according to location.[1]

Thirdly, a general essay such as this can easily come up with a comprehensive programme (a kind of ideal wish list) of all those elements that should characterize theological commentary. Yet any such programme needs to be tempered in practice by various recognitions. On the one hand, limitations

---

[1] It is instructive in this regard to compare my *The Theology of the Book of Genesis* (Cambridge: Cambridge University Press, 2009), in which I approach the biblical text as someone located primarily in biblical scholarship, with R. R. Reno, *Genesis* (Brazos Theological Commentary on the Bible; Grand Rapids, MI: Brazos, 2010), where Reno comes to the text primarily as a Christian theologian deeply rooted in classic Christian tradition. Each volume offers theological commentary—but there is not much overlap!

of space and time, and also contextual needs, may reasonably restrict the many possible dimensions of commentary. On the other hand, Old Testament texts themselves vary in their amenability to general concerns of theological commentary; for example, most genealogies simply offer less than most narratives—which is not a reason to neglect genealogies but rather to have appropriate differences of expectation according to varying literary genre.

## Preliminary Definition

Although I have already used the term "theological commentary," a little clarification as to what is, and is not, meant by the term may be appropriate; for the word "theology" is used in importantly different ways, and failure to define terminology can lead to confusion.

One monument of modern Old Testament scholarship is the multivolume *Theological Dictionary of the Old Testament.*[2] Here the term "theological" is used, in a way characteristic of much modern biblical scholarship, to denote a historical analysis of the religious terminology and concepts of the Old Testament set in relation to their world of origin. There is great value in such an exercise. Nonetheless, its understanding of "theology" is not that of this volume. Here the angle of vision is not the meaning of the Old Testament texts in relation to their world of origin (though that is not ignored)—which is in certain ways a looking behind the canon to a time when its constituent documents were written; rather the angle of vision is the meaning of the Old Testament texts in relation to Christian faith as a living reality—which is in important ways a looking ahead to that continuing faith in God to which the canon qua canon gives rise in the light of Christ.

In broad terms this difference in the understanding of "theology" relates to differences in overall approach to the biblical text—approaches which are often conveniently (though potentially misleadingly) given the shorthand designations of "historical–critical" and "canonical". What matters, however, is not the labeling attached, but rather the recognition that the meaning of "theology" is determined not least by the overall frame of reference within which it is used. Here the concern is to understand the biblical texts in relation to faith in God today.

## Three Distinctive Challenges Posed by the Old Testament

Some of the issues relating to the Old Testament and its theological interpretation relate equally to the New Testament. Nonetheless, there are at least three

---

[2] Edited by G. Johannes Botterweck and Helmer Ringgren (and, in later volumes, Heinz-Josef Fabry); English translation and edition: Grand Rapids, MI: Eerdmans, 1974–2006.

distinctive challenges that the Old Testament poses to its Christian commentators that are not posed by the New Testament.[3]

First, that collection of books that Christians call the Old Testament (a designation that obviously presupposes, and is a counterpart to, the New Testament) is a pre-Christian collection of books. All its constituent documents were written before ever there was a Christian faith, and the processes of selection, arrangement, and preservation as authoritative—that is the processes of the texts' becoming canonical—were mostly (whether or not entirely) completed before the rise of Christian faith. Whatever the issues that this posed for the early Church, in terms of relating Jesus in his life, death, and resurrection to existing scriptures, it poses a continuing challenge to Christians to recognize that what they seek to interpret Christianly was not originally Christian. This is one reason (among many) why issues of hermeneutics must always, in one form or other, be on the table. The task of theological commentary will be misunderstood and/or done badly if this pre-Christian character of the Old Testament is not borne in mind.

A second challenge, related to the first, is that the Old Testament's heritage is contested. Jews wrote and compiled these scriptures before ever there was a Christian faith, and, alongside Christian appropriation of these scriptures as the Old Testament, they continue as Jewish scripture (*Tanakh, Miqra*)) unbrokenly from ancient times until the present day. Unsurprisingly, Jews often interpret their scriptures rather differently than Christians do. Although differences of interpretation are inevitable, given the differing overall frames of reference rooted ultimately in differing stances toward Jesus, this does not mean that Christians should not still attend to, and learn from, Jewish interpretation where it is possible and appropriate.[4] Yet constructive attention to Jewish interpretation is notable for its absence in many modern Christian interpreters of the Old Testament. One looks in vain for it, or even any real recognition of its existence, in the monumental works of Old Testament Theology by Eichrodt and von Rad.[5] More recently, not least in the light of the Holocaust and growing cultural indifference to Jewish and Christian faiths alike, there has been much Christian rethinking of attitudes toward Jews, though no clear or consistent practice has emerged (probably unsurprisingly, given the complexity of the issues). Although respect for Jewish sensibilities is a major reason why both

[3]   Other challenges could include recognition of biblical Hebrew as being, in certain ways, a harder language to understand than Hellenistic/*Koine* Greek; this is because of its limited corpus and the relative lack of comparable ancient Hebrew usage beyond the canon.

[4]   Certainly my own work in theological commentary has been enormously enriched by insights from Jewish scholarship. I am particularly indebted to Jon Levenson, not least his wonderful *The Hebrew Bible, the Old Testament, and Historical Criticism* (Louisville, KY: Westminster/John Knox Press, 1993).

[5]   Walther Eichrodt, *Theology of the Old Testament*, 2 vols (trans. John Baker; London: SCM, 1961, 1967); Gerhard von Rad, *Old Testament Theology*, 2 vols (trans. D. Stalker; London: SCM, 1965, 1975).

Brueggemann and Rendtorff tend to bracket out reference to Jesus and the New Testament in their Old Testament Theologies,[6] their respect for Judaism does not lead them to interact with Jewish interpretations. However, ironically, Brevard Childs, who is sometimes criticized for unduly Christianizing the task of Old Testament interpretation, does frequently interact appreciatively with Jewish interpretation.[7] There is much still to be done in this area.

The third challenge is that already in pre-Christian times the Old Testament existed in two languages, Greek as well as Hebrew.[8] The Greek translation, the Septuagint, is arguably the first major work of translation in Western history; and it attests the need from earliest times to make the biblical content readily available in changing cultural and linguistic contexts. For our purposes, three points are significant. First, because the work of translation was pioneering (and as such an astonishing achievement) it was also rougher and less polished than one expects translations to be when translation is an established practice (and in places the translators appear to have struggled with a Hebrew text which was not only, of course, unpointed but also possibly unclearly written or damaged in some way); in places the Greek is simply difficult to read and make sense of as Greek. Secondly, although all translation is interpretation, some translations are more interpretive than others, and there is good reason at least sometimes to see the Greek translators as rendering texts in ways that deliberately made their content more accessible to the Hellenistic culture that the translation was serving. Thirdly, it was predominantly in Greek translation, rather than in Hebrew, that the Old Testament was read and appropriated both by the writers of the New Testament and by the Church Fathers. What then is the authoritative text of the Old Testament for the theological commentator? Hebrew or Greek?

The enduring problems were well brought out already in antiquity in a correspondence between Augustine and Jerome. Jerome, the scholar, has the scholarly instinct, when working on his translation of the Old Testament into Latin, to work from the Hebrew original ("*Hebraica veritas*") in preference to the Greek. Augustine, the thinker and pastor, upholds the importance of the Greek, not just because it was the form familiar to Christian congregations (who, then as now, often dislike certain kinds of change), but also because it had been fruitful and formative for Christian worship and theology and so was not lightly to be set aside.[9]

---

[6] Walter Brueggemann, *Theology of the Old Testament: Testimony, Dispute, Advocacy* (Minneapolis, MN: Fortress, 1997), pp. 89–93, Rolf Rendtorff, *The Canonical Hebrew Bible: A Theology of the Old Testament* (trans. David Orton; Leiden: Deo, 2005), pp. 740–756.

[7] This is most evident in his *Exodus* (London: SCM, 1974).

[8] For simplicity of presentation I subsume the Aramaic portions under the general category of Hebrew.

[9] See Mogens Müller, *The First Bible of the Church* (Journal for the Study of the Old Testament Supplement Series 206; Sheffield Academic Press: 1996), pp. 83–94.

To be sure, often nothing hangs on the difference between Hebrew and Greek. But sometimes something does. I have argued elsewhere that the meaning of the story of Cain and Abel (Genesis 4) differs fundamentally according to whether it is read in the Hebrew or the Greek—and that although the New Testament writers and most Christian tradition follow the lead of the Greek, the sense in the Hebrew is more searching.[10] A well-known New Testament example is the wording of Isaiah's commissioning (Isa. 6:9–10), a passage of such importance that it interprets Jesus's prime modes of communication: parables in the Synoptic Gospels (Mt. 13:10–17, Mk 4:10–12, Lk. 8:9–10) and signs in John's Gospel (Jn 12:37–40). In the Hebrew, the hard but clear sense of the text is that Isaiah's speaking to Israel will not be understood because his speaking in itself will be the cause of their unresponsiveness— "Keep listening, but do not comprehend . . . Make the mind of this people dull . . . so that they may not . . . comprehend" (NRSV). In the Greek, however, we find the more straightforward sense that Isaiah's speaking to Israel will not be understood because the people are already unresponsive— "You will listen by listening, but you will not understand . . . For this people's heart has grown fat . . . so that they might not . . . understand" (NETS). Although the wording in Mark, Luke, and John appears to follow the Hebrew, in Matthew the wording unambiguously follows the Greek (13:13–15)—and so there is more than one understanding of the reason why Jesus speaks in parables. Thus the New Testament implicitly acknowledges the authority of both the Hebrew and the Greek, and this is no doubt a good precedent for Christians to follow.[11] But it does not make for an easy life for the theological commentator if it is recognized that important passages in the Old Testament have more than one text-form and so more than one trajectory for interpretation.[12]

## Toward Articulating a Christian Frame of Reference for Theological Commentary

Much has been written on the issue of appropriate presuppositions for a biblical interpreter. Here I want to mention one: *expectations.* Theological interpreters approach the Bible with expectations that they do not have for any other book, even those by recognized moral and spiritual teachers. Often this is taken not to be in need of justification, as in the fascinating recent *Theology*

---

[10] See my *The Theology of the Book of Genesis*, pp. 88–101, and my "Exemplars of Faith in Hebrews 11: Abel" in *The Epistle to the Hebrews and Christian Theology* (eds, Richard Bauckham et al; Grand Rapids, MI: Eerdmans, 2009), pp. 353–363.

[11] A suggestive essay in this area is J. Ross Wagner, "The Septuagint and the 'Search for the Christian Bible'" in *Scripture's Doctrine and Theology's Bible* (eds, Markus Bockmuehl and Alan Torrance; Grand Rapids, MI: Baker Academic, 2008), pp. 17–28.

[12] See especially Michael Allen's essay on Exodus 3.

*of the Old Testament* by John Rogerson, who notes Bultmann's assumption for his *Theology of the New Testament*, that "these writings have something to say to the present, and makes that assumption the basis for his own work, as though it were self-evident and uncontroversial.[13] In a Christian culture that would be fine. But in contemporary post-Christian culture most questions of values, priorities, and authorities are contested. If one's working assumption is to be that the Old Testament has a contemporary signficance, which is not similarly shared by other ancient texts (Epic of Gilgamesh, Laws of Hammurabi, writings of Philo, etc), then what is its basis?[14] Hector Avalos, for example, has argued forcefully (though somewhat tendentiously) that "there is really nothing in the entire book Christians call 'the Bible' that is any more relevant than anything else written in the ancient world".[15] On what basis, then, can Christians appropriately continue to privilege the Old Testament in terms of their expectations?[16]

It is insufficient in the first instance to point to the content and claims within the text, for it could be responded that the Qur'an also has strong claims about God and life and yet Christians may simply shrug these off. Rather, the primary factor must surely be that down the ages Jews and Christians have approached these texts as giving truth about God and humanity, and we in some way identify with them,[17] and follow in their footsteps today. The historic and continuing existence of synagogue and church creates socially shared expectations for those who belong to them, or at least take them seriously (as do the mosque and Islamic culture for the Qur'an). Bible and church in this sense depend upon each other.

One important way of escaping some of the sterile Protestant/Catholic standoffs about the respective authority of Bible and church is to recast the issue in sociological terms—the church as a plausibility structure for the Bible. Peter Berger and Thomas Luckmann, for example, discuss what is humanly

---

[13] J. W. Rogerson, *A Theology of the Old Testament: Cultural Memory, Communication and Being Human* (London: SCPK, 2009), p. 2.

[14] Ibid., Rogerson's handling of the Old Testament, in terms of its enabling humanity to become more humane, suggests that, despite his title and his self-presentation as "an active Anglican priest" (p. 11), his working assumption may be primarily of the Old Testament as a literary classic with enduring insight into the human condition, comparable to that of Aeschylus or Shakespeare.

[15] Hector Avalos, *The End of Biblical Studies* (Amherst, NY: Prometheus Books, 2007), p. 22.

[16] I am not thinking here of the Old Testament as a major influence within historic Western culture (literature, art, music, etc), and the need to know the Old Testament and its historic reception in order to understand this culture. That is a significant, and increasingly common, reason for studying the Old Testament. But it is a mode of study that makes no assumption whatever about the contemporary significance of the Old Testament as in its own right still "having something to say."

[17] Given the complexities of history, and not least the often disreputable nature of church history, one's identification with previous generations can sometimes be far from straightforward, and may appropriately be selective.

necessary for someone to change their basic perception of the world, and with it their identity and allegiance, as in religious conversion (which includes, for our purposes, attitudes toward Scripture):

> The most important social condition is the availability of an effective plausibility structure, that is, a social base serving as the "laboratory" of transformation. This plausibility structure will be mediated to the individual by means of significant others, with whom he must establish strongly affective identification. No radical transformation of subjective reality (including, of course, identity) is possible without such identification, which inevitably replicates childhood experiences of emotional dependency on significant others. These significant others are the guides into the new reality.[18]

The importance of plausibility structures, and especially of the Church as a plausibility structure for Christian believing, has increasingly been recognized in recent years.[19] Without the historic and contemporary synagogue and church as plausibility structures where there are "significant others"—even if encountered informally in local embodiments such as family or friends or college—a necessary precondition for regarding the Old Testament as even in principle a meaningful, never mind enduringly truthful, witness to God and humanity will not be in place.[20]

A sense of the difference made by the expectation, derived from the continuing life of Jews and Christians, is well articulated by Brevard Childs:

> I do not come to the Old Testament to learn about someone else's God, but about the God we confess, who has made himself known to Israel, to Abraham, Isaac and to Jacob. I do not approach some ancient concept, some mythological construct akin to Zeus or Moloch, but our God, our Father. The Old Testament bears witness that God revealed himself to Abraham, and we confess that he has broken into our lives. I do not come to the Old Testament to be informed about some strange religious phenomenon, but in faith I strive for knowledge as I seek to understand ourselves in the light of God's self-disclosure. In the context of the church's scripture I seek to be pointed to our God who has made himself known, is making himself known, and will make himself known. . . . Thus, I cannot act as if I were living at the

---

[18] Peter L. Berger and Thomas Luckmann, *The Social Construction of Reality: A Treatise in the Sociology of Knowledge* (Anchor Books; New York: Doubleday, 1967), p. 157.

[19] See Lesslie Newbigin, *The Gospel in a Pluralist Society* (London: SPCK, 1989), pp. 222–233.

[20] A foundational essay for recognizing the implications of the social character of knowledge in relation to biblical study is Jon D. Levenson, "Historical Criticism and the Fate of the Enlightenment Project," in his *Hebrew Bible* [n.4], pp. 106–126.

beginning of Israel's history, but as one who already knows the story, and who has entered into the middle of an activity of faith long in progress.[21]

One instructive textual focus for this whole issue of approach and assumption can be seen in the convention that the Hebrew term for deity, *)elohim*, when predicated of Y<small>HWH</small>,[22] should be rendered "God," not "god," a convention present in all standard modern English translations of the Bible. This convention of capitalization is not present in Hebrew manuscripts (which have no capital letters), and so is introduced into translation in the light of historic Jewish and Christian belief that the biblical deity is indeed the true God. To be sure, sometimes this point is made in the Hebrew text by the use of the definite article, *ha*, in conjunction with *)elohim*. Thus Moses, the speaking voice in Deuteronomy, makes the point that what Y<small>HWH</small> has done for Israel is to enable them "to know that Y<small>HWH</small> is God; there is no other" (4:35,39, *yada( ki yhwh hu) ha)elohim )en (od)*.[23] A paradigmatic narrative exemplification of this is the encounter between Elijah and the prophets of Baal on Mt Carmel, where at the climax of the story the people of Israel acknowledge, with repetition for emphasis, that "Y<small>HWH</small> indeed is God (*yhwh hu) ha)elohim*)" (1 Kgs 18:39). Correspondingly, Solomon, at the dedication of the temple, prays that this acknowledgement, that "Y<small>HWH</small> indeed is God; there is no other (*yhwh hu) ha) elohim )en (od*)" (1 Kgs. 8:60) will be made by "all the peoples of the earth"— that is, the definitive reality of Israel's deity will receive universal recognition. Jews and Christians in their faith and practice down the ages have in principle sought to realize that recognition of God of which the Old Testament speaks. This convention of rendering all uses of *)elohim*, even without the definite article, as "God" is, ironically, still accepted by many Christian scholars who are strongly critical of renewed theological interpretation on the grounds that it brings to the text assumptions that are not in the text itself and so is likely to skew and/or prejudge the interpretation of the text[24]—though unsurprisingly scholars without religious affiliation are increasingly abandoning the

---

[21] Brevard S. Childs, *Old Testament Theology in a Canonical Context* (London: SCM, 1985), pp. 28–29.

[22] Decisions about how best to render the tetragrammaton are closely related to this whole issue. My preference for following historic Jewish practice of non-pronunciation of the name, or using an alternative, most commonly capitalized L<small>ORD</small>, is in significant part for reverential reasons, though I think it is also helpful in relation to contemporary debates about the nature of God and the intrinsic limitations of human language in speaking appropriately of God.

[23] This formulation is a kind of Old Testament equivalent to the Pauline summary formulation in the New Testament, "to believe that Jesus Christ is Lord" (*pisteuein hoti kyrios Iesous Christos*).

[24] This is a major concern in John Barton, *The Nature of Biblical Criticism* (Louisville, KY: Westminster John Knox, 2007), especially pp. 137–186, to which I have responded in my "Biblical Criticism and Religious Belief," *Journal of Theological Interpretation* 2, no. 1 (2008), pp. 71–100.

convention. This reminds that one's reading of the Old Testament text may be more complexly intertwined with its historic and continuing reception than is commonly recognized.

In a contemporary cultural context, I think there is real value in setting theological interpretation of the Old Testament within this overall frame of reference of expectations generated by the social nature of knowledge in relation to the enduring thought and practice of synagogue and church. This should enable one to make most sense both of theological commentary in itself and of its relationships to alternative approaches.

## Differing Approaches to the Old Testament

The next major issue for establishing an appropriate frame of reference for theological commentary relates to the "distinctive challenge" mentioned near the outset of this chapter, the pre-Christian nature of Israel's scriptures, and so what is necessary to read pre-Christian texts Christianly.

The classic Christian approach is exemplified in the paradigmatic story of the road to Emmaus, where the risen Jesus expounds Israel's scriptures: "beginning with Moses and all the prophets he interpreted the things about himself in all the scriptures" (Lk. 24:27).[25] On this basis—that in some real sense it is Jesus of whom Israel's scriptures speak—the church developed reading strategies for Israel's scriptures as Old Testament in relation to the New Testament. The Fathers were well aware that much of the prima facie sense of the Old Testament did not obviously relate to Jesus, but they had no difficulty in moving into metaphorical and analogical modes of reading— historically depicted by the easily misunderstood term "allegory"—that could enable Christian reading to take place. One prime reading strategy was to frame the Old Testament within a pattern of *promise and fulfillment*—thereby to read the Old Testament as promising and looking forward to Christ, and remaining the necessary complement to the New Testament for understanding how Jesus fulfills God's promises and purposes. Another prime reading strategy was *typology/figuration*—whereby analogies to, and adumbrations of, God's self-revelation in Jesus were looked for, and found, within the Old Testament; if the one true God, the God of Israel, has definitively revealed Himself in Jesus, then, whatever recognition should rightly be made of the "many and varied" modes of divine self-revelation (Heb. 1:1), it should be appropriate to expect a fundamental consistency throughout the canonical portrayal of God and His

---

[25] I have discussed the hermeneutical significance of this story more fully in my *The Bible, Theology, and Faith* (Cambridge: Cambridge University Press, 2000), pp. 45–70.

dealings with His creation.[26] At their best, these classic approaches embody a deep canonical logic and so rightly still, in one form or other, are represented in Christian liturgies and feature in much preaching and Bible study. At their worst, however, the Old Testament could be too easily assimilated to concerns that are far removed from it.[27]

This approach was problematized in major ways in the context of the Enlightenment, for various and complex reasons.[28] The predominant scholarly approach increasingly became a distancing of the Old Testament from Christian theology (often unhelpfully characterized by the shorthand "dogma") so that its historical distinctiveness could be appreciated in its own right. This basic stance was variously understood and practiced. For some, it was a way of removing biblical authority from the public arena and reconceiving the Bible as, at most, a significant cultural monument. Yet for many scholars an ancient-historical approach became a way of enriching a reading of the familiar texts, as a fresh appreciation of ancient context (with a concomitant rediscovery of the wider ANE world), and of likely meaning in that context, enabled the material quite simply to be better understood.

However, the basic sense of the value of understanding Old Testament texts in their ancient, pre-Christian, contexts rapidly complexified. A growing

---

[26] The Christian approach to Israel's scriptures as Old Testament, an issue often thought to be without real analogy, in fact has a striking precedent already within the Old Testament, specifically in the Pentateuch. Here Israel, from the perspective of knowing God as YHWH, has appropriated the patriarchal traditions in which, as Exod. 6:2–3 clearly says and Exod. 3:13–15 strongly implies, God was not yet known at YHWH. This appropriation is now well-embedded within the textual tradition, so that God is depicted as YHWH within Genesis—a feature which had puzzled and challenged attentive readers of Exodus 3 and 6 from long before modern pentateuchal criticism. There remain, however, sufficient pointers within the text so that it is still possible to see something of the processes of appropriation, and these processes interestingly embody the interpretive strategies both of promise and fulfillment and of typology/figuration. See my *The Old Testament of the Old Testament* (Overtures to Biblical Theology; Minneapolis, MN: Fortress, 1992; repr. Eugene, OR: Wipf & Stock, 2001), esp. pp. 105–146, and Jon D. Levenson, "The Conversion of Abraham to Judaism, Christianity, and Islam" in *The Idea of Biblical Interpretation: Essays in Honor of James L. Kugel* (eds, Hindy Najman and Judith Newman; Leiden & Boston: Brill, 2004), pp. 3–39 (esp. pp. 3–18).

[27] One hugely influential misreading comes from Augustine, who found his prime textual warrant for a doctrine of double predestination in the divine oracle given to Rebekah (Gen. 25:23), which is the sole biblical passage where a differentiating divine decision about the future of two people is made prior to birth. Paul's acute reading of the logic of this, that it shows that divine choice is not dependent upon human action or deserving (Rom. 9:10–12), of course mediated Genesis to Augustine but hardly warrants the doctrine of double predestination that Augustine formulated, a doctrine that has arguably had seriously negative effects on Christian thought and life; see Ellen Charry, "Rebecca's Twins: Augustine on Election in Genesis" in *Genesis and Christian Theology* (eds, Nathan MacDonald et al; Grand Rapids, MI: Eerdmans, 2011).

[28] A fresh and insightful presentation of many of the issues at stake is Michael C. Legaspi, *The Death of Scripture and the Rise of Biblical Studies* (Oxford Studies in Historical Theology; New York: Oxford University Press, 2010).

recognition of the likely intrinsic complexity within many texts—that is, that much material had developed over time, had already been recontextualized, and had been incorporated into sequences that initially looked straightforward but were in fact composite—led to an increasing dismantling both of the literary sequence of the biblical books, and of the texts themselves, in favor of relating all content to its supposed original contexts (which were often depicted with generous amounts of imagination and hypothesis, given the paucity of evidence). The result was a multiplicity of distinct voices, arranged in a startling sequence (e.g. the reversal, in large measure, of the sequence of law and prophets), with a scholarly emphasis upon historical development and difference over time, all of which was increasingly hard to relate to traditional ways of understanding the canon. Certainly, regular and fruitful attempts were made to be theologically constructive within this frame of reference, from, say, George Adam Smith's vigorous portrayal of the prophets[29] to von Rad's portrayal of the Yahwist and various essays on the "kerygma" of the different strands of the Pentateuch.[30] Nonetheless, major questions remained about what constituted "theology" in this frame of reference and how, if at all, it differed from historical accounts of Israelite religious thought and practice.

More recently, this ancient-historical frame of reference has been transformed by at least three major factors, factors which for our purposes significantly, even if no doubt unintentionally, converge. First, literary approaches to the biblical texts have argued for the intrinsic meaningfulness of texts in themselves, even if historically composite in formation (though at least sometimes literary readings, by virtue of greater sensitivity to the dynamics within texts, have undermined arguments for viewing texts as composite). Literary categories such as the narrator and the implied reader mean that one no longer has to be constrained by the historical categories of author and original audience, and fresh vistas for reading are thereby opened up.

Secondly, a renewed interest in the phenomenon of canon, as promoted primarily by Brevard Childs,[31] has, among other things, led to a different angle of vision on the Old Testament. In this light the canon is not a *problem* (as it has been for the ancient historian to whom it has obscured the nature and course of Israel's history and religious development and so has needed to be abandoned in favor of reordering and reinterpreting its content) but a *resource*. That is to say, even if the processes of canonical compilation and formation

---

[29] *The Book of Isaiah*, 2 vols (Expositor's Bible; London: Hodder & Stoughton, 1897), *The Book of the Twelve Prophets*, 2 vols (Expositor's Bible; London: Hodder & Stoughton, 1898).

[30] Gerhard von Rad, *Genesis* (Old Testament Library; trans. John Marks; 3rd edn; London: SCM, 1972); see especially the Introduction. The "kerygma" essays are conveniently collected and contextualized in Walter Brueggemann and Hans Walter Wolff, *The Vitality of Old Testament Traditions* (Atlanta, GA: John Knox, 1975).

[31] The best account of Childs's concerns is Daniel Driver, *Brevard Childs: Biblical Theologian* (Forschungen zum Alten Testament II/46; Tübingen: Mohr Siebeck, 2010).

have obscured the underlying history, they may have done so for instructional purposes, seeking to render Israel's traditions in such a way as to make their hard-won insights into God's nature and purposes most accessible to future generations. Even if it was not a priority in much of Israelite and Judahite religion in antiquity "to know that YHWH is God; there is no other," that should nonetheless be the priority in future for all those who seek to enter into that knowledge of God that has been recognized as definitive for Israel—and the point of the canon and the way it has shaped the received material is to enable that to happen.

Such a "canonical approach" does not deny the likely complexities underlying the formation of the canonical texts or that the processes leading to the familiar portrayal of Israel's history and religion would most likely have been sharply contested.[32] Nonetheless, its focus is not on "the world behind the text," that is the concern of the ancient historian, but rather on "the world within the text," that is the priorities and norms now portrayed and promoted, and on "the world in front of the text," that is the continuing life of communities of faith, both Jewish and Christian, which have sought to realize, in their various ways, those existential realities of which the Old Testament speaks. Thus, for reasons distinct from the literary approach, there is attention to the Old Testament text in its "received" form; and, among other things, this not only makes it easier to rejoin conversation with premodern readers, who also read the text in its received form, but it also gives reason to attend to the theological construals made by such readers as they sought in their own contexts to understand that of which the texts speak.[33]

Thirdly, extensive work in hermeneutics has brought a richer and more complex articulation of what is necessary to read the Old Testament well. One significant factor, among many, has been an emphasis upon the necessary contribution of the reader to the reading of the text. Decisions have to be made about how to construe material that may be ambiguous, or containing gaps and silences, and also, fundamentally, how to understand its subject matter. Readers must use knowledge, imagination, and judgment, and however much these may rightly be informed by knowledge of the ancient world, they will also rightly be informed by understanding of the contemporary world. As Nicholas Lash puts it:

If the questions to which ancient authors sought to respond in terms available to them within their cultural horizons are to be "heard" today with

---

[32] A good short account is Christopher Seitz, "Canonical Approach" in *Dictionary for Theological Interpretation of the Bible* (eds, Kevin Vanhoozer et al; Grand Rapids, MI: Baker Academic, 2005), pp. 100–102.

[33] An excellent entrée to the interpretive value of reception history is John Thompson, *Reading the Bible with the Dead* (Grand Rapids, MI: Eerdmans, 2007). Among other things, Thompson shows how frequently the concerns of modern feminists were anticipated by thoughtful premodern readers.

something like their original force and urgency, they have first to be "heard" as questions that challenge us with comparable seriousness. And if they are to be thus heard, they must first be articulated in terms available to us within *our* cultural horizons. There is thus a sense in which the articulation of what the text might "mean" today, is a necessary condition of hearing what that text "originally meant."[34]

Of course, this has always been so, and good historians, not least, have generally acknowledged it. Nonetheless, with regard to many a debate about Old Testament interpretation, it seems increasingly odd that (so the argument has often gone) a scholar's contemporary understanding of politics and psychology can be straightforwardly brought to bear upon interpreting a text, while a scholar's religious and theological understandings have to be bracketed out. Should it not rather be said that *all* facets of contemporary understanding may in principle be helpful for understanding biblical texts, as long as they are employed in a heuristic and disciplined way? As such, however much theological understandings have developed and changed over time, it should hardly be controversial to argue that living within a Christian frame of reference, which seeks to realize those existential realities of which the Bible speaks, and whose patterns of thought and practices of life have developed in continuity with the biblical accounts, ought in principle to be illuminating for understanding much (even if by no means all) of which the biblical, including the Old Testament, writers speak; for it is the intrinsic nature of the subject matter, rather than its historical development, that is the focus of interest. Thus a contemporary ecclesial frame of reference may have its own potential contribution in various ways. It can become appropriate to work again with the ancient notion of a "rule of faith" to frame one's reading.[35] Additionally, as has been well said, "the interpretation of Scripture is a difficult task *not* because of the technical demands of biblical scholarship but because of the importance of character for wise readings."[36]

[34] "What Might Martyrdom Mean?" in his *Theology on the Way to Emmaus* (London: SCM, 1986), pp. 75–92 (p. 81). A suggestive discussion, which models the kind of major rethinking that may be needed to realize Lash's point in contemporary Western culture where "God" tends to be thinned down and marginalized, is Rob Barrett, *Disloyalty and Destruction: Religion and Politics in Deuteronomy and the Modern World* (Library of Hebrew Bible and Old Testament Studies 511; London: T&T Clark, 2009).
[35] See Kathryn Greene-McCreight, "Rule of Faith" in *Dictionary* [n.32], pp. 703–704; also my *Bible* [n.25], pp. 38–44 (reprinted in *Old Testament Theology: Flowering and Future* (ed. Ben Ollenburger; Winona Lake: Eisenbrauns, 2004), pp. 464–469).
[36] Stephen Fowl and L. Gregory Jones, *Reading in Communion* (London: SPCK, 1991), p. 49. A fascinating exploration of qualities appropriate to its readers that is related to the Old Testament's own priorities is Richard Briggs, *The Virtuous Reader: Old Testament Narrative and Interpretive Virtue* (Studies in Theological Interpretation; Grand Rapids, MI: Baker Academic, 2010).

## Conclusions

All this brings us back to our starting point, that the present project of theological commentary is premised upon the in-principle fruitfulness of bringing insights from Christian theology and practice to bear upon the reading of the Old and New Testaments. However, certain clarifications can now be made.

First, there are many different things that may legitimately be done with the biblical text. In a premodern context proposals for "theological commentary" would have sounded odd—when Scripture and continuing faith were thoroughly integrated, what other kind of commentary was there? Now, however, the recognition that one can approach the Old Testament in ways that do not presuppose its integration with its Christian reception makes for productive diversity of approach and goal. Practitioners of theological commentary are explicitly concerned with reading the biblical text in ways that should more or less directly contribute to nourishing the life of the church—not practising homiletics, but so working at the subject matter of the text that preachers (among others) should have access to a penetrating understanding of that of which the text speaks. They should not be denigrating other ways of approaching the text, insofar as they relate to legitimate goals. Most obviously, one staple of biblical scholarship is the provision of high quality information about textual criticism and philology, as part of establishing what constitutes the text and what it says—the kind of material that one expects (among other things) to find in commentary series such as the *International Critical Commentary* or *Hermeneia*. Theological commentary presupposes that such work is being carried on, and is available to draw on, and is likely itself to contribute to such work only in an occasional ad hoc way, if at all.

Secondly, although it is a basic principle of interpretation that one should "interpret in context," it is clear that there are many different possible contexts. Already within their Old Testament frame of reference many texts have been recontextualized.[37] And when Israel's scriptures are themselves recontextualized in relation to the New Testament and historic Christian traditions (Protestant, Catholic, Orthodox, themselves all variegated) and in relation to the contemporary world, then theological interpreters will always have a

[37] The Psalms are a prime example. It seems clear from the headings (Asaph, Korahites, etc) that originally separate collections have been brought together, with original setting lost. Preexilic psalms about king and ark are preserved and considered meaningful in the post-exilic collection that is the psalter even though there was no longer a king or an ark—as also in all use of the psalter down the ages! If some of the psalm headings, especially those specifying incidents in the life of David, relate not to context of origin but to context for interpretation (as persuasively argued by Brevard Childs, "Psalm Titles and Midrashic Exegesis," *Journal of Semitic Studies* 16 (1971), pp. 137–150), then psalms originally anonymous and generalized have received a specific imaginative focus, which in turn opens the way to their recontextualization within a messianic frame of reference.

plurality of possible contexts. The notion of a "rule of faith" to guide theological commentators, far from prejudging and skewing interpretation (so as to make it conform to some traditional reading or dogmatic norm), in fact should give theological commentators freedom to decide on their approach both in terms of how best to do justice to their subject matter and in terms of their overall purpose and goal,[38] in accordance with their general Christian understanding of "how things go" (an understanding which, of course, varies between Christians, and should always entail listening and learning). Sometimes commentators may stay with the Old Testament material in its pre-Christian frame of reference, but they may also develop its resonances in other contexts as appropriate.[39]

In short, theological commentary should open up ways of reintegrating the Old Testament with contemporary faith and life. As such it is both unpredictable and a task constantly to be renewed.

---

[38] On this general issue, there are wise words in Ellen Davis, *Wondrous Depth: Preaching the Old Testament* (Louisville: Westminster John Knox, 2005), p. 72.

[39] For example, the opening narrative about Job (1:1–2:10) poses the issue of whether relationship with God ("fear of God") can be disinterested—an issue with wide resonance on its own terms, and interesting to relate to the rest of the book of Job. However, it could also be related to Jesus' understanding of his being Son of God (as in my *Bible* [n.25], chapter.6), to Carmelite spirituality with its suspicion of self-seeking even in religious experience, and to modern hermeneutics of suspicion as in Marx, Freud, and Nietzsche.

Chapter 12

# Theological Interpretation of Scripture: Yes, But . . .

## D. A. Carson

Theological Interpretation of Scripture (TIS) is partly disparate movement, partly a call to reformation in biblical interpretation, partly a disorganized array of methodological commitments in hermeneutics, partly a serious enterprise and partly (I suspect) a fad. Different writers speak of TIS in fairly diverse ways. One might even argue that some people who offer the best theological interpretation of Scripture (note the lowercase letters) have very little connection with the movement known as TIS: one need search no farther than the honoree of this volume, whose astonishing range of expertise includes competent exegesis of the documents of both Testaments, an impressive grasp of the history of interpretation, a deep understanding of many nuances in the patristic period, in the Reformation age, and in contemporary (especially European) theology, and whose interpretation of Scripture is never flaccid or narrowly historical, but invariably profoundly theological. If all who align themselves with TIS were committed to pursuing the kind of theological interpretation of Scripture exemplified in the writings of Henri Blocher (most of whose work, sadly, has never been translated into English), the chapter I am now writing would be very different.

Another writer who does not connect his work with TIS but who is traveling down a parallel path is Peter Leithart,[1] who prefers to speak of entering into the depths of the text. Always evocative and sometimes provocative, Leithart provides another parallel to the TIS tradition: his actual handling of biblical texts, while invariably stimulating, is less frequently convincing.[2]

As I worked to canvas the literature, I had expected to write something that said "Yes" to an array of important points, and then to introduce my list of objections or questions with "But"—and indeed, not a few have written essays

---

[1] See especially his *Deep Exegesis: The Mystery of Reading Scripture* (Waco, TX: Baylor University, 2009).

[2] See, for example, his work *The Epistles of John Through New Eyes: From Behind the Veil* (Monroe, LA: Athanasius, 2009). I have interacted with this work in my forthcoming commentary in the NIGTC series.

organized more or less in that fashion.[3] But as I worked on the material, I became dissatisfied with this way of organizing my reflections because the "Yes" and "But" components are closely intertwined. In other words, it is not that there are good points and more questionable points in TIS, nicely distinguishable, but rather that along every axis the good and the questionable are almost inextricably entangled. So in what follows, instead of two lists I have argued for a *sic et non* for each entry. The result, I fear, is rather messy—but so is TIS.

According to its proponents, TIS is both young and old. Apart from its use by Stephen Fowl in 1997,[4] the expression "theological interpretation of Scripture" is singularly elusive in the literature that predates 2005. Yet as the subtitle of Treier's introduction to the subject makes clear, proponents think of the movement less as an innovation than as a recovery of Christian practice.[5] This claim reflects one of the trends that has led to TIS: dissatisfaction with a great deal of contemporary exegesis, not least historical-critical methods that are enslaved by philosophical naturalism, and extravagantly speculative interpretations driven by contemporary agendas (e.g., homosexual readings of Scripture). Many desire to see more exegetical and theological continuity with the pre-Enlightenment church. Other motivations behind the rise of TIS— certainly not an exhaustive list—include suspicion of grammatical-historical methods (judged to be mechanistic and reductionistic), the sensibilities of the Yale School (especially Lindbeck), and a desire to work out how a faith-driven emphasis on the freedom of God will relativize all hermeneutical methods as believers apprehend the living Truth (think Barth).

In what follows, I shall provide six propositions and in each case offer my "Yes, but . . . "

**Proposition One:** TIS is an attempt to transcend the barren exegeses generated by historical-critical methods, and especially those readings of Scripture that are "historical" in the sense that they are frankly anti-supernatural interpretations determined by post-Enlightenment assumptions about the nature of history.

**Yes:** This is one of the important arguments in the influential book by Richard Topping.[6] Should the secular hermeneutical categories of habitual

---

[3]  For example, Charlie Trimm, "Evangelicals, Theology, and Biblical Interpretation: Reflections on the Theological Interpretation of Scripture," *Bulletin for Biblical Research* 20 (2010), 311–330; Gregg R. Allison, "Theological Interpretation of Scripture: An Introduction and Preliminary Evaluation," *Southern Baptist Journal of Theology* 14/2 (2010), 28–36.

[4]  Stephen E. Fowl (ed.), *The Theological Interpretation of Scripture: Classic and Contemporary Readings* (Blackwell Readings in Modern Theology: Cambridge: Blackwell, 1997).

[5]  Daniel J. Treier, *Introducing Theological Interpretation of Scripture: Recovering a Christian Practice* (Grand Rapids, MI: Baker, 2008). Cf. also Kevin J. Vanhoozer (gen.ed.), *Dictionary for Theological Interpretation of the Bible* (Grand Rapids, MI: Baker, 2005).

[6]  Richard R. Topping, *Revelation, Scripture and Church: Theological Hermeneutic Thought of James Barr, Paul Ricoeur, and Hans Frei* (Aldershot: Ashgate, 2007). Cf. also Mark Alan

naturalism constrain our reading of the Bible, or should we read the Bible as Christians? Certainly it is easy to think of excellent targets for the criticism that TIS levels. One need only think of, say, the anti-supernaturalism of Rudolf Bultmann in the last century, or of Heikki Räisänen at the end of that century and in ours. But those are easy targets. More subtle are the many writers who are not anti-supernaturalists but whose exegetical work feels as if it is grounded in anti-supernaturalism. To cite Schlossberg:

> If we wish to consider the Babylonian captivity of the kingdom of Judah in 587 B.C., we shall find sufficient documentation and archaeological evidence to speak of the political, economic, social, and military causes of the debacle. But the Hebrew prophets said that it took place because God's judgment had fallen on the Judeans for their idolatry and wickedness. From that perspective, the "causes" that the historian's explanation advances are not causes at all, but effects, and are thought to be causes only because of the meta-historical commitments that the historian brings to the evidence.[7]

Still more subtle are the ways in which many biblical interpreters are pretty careful with individual texts, even listening attentively to their attestations of supernaturalism, yet exhibit no interest in (and not a little suspicion of) putting the biblical texts together under the conviction that one Mind finally stands behind all of Scripture. TIS stands for the unity of the Bible, a unity often lost in the world of biblical scholarship that has moved downward and inward from biblical theology to the theology of the two respective Testaments to the theology of the individual corpora of each Testament to the theology of the putative sources (real and imagined) of each corpus. Atomistic readings reign.

Insofar, then, as TIS challenges these common habits of mind in the guild of biblical scholars, it stands within the circle of many Christians who have leveled similar criticisms toward some trends across the last quarter-millennium.

**But. . . .** This emphasis in TIS is often cast in terms of the conflict between history and theology, with history made out to be the villain. One understands why this is so, not least when reading, say, Räisänen's insistence that the project of New Testament theology should be replaced by (1) "a history of early Christian thought" from a strictly neutral vantage point,[8] and (2) an examination of the history of the influence of the New Testament from a philosophical

Bowald, *Rendering the Word in Theological Hermeneutics* (Aldershot: Ashgate, 2007); Richard B. Hays, "Reading the Bible with Eyes of Faith: The Practice of Theological Exegesis," *Journal of Theological Interpretation* 1 (2007), 5–21.

[7] Herbert Schlossberg, *Idols for Destruction: Christian Faith and Its Confrontation with American Society* (Nashville: Thomas Nelson, 1983), 22; cited also in Hans Madueme, "Review Article: Theological Interpretation After Barth," *Journal of Theological Interpretation* 3 (2009), 143.

[8] Heikki Räisänen, *Beyond New Testament Theology* (2nd edn; London: SCM, 2009), 209, self-consciously returning to the agenda of W. Wrede in 1897.

perspective shaped by our awareness of religious pluralism. Yet surely it is not history that is the problem, but a kind of naturalistic history.

In fact, there are two overlapping dangers to avoid. *First,* many biblical scholars use the word "history" to refer to what has happened in the past, or to reports of what has happened in the past, on the assumption that the only way in which we may legitimately claim any knowledge of such past events is that they belong exclusively to the natural world. This does not mean, for example, that they deny that Jesus rose from the dead in some literal sense (i.e., that Jesus' pre-death body, complete with stigmata, has some real connection with the body that rose from the tomb, which was thereafter empty), but only that Jesus' resurrection cannot claim to be an *historical* event: it is an "event" accessible only to "faith."[9] This is rather different from thinking that "history" refers to what has actually happened in the past, or to reports of what has actually happened in the past, regardless of whether the putative past events belong exclusively to the natural realm or not. In this sense, Jesus' resurrection *is* an historical event, and is accessible to historians in much the same way that all past events are accessible to historians—through witnesses of various sorts. The issues are so *theologically* important that I would have thought that theological interpretation would be careful not to cast itself over against historical interpretation, but to reflect more profoundly on how in Scripture many revelatory claims about God are grounded in history (in the second sense).

*Second,* one can make a case that the distinctiveness of New Testament treatment of the Old turns in part on a certain *historical* reading of the earlier biblical documents—and that this *historical* reading is determinative for a great deal of *theological* interpretation. Numerous scholars, of course, have rightly pointed out that New Testament writers commonly deploy many of the same exegetical techniques and hermeneutical assumptions that one finds among the rabbinic *middoth.* Nevertheless, the more we underline the similarities between early Christian readings of the Old Testament and early non-Christian Jewish readings of (what Christians call) the Old Testament, the more hardpressed we are to explain why their readings of the same text issue in such different theologies. To make the matter more concrete, what are the hermeneutical differences between the way Paul read the Hebrew Scriptures before his Damascus Road experience and the way he read the Hebrew Scriptures after his Damascus Road experience? It is correct to say that the Christian Paul read those Scriptures through the lens of the resurrected Christ—but that tells us what triggers the hermeneutical shift, not what the shift itself is.

---

[9]   We are tripping closely to distinctions that some theologians have made between *Geschichte* and *Historie,* distinctions that have bedeviled discussion of the nature of "salvation history": see especially Robert W. Yarbrough, *The Salvation Historical Fallacy? Reassessing the History of New Testament Theology* (History of Biblical Interpretation 2; Leidendorp: Deo, 2004).

Arguably, two or three hermeneutical shifts can be identified, but I shall mention only one. Unlike unconverted Jews who tended to read the Hebrew Scriptures in such a way that *Torah* was elevated to a point of hermeneutical control, Christians tended to read those same Scriptures by underscoring *historical* sequence. Thus Paul in Galatians 3 emphasizes the promise given to Abraham *before* the giving of the law, a promise received by faith—and he insists that the law, when it was *later* given, could not annul the promise, nor could it overturn the fact that Abraham was justified before God *before* the law was given. He concludes that the law must therefore have *other* functions. In Heb. 4:1-13, *Auctor* observes that in Psalm 95 God is still offering "rest" to his covenant people, even after some of them, at least, have entered into the "rest" of the promised land, so he concludes that entrance into the promised land could not have been the ultimate rest God envisaged, since he *later* beckons them still to enter God's rest. Reflection on the fact that it is *God's* rest that is the ultimate appeal ("*my* rest," God says in Psalm 95), *Auctor* builds a trajectory from God's rest at the end of creation week (Genesis 2) through sabbath, entry into the promised land, and the promise of Psalm 95, to show that in his own day the promise of some greater rest than that of entering Canaan still stands. In Hebrews 7, *Auctor* argues that the announcement of a Melchizedekian priest-king in Psalm 110, *after* the establishment of the Levitical priest and the *Torah*'s insistence that priest and king belong to separate tribes and must never be the same person, shows that God himself did not envisage *Torah*'s arrangements for priest and king to be permanent. And if you change the regulations regarding the priest, you transform the entire law-covenant, for the law-covenant is hugely bound up with the priestly arrangements (including tabernacle, sacrifices, the significance of *yom kippur*, and so forth). In other words, reading Psalm 110 in its sequence *after* the giving of the law establishes that the entire law-covenant is in principle obsolete once Psalm 110 is written. A similar conclusion is drawn from historical reasoning in Hebrews 8: the promise of a *new* covenant in the time of Jeremiah, long *after* the giving of the law, renders the law obsolescent in principle: it is bound to pass away (8:13).

The point is that these (and numerous other) New Testament readings of the Old Testament Scriptures turn on *historical* distinctions (not least sequence in time to establish continuity and discontinuity) in order to establish *theological* instruction (what God's purposes were in the giving of the law, the status in God's mind of that law-covenant in *Auctor*'s day, the way in which it points forward to something different and greater, ultimately fulfilled in Jesus).[10] Theological interpretation is here tightly intertwined with subtle

---

[10] In fact, this kind of reading of the Old Testament by several New Testament writers stands behind a dramatic tension in the New Testament texts: the same gospel that is often said to be prophesied in the Old and fulfilled in the New is often said to be hidden in the Old and revealed in the New (i.e., before Jesus came, this gospel, or some aspect of it, was a musthvrion). The gospel was, as it were, hidden in plain sight, and seeing the Old

historical reading of biblical texts. I am grateful that the ablest TIS supporters recognize many of the typological ways in which Old Testament texts
point forward to Jesus.[11] It is good to read the words of Vanhoozer: "The Old
Testament testifies to the same drama of redemption as the New Testament,
hence the church rightly reads both Testaments together, two parts of a single authoritative script."[12] Of course, this is not an exclusive distinctive of a
movement called TIS. Countless confessional evangelicals have argued along
these lines for a long time. It is appropriate to speak of "the same drama of
redemption" across the entire Bible. Yet this drama embraces points of continuity and discontinuity, of announced obsolescence of some parts as they
point to "new" parts—and some of these distinctions are discoverable by the
kind of exegesis that listens while the text makes *historical* distinctions. It
would be reassuring to hear proponents of TIS who warn against historical
criticism express appreciation of the rightful role it may play.

For at least some proponents of TIS, to foster a clash between theology and
history is in danger of approaching the issues with a meat cleaver when a scal-
pel is needed. To push for the unity of Scripture is a grand thing, but it is one
thing to argue that all of Scripture is finally in support of a unified theology
and another thing to argue that that unified theology is precisely what unifies
the Bible. The ways in which the unity of Scripture should be defended are
subtle and multifaceted, and embrace distinctions historical, genre-related,
author-related, and other distinctions that cannot rightly be skated over in the
rush toward theological unity. TIS shows at least some sensitivity to genre; so
far it has shown less sensitivity to history. (I shall return to further reflections
on the role of history in the third proposition, below.)

**Proposition Two:** More broadly, TIS aims to bring biblical studies and
theology closer together.

---

Testament text through Jesus Messiah and his cross and resurrection enables believers
to see patterns in the Old Testament documents—often patterns established by historical sequence—that they had not seen before becoming Christians. The trajectories they
thus trace out drive them to conclude that Jesus the Messiah is simultaneously Davidic
king and legitimate priest, triumphant conqueror and suffering servant, and so forth,
and that these *theological* conclusions *are truly grounded in the older Scriptures even if they were
not fully seen until the coming of Jesus.* In other words, massive theological conclusions are
grounded in a complex reading of the Old Testament Scriptures that is steeped in historical nuance. I have tried to unpack some of these connections in "Mystery and Fulfillment:
Toward a More Comprehensive Paradigm of Paul's Understanding of the Old and the
New," in *Justification and Variegated Nomism*, vol. 2, *The Paradoxes of Paul* (WUNT 181; eds,
D. A. Carson, Peter T. O'Brien, and Mark A. Seifrid; Tübingen: Mohr Siebeck, 2004),
393–436.

[11] For example, Peter Leithart, *1 & 2 Kings* (Brazos Theological Commentary on the Bible;
Grand Rapids, MI: Brazos, 2006).

[12] Kevin J. Vanhoozer, "Ten Theses on the Theological Interpretation of Scripture," *Modern
Reformation* 19/4 (July/Aug 2010), 17.

**Yes:** Certainly there is a fair bit of antipathy between biblical scholars and theologians,[13] not least because their respective disciplines seem to pull in quite different directions. Writing from a Catholic perspective, Reno observes:

> For the accordance of doctrine and Scripture is by no means obvious. At times, what Scripture says is opaque, but doctrine is clear. At other times, what the Church teaches is either puzzling or undeveloped, but the plain sense of Scripture seems perspicuous and compelling. At still other times, the Bible seems to blatantly contradict dogmatic claims, or strike at oblique angles, or even hover with perplexing irrelevance. Just think of the Catholic doctrines of the Immaculate Conception and the bodily Assumption of Mary.[14]

The challenge is not exclusively Catholic, of course. In the wake of the Reformation, Protestants have customarily thought of sanctification as that process by which Christians become increasingly conformed to Jesus Christ, that process by which they grow into more holiness, even if that process will not be complete until the consummation. That is the controlling usage of "sanctification" in Protestant theology. Close study of Pauline (indeed, New Testament usage) shows that a high proportion of the occurrences of the noun refer instead to what is sometimes called positional sanctification or definitional sanctification.[15] People may be set aside for God, holy or sanctified in that sense (in a not-dissimilar way that the shovel that takes the ash away from the altar in the Old Testament is said to be sanctified) without demonstrating characteristics of personal holy behavior.[16]

Other examples concern both Protestants and Catholics. Shall we continue to defend the eternal generation of the Son? In the past, however, that doctrine was commonly tied to the word μονογενής~. A large majority of philologians today holds that the word does not mean "only begotten" but "unique" or even "unique and beloved" (note the usage in Heb. 11:17). So on what does the eternal generation of the Son rest? Or again: from the third century on, Mary was called θεοτόκος, "God-bearer," often loosely rendered "Mother of

---

[13] In this chapter I shall use "theologians" as a shorthand for "systematic theologians" or "dogmatic theologians," and "theology" as a shorthand for "systematic theology" or "dogmatic theology." That reflects dominant usage in North America. Readers in, say, the United Kingdom, use "theology" and "theologians" as the large categories that *include* subsidiary disciplines such as biblical exegesis, historical theology, and so forth.

[14] R. R. Reno, "A Richer Bible," *First Things,* 205 (Aug/Sept 2010), 41.

[15] See David Peterson, *Possessed by God: A New Testament Theology of Sanctification and Holiness* (NSBT 1; Leicester: IVP, 1995).

[16] I have teased out this example a little more in "'A Holy Nation': The Church's High Calling," in *Holy, Holy, Holy: Proclaiming the Perfections of God* (Orlando, FL: Reformation Trust, 2010), 73–89.

God." Neither expression is found in the Bible. Should it be defended, or not? If so, why? If not, why not?

It is easy to multiply examples. So how can one not be concerned to bring biblical exegesis and theology closer together?

The broader problem is that a great deal of popular preaching and teaching uses the Bible as a pegboard on which to hang a fair bit of Christianized pop psychology or moralizing encouragement, with very little effort to teach the faithful, from the Bible, the massive doctrines of historic confessional Christianity. Surely we ought to expend effort to bring the Bible and theology closer together.

**But. . . .** The illustrations I used are not all of a piece. When they are analyzed, they disclose that the ways in which Scripture and theology are likely to be brought together will differ strongly in different theological traditions. For Reno, the authority of the Catholic magisterium is not inferior to the authority of Scripture. It will not occur to a devout and faithful Catholic that the Church might be wrong in its teaching regarding the immaculate conception and the assumption of Mary or that they should be corrected by Scripture. What "bringing the Bible and theology together" means in such instances will be quite different for the Catholic and the Protestant. The promulgation of the doctrine of the bodily assumption of Mary took place in 1950. Even on the most generous tracing of the history of doctrine, it is difficult to affirm that this doctrine was universally believed in Catholic heritage across the centuries. It is extraordinarily difficult to tie it to serious interpretation of Scripture. From a non-Catholic perspective, if this is what is meant by the theological interpretation of Scripture, biblical scholars have the right to be skeptical of TIS. Surely a distinction must be made between a richer reading of Scripture that deploys more than historical-critical methods to find doctrine in Scripture that fair-minded readers can see is truly there once the blinkers of a reductionistic method are removed, and another thing to impose one's doctrine on Scripture in the name of bringing Scripture and theology together.

One must ask if the example of sanctification is of the same order, apart from the absence of a Protestant magisterium. Does the Protestant doctrine of sanctification function so authoritatively in various confessional Protestant communities that within those communities it is being imposed on Scripture? The answer must be carefully nuanced. There are passages in the New Testament in which the doctrine of sanctification is clearly taught even though the word sanctification does not appear. One thinks, for example, of Philippians 3, in which Paul does not think of himself as having arrived at his goal, but is self-consciously pressing on to maturity, to a greater knowledge of Christ and fellowship in his suffering and power. In other words, here is sanctification without (the word) "sanctification." It appears that the doctrine of sanctification is amply attested in the New Testament even when the word is not found, while the passages in the New Testament that use the word frequently use it in a way rather different from its usage in Protestant theology. On this topic, the domain of discourse of the Bible (in particular, of the part of the Bible written by Paul) is different from the domain of discourse in much confessional Protestant theology. If one reads such theology into all the passages where Paul uses the word "sanctification," inevitably one will be imposing one's theology (no matter how confessionally defensible) onto the biblical text. On the other hand, if one demonstrates how the confessional standards on this subject can be shown to reflect biblical (including Pauline) teaching even where the word "sanctification" is not used, and if one carefully notes how vocabulary usage in different domains of discourse can be quite disparate, it might be quite possible (and surely highly desirable) to bring the Bible and theology closer together. Note, however, that this desideratum is not being achieved by a methodological device called TIS that enables us to read the Bible more theologically. It is being achieved by patient and careful reading of both biblical and later theological texts, observing their distinctive vocabularies and emphases. And of course the subject becomes more complex yet when we integrate the different ways the Bible deploys the holiness word-group in both Testaments.

As for the third example introduced above, if the eternal generation of the Son is detached (as it should be) from μονογενής, it may nevertheless remain attached to Scripture in a passage such as Jn 5:26. This admittedly difficult verse occurs in an extended section dealing with the relationships between the Father and the Son (5:16-30). On the one hand, the Son can do nothing by himself; on the other hand, whatever the Father does, the Son also does (5:19). Within this discussion, the text affirms that God has "life in himself" (5:36). The expression is slightly odd. It appears to mean more than that he has life: rather, he has life that does not depend on another, he has self-originating life. He is self-existent. If that is the meaning, how is the rest of the verse to be understood? "For as the Father has life in himself, so he has granted the Son also to have life in himself" (5:36). If the text had said, "For as the Father has life in himself, so he has granted the Son to have life," the logic would be plain, but the Son would certainly not be identifiable with God in any sense. Conversely, if the text had said, "For as the Father has life in himself, so also the Son has life in himself," the self-existence of the Son would be preserved, but it would be difficult to avoid theism. Instead, we are told that "as the Father has life in himself, so he has *granted* the Son also to have life in himself." How does one *grant* "life-in-himself," self-originating life as God has self-originating life? If it is granted, how is it self-originating? Of the many solutions commonly offered, that one is best which argues that this is an *eternal* grant. That reading certainly seems to fit best with the rest of the passage. If it is correct, the notion of the eternal generation of the Son might be connected with the Scriptures through this passage.

The final example, concerning θεοτόκος or "Mother of God," is a little different again. In most of the early usages, up to and including the sixth century, the expression said relatively little about Mary and a great deal about Jesus. Was the baby whom Mary bore *already* truly God? If so, she was the God-bearer. The issues were primarily Christological. When that topic was no longer disputed, the title, in line with increasing focus on Marian theology, came to say much more about Mary than about Jesus. From the perspective of a Christian who holds that Scripture sets bounds to what may truly be said to be Christian doctrine, there are some understandings of θεοτόκος that I am happy to affirm as in line with Scripture (even if the word is not applied to Mary), and other understandings I must disavow. Once again, how one brings Scripture and theology together turns on an array of other commitments that must not be sidelined because of some sort of hegemonic view of TIS.

**Proposition Three:** TIS accords greater credibility to pre-critical exegesis—patristic, medieval, reformational—than to contemporary exegesis, and especially to patristic readings.

**Yes:** We have returned to the element of TIS that claims it is not new but is returning to older ways of reading the Bible that yielded far great theological richness than do contemporary historical-critical and grammatical-critical exegeses. One worries about interpreters who are always striving to find something *new* in Scripture but who rarely take the time to show how their readings are nestled within the massive confessional heritage of historic Christianity. The influential essay by D. S. Yeago has powerfully argued that the church's confessional traditions will provide hermeneutical aid, not hindrance, to responsible theological tradition.[17] How could we possibly imagine that we have nothing to learn from generations of believers before us who devoted their lives to studying and meditating on the Scriptures we are reading?

At heart is a self-conscious return to the *analogia fidei*, the "analogy of the faith" or the "rule of faith" (early summary of fundamental Christian beliefs), as well as to an array of creeds and confessions. Not a few TIS writers assert that the *analogia fidei* is one of its central interpretive principles. Thus Treier, introducing TIS and referring to his own description of the new Brazos Theological Commentary on the Bible series, writes:

The series "presupposes that the doctrinal tradition of the church can serve as a living and reliable basis for exegesis." This tradition, more specifically, is that doctrine surrounding the Nicene Creed. The series promotes "intra-textual analysis" as its "key method," along with drawing upon "the liturgical practices and spiritual disciplines of the church as a secondary dimension

[17] "The New Testament and the Nicene Dogma: A Contribution to the Recovery of Theological Exegesis," in *The Theological Interpretation of Scripture: Classic and Contemporary Readings* (ed. Stephen S. Fowl; Blackwell Readings in Modern Theology; Oxford: Blackwell, 1997).

of the canonical context for exegesis of scriptural texts." Such an approach can lead to various senses of Scripture, including "allegorical" readings, and requires that contributors engage the history of exegesis, not in order to provide readers with a summary of past interpretation, but in order to shape exegetical judgments in conversation with the tradition.[18]

Within measure, even Treier's self-conscious stepping beyond mere *Rezeptiongeschichte* ("not in order to provide readers with a summary of past interpretation") is a helpful reminder not only of our *doctrinal* indebtedness to the past but of our *methodological* indebtedness to the past.

**But. . . .** Numerous qualifications cry out for a hearing. It may be organizationally helpful to serialize them.

(1) Depending on which sector of the defenders of TIS is speaking, it is not entirely clear why so much emphasis is placed on the patristic period. For many Catholics, the appeal to the magisterial authority expressed through the first seven (ecumenical) councils may be part of the reason; for many others, a similar appeal is made to the Great Tradition. Both parties sometimes write as if either (a) these ecumenical councils share the authority of Scripture, or (b) at very least they are not to be questioned because they were both ecumenical and much closer to Christ and his apostles than we are; and so, further, (c) they constitute all that is necessary to establish a confessional bond of true Christians today—a stance which, of course, marginalizes the Reformation standards.

No informed confessional evangelical will agree to (a): there is an ontological gap between the books of the Bible and all other documents. That the early councils were ecumenical—so (b)—is something for which to be grateful, and warrants that Christians everywhere should pay the more careful attention to them, but even council documents and creeds must be tested by Scripture, not the reverse (even while we quickly insist that this must not be taken as a glib formula, since what the Scriptures are truly saying may be adequately summed up in creeds and confessions on this point or that, and we who interpret Scripture enjoy no *tabula rasa* approach to biblical interpretation but necessarily interpret out of a framework which *itself* must constantly be tested). Moreover, the church has sometimes charged ahead toward false teaching that was corrected by heroic people who challenged the consensus: one thinks of Athanasius' *contra mundum* or Luther's "Here I stand."

The fact that the fathers were closer to the events described in the New Testament and to the time of writing of those documents is almost irrelevant. Most of them were, after all, hundreds of years removed. In the patristic period as in all others, there were better interpreters (John Chrysostom,

---

[18] Ibid, 40.

Augustine) and worse interpreters (Origen). Some years ago I set myself the
task of reading Origen's massive commentary on Romans. The Greek original
is no longer extant; I read it either in Rufinus' Latin version or in the magnificent English translation of Rufinus by Thomas Scheck while Scheck's work
was still in manuscript form.[19] With the best will in the world, I find it difficult
to imagine that many would be so bold as to claim that Origen understands
what biblical texts are actually saying as well as Chrysostom does, or as well as,
say, John Calvin understood Romans in the Reformation period, or Joseph
Fitzmyer does today. And in any case, in response to (c), why should we think
the Great Tradition is a *sufficient* ground for a common Christian front? One
could make a serious case that it provides a *necessary* ground, but *sufficient*? Are
we to think that no serious aberrations would or could ever be introduced into
the life and thought of the church after the patristic period? If so, why are
proponents of TIS so eager to correct errors that they adjudge to be egregious
today? Does the fact that the issues surrounding the Reformation had more
to do with authority and justification and less to do with Christology and the
Trinity make them any less intrinsically important? Many have observed that
the church's thought may remain relatively fuzzy in this or that doctrinal area
until it is challenged by something clearly aberrant and strongly opposed to
the Christian heritage. Does the mere *sequence* of such aberrations, and therefore of the theological work undertaken in consequence, have any necessary
bearing on the importance of the topic—Christology in the patristic period,
the threat of Islam in the time of Aquinas, justification in the sixteenth century? It is not that the Fathers of the early centuries wrote nothing about justification.[20] Rather, because they were not deeply and perennially challenged
in that arena, they devoted less attention to it, and consequently strove less for
consistency and widespread agreement. More importantly yet, if one is looking for excellent models of how the patristic and medieval fathers *should* be
cited and used abundantly if discerningly, one could do a great deal worse
than begin with Luther, Calvin, and other Reformers. The links between
Calvin and Thomas Aquinas have frequently been probed, and his grasp of
patristic sources is wholly admirable. So why the frequent marginalization of
Reformational voices in TIS literature?

Nothing I have just said justifies failing to listen attentively to, and learn
from, believers in these pre-critical eras. By and large, however, TIS supporters do not address these questions, and their implicit answers are often vague
and troubling.

(2) In his support for TIS, Treier, as we have seen, includes allegorical readings of Scripture among the approaches he is willing to support. Unfortunately,

---

[19] Thomas P. Scheck, ed. and trans., *Commentary on the Epistle to the Romans* (2 vols.;
Washington: Catholic University of America Press, 2001–2002).
[20] Cf. Thomas C. Oden, *The Justification Reader* (Grand Rapids, MI: Eerdmans, 2002).

he gives no hint at what he means by allegory. Many in the orthodox heritage embrace figurative allegory, narrative allegory, and typological allegory. Would Treier do so? Is he adopting the fourfold readings much loved in the Middle Ages—literal, moral, tropological, and allegorical? Would he try to deploy all four readings in every text, as advocated by many in the pre-critical eras? If we are to learn from the last big wave of pre-critical thinkers (the Reformers) and not only the first big wave (the Fathers), what shall we make of the Reformers' rejection of the fourfold interpretive scheme? Isn't the pre-critical *versus* post-Enlightenment polarity a hopeless reductionism?

More narrowly, is Treier thinking of allegory in nothing more than the sense deployed in Gal. 4:24 (ἅτινά ἐστιν ἀλληγορούμενα)? Whether designated figurative or typological, who would want to deny the existence of allegory *in this sense*? In his book on parables, New Testament scholar Craig Blomberg insists that Jesus himself interprets at least some of his own parables in an allegorical fashion.[21] I remain unpersuaded that allegory is the best category for what is going on in the parables, but if one accepts it, is that all that Treier means? If so, we do not need to appeal to patristic exegesis to warrant allegorical interpretation. On the other hand, more sophisticated treatments of allegory do not simply look for the figurative elements in narrative parables or the typological patterns in narrative literature (as in Galatians 4). Rather, they argue that the distinctive element of allegory is that it requires an interpretive grid not grounded in the text at hand, an extratextual grid.[22] When Philo tells us that the respective meanings of the patriarchs Abraham, Isaac, and Jacob are the three fundamental principles of a Greek education, with the best will in the world it is difficult to see how this conclusion derives from the text of Genesis. An extratextual grid has been superimposed on the text. What, then, is the warrant justifying this kind of allegorical reading of Scripture—dependent on an extra-biblical grid? Nor will it do to argue that the *analogia fidei* might be a legitimate extratextual grid, for the *analogia fidei* itself must be shown to be grounded in the text of Scripture. Moreover, the *analogia fidei* functions better to provide boundary interpretations than to stipulate that a specific component of the *analogia fidei* is found in a particular biblical passage, *absent any textual evidence of any kind*. Speaking of learning from past thinkers of the

---

[21] Craig Blomberg, *Interpreting the Parables* (Downers Grove: InterVarsity, 1990); cf. also his essay, "The Parables of Jesus: Current Trends and Needs in Research," in *Studying the Historical Jesus: Evaluations of the State of Current Research* (eds, Bruce Chilton and Craig A. Evans; Leiden: Brill, 1994), 231–254.

[22] That is why Hans Weder, *Die Gleichnisse Jesu als Metaphern: Traditions und redaktionsgeschichtliche Analysen und Interpretationen* (2nd edn; **Forschungen zur Religion und Literatur des AT und NT** 120; Göttingen: Vandenhoeck und Ruprecht, 1980), observes that the figurative (allegorical?) elements attached to the details of the parable of the soils are intrinsic to the narrative and draw their force out of the narrative, rather than depending on an extratextual grid. If the extratextual grid is the criterion for allegory, the parables are not allegorical.

pre-critical eras, one begins to grow in respect for the Reformers who thought their way clear of fuzzy notions of allegory to a greater dependence on "literal" interpretation (without losing a sophisticated grasp of metaphorical language), and less of TIS support for unspecified allegory.

(3) Perhaps this is the place to enter a small demurral against the way the Enlightenment becomes a whipping boy in TIS, with everything before it being called "pre-critical" and therefore approved, and everything from the Enlightenment on generally frowned upon. I have already suggested that a little discretionary frowning toward the pre-critical side of this divide might not be out of place. Now we must remind ourselves of several things that suggest there should be a little *less* frowning on the Enlightenment side.

*First,* the Enlightenment is regularly treated in the TIS movement as a unified period characterized by philosophical naturalism, religious and theological skepticism, and the creation of an array of subject/object problems. All these points can be challenged. The Enlightenment had a different face in France than in England. In its early decades its was the playground of Christians as much as the playground of others. Philosophical naturalism rules widely today, but in the beginning of the Enlightenment it was not so. One should recall, for instance, that the influential Tübingen School is, after all, the product of the nineteenth century. There is a distinctly ahistorical feel to the way the Enlightenment is treated by TIS authors. It is more of a symbol for what they do not like than an accurate representation.

*Second,* insofar as rising naturalism and atomistic interpretations do increasingly prevail (especially in Western academic circles), and insofar as confessional Christians tried to engage these developments, they are often tarred by TIS supporters with the same dismissive brush as their more skeptical contemporaries on the ground that they too have been infected by "the Enlightenment." What is needed, we are told, is a return to pre-critical exegesis so as to take the Bible out of the academy and return it to the church.

*Of course* the Bible is the church's Bible, not the academy's Bible, if by that is meant that the Bible is for the people of God, not for people who constantly try to pull it apart in the framework of an unyielding naturalism. Yet the onslaught against the Bible has been so sustained and so rigorous that Christians—people in the church—serving in the academy (for the disjunction between the church and the academy cannot be made as absolute as TIS supporters seem to think) who stood up to these trends should surely be thanked and honored, not rebuked for being post-Enlightenment thinkers who fail to appreciate pre-critical exegesis. At the least, this smacks of ingratitude.

*Third,* are there not *some* interpretive gains generated by the Enlightenment, gains that contributed to more accurate interpretation and therefore to theology that was better grounded in the text of Scripture? Yes, one remembers all the destructive trajectories. Yet is it not the part of both courtesy and accuracy to remember substantial valuable contributions—in philology, for instance, in text criticism as the finds of the nineteenth and twentieth centuries were explored, in biblical theology? Does one really want to write off, say, an Adolf Schlatter, suggesting that what the poor man really needed was some instruction from TIS proponents so that both his methods and his theology might be enriched?

*Fourth,* the approach of TIS to historical matters is complicated by two other factors. (a) TIS objects, as we have seen, to *historical*-critical methods of interpretation (especially insofar as those methods default to an assumed philosophical naturalism) and wants to leap back *in history* to earlier periods in order to lean on a more *theologically* orientated and less *historically* orientated approach to reading Scripture. Well and good. But sometimes today the expression "historical-criticism" refers to a grab bag of methods that have little to do with history and a great deal to do with naturalism. The older historical criticism—including source criticism, redaction criticism, tradition criticism, even social-scientific criticism—claimed to be unpacking history disclosed in the text as the text coughed up its secrets to these new "scientific" methods. The newer criticisms—for example, feminist criticism, postcolonial criticism, audience criticism—are simply not interested in the same sort of *historical* questions. In other words, TIS should more clearly warn against naturalism and against history grounded in naturalism, rather than against history per se. (b) On the basis of how the New Testament writers injected *historical* sensitivity into their reading of the Old Testament documents (discussed in Proposition One, above), one might ask how long such historical sensitivity persisted in the early church. With time this historically grounded typology gave way to a more thematically controlled typology: presbyters became priests, the eucharist became a sacrifice, the table an altar—all calling to mind Old Testament antecedents without the New Testament's assorted grids for establishing continuity and discontinuity. Some measure of the older historically grounded typology resurfaces in the Reformation. It receives a further boost in the rise of the biblical theology movement (whose origin is often pegged to Johann Philipp Gabler's inaugural address at the University of Altdorf in 1787). Sadly, the rising wave of naturalism gradually destroyed much of biblical theology as it pursued distinctions among biblical books and corpora while losing the big picture: biblical theology became thoroughly atomistic biblical theologies. Yet there were remarkable exceptions. The line through Johann C. K. von Hofmann in the nineteenth century (1810–1877) takes us directly to Adolf Schlatter and Geerhardus Vos in the twentieth century, and beyond—voices graced with responsible exegesis, theological confessionalism, historical awareness, sensitivity to the way the writers of the New Testament appealed to historical sequence to establish their conclusions regarding continuity and discontinuity between the Testaments, and much more. Today, however, we are drifting in Western culture toward a *reduced* appreciation of history, a reduced grasp of chronology, sequence, development. Even when we *do* seem to be extolling the virtues of the past, it has more to do with nostalgia than historical rigor. As Gillis Harp observes (building on Christopher Lasch), there is an approach to history that wallows in nostalgia but does not really engage the past seriously. It "actually reflects a dismissive attitude to the past."[23] In more skeptical moments, I wonder if TIS falls into this nostalgic approach to history, rather than letting past and present seriously engage one another. In other words, I wonder if TIS owes something of its impetus to the ahistorical fads of the day.

**Proposition Four:** TIS aims to be God-centered as opposed to human-centered (including human-hermeneutical-rules-centered).

**Yes:** Potentially there is something both lovely and healthy about this emphasis. Reading the Bible primarily to uncover what the mighty _I_ can get out of it is certainly skewing the biblical focus on the glory of God. Moreover, if hermeneutical rules somehow function so as to box God in, to domesticate God, one wants to applaud TIS. Readers should be approaching the text not as its master but as its servant;[24] one should not so much seek to master Scripture as be mastered by it, and especially be mastered by the God whose Word it is. There is a sense in which such reading partakes of a bold "I am not ashamed of the gospel," instead of hiding behind a panoply of scholarly conventions while projecting an impression of objective scholarly distance.

**But . . .** An array of caveats springs to mind.

(1) The flight from rules that merely domesticate God is a good thing, but surely one must beware of the pressure from the many in this twenty-first century world who want faith to be purely subjective, all in the name of making God so "big."

(2) It would be good if more TIS supporters recognized how many others from confessional evangelicalism write much of their material entirely within this same confessional world that TIS is advocating. These believers might interact with some critical thought on the Bible while playing the "game" and keeping in line with the hermeneutical stances of some secularists in order to make some useful points about, say, source criticism in John or Isaiah. Their heart, however, is disclosed in their more usual contributions. In my own small world, all the contributors to New Studies in Biblical Theology and in the Pillar New Testament Commentary series are expected to write in conscious submission to the text, in joyful conformity to confessional Christianity, as a believer to believers. If others want to

---

[23] Gillis Harp, "Taking History Seriously in an Ahistorical Age," _Modern Reformation_ 17/5 (Sept/Oct 2005), 35.

[24] Cf. Kevin J. Vanhoozer, "Imprisoned or Free? Text, Status, and Theological Interpretation in the Master/Slave Discourse of Philemon," in _Reading Scripture with the Church: Toward a Hermeneutic for Theological Interpretation_ (eds, A. K. M. Adam, Stephen E. Fowl, Kevin J. Vanhoozer, and Francis Watson; Grand Rapids, MI: Baker, 2006), 92.

listen in, well and good—but the writers are certainly not pretending to be neutral masters of the text. On many fronts, TIS supporters would do well to sound a little less as if they are singing a chorus from Elijah: "And we, we only, are left."

(3) While the refusal to allow hermeneutical rules to box God in is salutary, suspicion of all hermeneutical rules or principles is shortsighted, and even stands over against the bias in TIS toward the church fathers. Augustine, after all, lists an array of interpretive rules that mirror not a few contemporary rules—and of course he simultaneously insists that Bible readers be reverent and confessionally informed.[25] Principles that emerge from the reading of *any* text (e.g., syntax of the language) need to be learned; numerous other interpretive principles will emerge *from the text itself.* If they emerge from the text, and if the interpreter does not insist that these interpretive rules are exhaustive, it is hard to imagine why anyone would think they might box God in. Surely, rather, they honor the God who has chosen to communicate with us precisely through such human texts.

(4) The concern to be God-centered cannot be faulted. It is then deployed to warrant that biblical interpretation take place in the church and for the church, which alone maintains this God-centeredness, not the academy. We have already considered that interpreting the Bible within the church might simply mean moving within the contours of the *analogia fidei,* and tried to think through what this should and should not look like. But some TIS writers understand clauses such as "biblical interpretation [must] take place *in the church and for the church*" to mean something like "among Christian believers" and "for Christian believers." At one level this is exactly right. The Bible is for Christians, and Christians are the ones who, precisely because they want to hear the voice of God, should be reading it and interpreting it.

Nevertheless: (a) Christians interact with non-Christians. Anyone who has been in ministry near a major university with a biblical or religious studies department will have stories to tell about students who are facing complicated questions about the Bible that do not arise from the believing community but ultimately from the academic world. Not to engage with them and respond to them thoughtfully and carefully is a terrible mistake. When TIS supporters write in antithetical terms about interpreting the Bible in the church and not in the academy, they sometimes begin to sound as if they are advocating a hermetically sealed-off huddle.

(b) When some TIS supporters speak of interpretation in the church and not in the academy, they overlook the fact that all or almost all of them work

---

[25] *De Doctrina Christiana,* book II.

in the academy. Of course, they might protest that they also belong to the church. But that is the point: church and academy are not completely disjunctive. Certainly these scholars are writing *for* the academy: TIS as a movement has not, by and large, so far penetrated the church. But if the fundamental antithesis is not between the academy and the church, what is it? That brings us to the next observation.

(c) The TIS movement is far from united theologically. Its supporters can be found among at least four groups: Roman Catholics, confessional evangelicals, Barthians, and chastened liberals. Although on some matters they share common theological commitments—Trinitarianism, for instance, to which I will return in a moment—on many matters fundamental to TIS they actually mean something quite different from group to group. Earlier I showed how an appeal to the *analogia fidei* looks quite different for Catholics than it does for confessional evangelicals. It would be easy to show that the Christian's or the church's understanding of the authority and truthfulness of Scripture is rather different for chastened liberals and for confessional evangelicals and traditional Catholics. On the point now at hand, what it means to appeal to God over against hermeneutical rules will at some point be rather different for confessional evangelicals and for Barthians.[26] Madueme goes so far as to hint that Barth is a source of many of the present problems in TIS: Barth's "greatest weakness as a resource for theological interpretation is a consistent ambivalence on the relationship between history and theology. To the extent that Scripture is not only a theological but also a historical entity, this gives rise to a related ambivalence between theology and Scripture."[27] In any case, TIS is a frustratingly disparate movement—frustrating not simply because it is disparate, but because its proponents tend to stand shoulder to shoulder as they confront that which is not TIS, while failing to acknowledge and wrestle with the very substantial disparity within their own ranks and which is sending off its proponents in different directions.

**Proposition Five:** TIS commonly insists we ought to read Scripture through Trinitarian lenses.

**Yes:** As a response to bland theism, this is a welcome relief. It is articulated in a variety of ways. Here is Vanhoozer: "The nature and function of the Bible

[26] Even to begin to justify this last point would immediately double the length of this paper. Despite the arguments of some Barthians to the contrary, Barth's understanding of the nature of Scripture is a long way removed from that of traditional confessionalism. On the latter, cf. John D. Woodbridge, *Biblical Authority* (Grand Rapids, MI: Zondervan, 1982). On Barth's views, one of his most informed and attractive representatives is John Webster, *Holy Scripture: A Dogmatic Sketch* (Cambridge: University Press, 2003), with which I attempted to interact in D. A. Carson, "Three More Books on the Bible: A Critical Review," *Trinity Journal* 27 (2006), 1–62. I am indebted to the honoree of this volume for some private communications that have clarified my thinking on some of these matters.

[27] Hans Madueme, "Review Article: Theological Interpretation after Barth," *JTI* 3 (2009), 155.

are insufficiently grasped unless and until we see the Bible as an element in the economy of triune discourse. Those who approach the Bible as Scripture must not abstract it from the Father who ultimately authors it, the Son to whom it witnesses, and the Spirit who inspired and illumines it."[28] Of course, all sides will (or at least should) concur that one ought not read the exact formulations of fourth-century Trinitarianism, with their careful distinctions between substance and person, back into the biblical documents: that would be anachronistic. But most scholars in the secular academy make this true observation about the danger of anachronism, and then fail to find *any* Trinitarianism in Scripture. Still less do they integrate Trinitarian thought into a doctrine of Scripture, with implications for its interpretation.

**But. . . .** Recent years have witnessed an explosion of books and papers on the doctrine of the Trinity. Much of this is salutary, though a case could be made that some writers are trying to squeeze too much theological freight into the doctrine, as judged by the extent to which they fly beyond anything attested by or hinted at within Scripture. (Thus we have returned to the question of which TIS supporters are nurtured by the finality of Scripture's magisterial authority.)

But one should not fail to ask, "Why the Trinity as a, or even the, lens through which to read Scripture? Why not something else?" It may be because the doctrine of the Trinity was central to debates in the patristic period, and we have already observed how much stress TIS supporters place on the church fathers. Still, one cannot help but ask, why not read the Bible in the light of Jesus' resurrection, as Hays engagingly suggests?[29] Or in the light of the gospel, easily warranted by studying the contexts of all the uses of the εὐαγγέλιον word-group? Or in the light of the consummation, as Steinmetz argues, since when we have read the end of the story, we cannot, indeed we should not, reread it as if we do not know[30] the end? Or, more comprehensively, in the light of Christ, the ultimate Word?

In short, one detects undigested proposals running through TIS.

**Proposition Six:** TIS tends to see Scripture less as a set of propositions disclosing God than as the story of God and his saving plan of redemption.

**Yes:** Once again the best side of TIS is a great deal less creative than it claims. The best proponents of biblical theology have been making much the

---

[28] Kevin J. Vanhoozer, "Ten Theses on the Theological Interpretation of Scripture," *Modern Reformation* 19/4 (July/Aug 2010), 17. See further his "Triune Discourse: Theological Reflections on the Claim that God Speaks," in *Trinitarian Theology for the Church: Scripture, Community, Worship* (eds, David Lauber and Daniel J. Treier.; Downers Grove, IL: InterVarsity, 2009), 25–78.

[29] Richard B. Hays, "Reading Scripture in Light of the Resurrection," in *The Art of Reading Scripture* (eds, Ellen F. Davis and Richard B. Hays; Grand Rapids, MI: Eerdmans, 203), 216–238.

[30] David C. Steinmetz, "Uncovering the Second Narrative: Detective Fiction and the Construction of Historical Method," in *The Art of Reading Scripture*, 54–67.

same appeal for a long time. Today the only voices that will seriously doubt this claim are the most secular ones. These voices deny that there is but one story of God, one saving plan of redemption, that runs through the Bible. So it is doubtless helpful to be reminded of the unity of the Bible's storyline, what Bauckham is not afraid to call its metanarrative.[31]

**But. . . .** Two caveats suggest themselves. *First*, one tires of the endless swipes at propositions. *Of course* the Bible has more than propositions: riddles, narratives, commands, letters (which of course hold many propositions), proverbs, lament, and so forth. But anyone can see that the Bible is not lacking in propositions. Even behind other forms—say, lament—assorted propositions lurk, just as behind many of the Bible's propositions, other things may lurk—for example, praise, denunciation, warning, and so forth.

Second, and more importantly, if one rightly concludes that there is a central storyline to the Bible and tries to use it in ways that enrich our theological understanding of Scripture, it does not necessarily follow that one is reading that storyline richly and well. Moreover, failure to do so will have deleterious effects on the theology we construct as a result of our (flawed) understanding of that storyline. To take an easy and common example, several recent attempts at summarizing the Old Testament's storyline ably depict God graciously pursuing his rebellious image-bearers across the turning points in redemptive history, climaxing in the sending of his Son. Yet not a word is spoken of the six hundred times, mostly in narrative context, in which God is said to be angry with his covenant people, threatening them with judgment. In other words, the storyline itself depicts God as simultaneously standing over against his people in wrath and standing over against them in love and mercy. Failure to track out these intertwining themes results in a radically different reading of Jesus, his cross and resurrection, the consummation, and ultimately what we think the gospel achieves. In short, observing the storyline does not guarantee accurate reading of it.


## Concluding Reflections

A colleague and friend, Graham Cole, has written a paper[32] developing a model he has used in the classroom. He speaks of four levels of interpreting biblical texts. At the first level, the Bible itself must be understood exegetically, within its literary and historical contexts, with appropriate attention devoted to literary genre, attempting to unfold authorial intent so far as it is disclosed in the text. At level 2, the text must be understood within the whole of biblical

---

[31]  Richard Bauckham, "Reading Scripture as a Coherent Story," *The Art of Reading Scripture*, edited by Richard Hags and Hellen Dau. Grand Rapids: Earchmas, 2003, pp. 38–53.

[32]  Forthcoming.

theology, including where it fits into and what it contributes to the unfolding storyline and its theology. At level 3, the theological structures found in the text are brought to bear upon, and understood in concert with, other major theological emphases derived from Scripture. At level 4, all teachings derived (or ostensibly derived) from the biblical text are subjected to and modified by a larger hermeneutical proposal (e.g., Trinitarian action, God's love and freedom, or something vague such as "what was disclosed in Jesus"). Traditional interpreters of Scripture who hold the Bible as the Word of God tend to operate at levels 1 and 2, with the strongest of them making excursions now and then into level 3.

So far, many if not most supporters of TIS operate at levels 3 and 4. One suspects that one of the reasons why the Brazos Theological Commentary on the Bible has, in several of its volumes, proved so unsatisfying is that its writers were operating at levels 3 and 4 while trying to give the impression they were operating at levels 1 and 2. Because readers could not forge the actual connections between text and theology ostensibly derived from a *commentary* on the text, they balked—and rightly so. For what is really needed is work that shows how levels 1, 2, and 3 *should* be tied together. One should indulge in level 4 only with the greatest caution, and only after the writer has done a lot of work on the first three levels.

As I am writing this, I have not, of course, read the contributions to this volume that focus on the interpretation of specific sample biblical passages. Perhaps some of them will be the breakthrough essays that achieve genuine historical and theological integration under the authority of Scripture. At this moment, however, I am inclined to think that what is most valuable in TIS (and much is), is not new; what is new in TIS varies from ambiguous to mistaken, depending in part on the theological location of the interpreter.

# Index of Scriptures

# Index of Names